HANDBOOK OF EVANGELICAL THEOLOGY

Robert P. Lightner

HANDBOOK OF EVANGELICAL THEOLOGY

A Historical, Biblical, and Contemporary Survey and Review

kregel
PUBLICATIONS

Grand Rapids, MI 49501

Handbook of Evangelical Theology by Robert P. Lightner

Copyright © 1995 by Robert P. Lightner

Published in 1995 by Kregel Publications, a division of Kregel, Inc., P. O. Box 2607, Grand Rapids, MI 49501. Kregel Publications provides trusted, biblical publications for Christian growth and service. Your comments and suggestions are valued.

Cover Design: Alan G. Hartman

Library of Congress Cataloging-in-Publication Data
Lightner, Robert P.
[Evangelical theology]
    Handbook of evangelical theology / Robert P. Lightner.
       p. cm.
    Originally published: Evangelical theology. Grand Rapids, MI: Baker Book House, 1986.
    Includes bibliographical references and indexes.
    1. Theology, Doctrinal. 2. Evangelicalism. I. Title.
BT75.2.L49   1995   230'.046—dc20   93-16510
                                   CIP

ISBN 0-8254-3145-x (paperback)

3 4 5 6 7 / 08 07 06 05 04

Printed in the United States of America

To
John F. Walvoord
international theologian,
seminary president,
stalwart of the faith

Acknowledgments

My thanks to Dallas Theological Seminary for granting a leave of absence from my seminary duties to write this book.

I am indebted to publishers of some of my previous books for granting permission to utilize material in those volumes in this one.

I owe special thanks to Dr. Gordon Lewis of Conservative Baptist Theological Seminary, Denver, and Dr. Paul Nevin of Moody Bible Institute, Chicago, for critically reading the manuscript and making many helpful suggestions.

Contents

Introduction

This book has been carefully titled. It is a survey and review of evangelical theology and is not intended to be a full-orbed work of systematic theology, though it does, of course, deal with all the fundamental doctrines of the historic Christian faith. Each of these is approached from a theocentric perspective indicated by the chapter titles.

The term *evangelical* is used rather widely today. My readers, therefore, need to understand the meaning I attach to it in this book.

Evangel is a biblical word meaning "gospel" or "glad tidings" and is attached to each of the Gospels in the New Testament. Evangel denotes more than the good news of deliverance from sin, since those Gospels contain more than that. What must one believe to be classified legitimately as an evangelical?

The divine inspiration and authority of the Bible is a major doctrinal belief of evangelicals, but it does not stand alone. Other essential beliefs have been summarized by Harold Lindsell:

> (1) . . . God is a Trinity, one in essence, subsisting in three persons, the Father, the Son, and the Holy Spirit; (2) . . . Jesus is the incarnate, virgin-born Son of God, sinless, holy, and the vicarious substitute for man's transgressions; (3) . . . Adam was the first man, he sinned in the garden of Eden and his transgression wrought disaster for the human race; (4) . . . Jesus rose in bodily form from the grave, ascended into heaven, and is coming again personally, visibly, and in power and great glory; (5)

1

. . . salvation is by faith alone, without works of righteousness; (6)
. . . there is a heaven and a hell.[1]

With this summary, which elaborates the five fundamentals set forth at the turn of the century by those opposing liberal theology, I concur.

Theology, from the Greek *theos* (God) and *logos* (word), is in its broadest meaning a word about God. As a science it includes three major areas: biblical, historical, and systematic. This book is a study primarily in the area of systematics but also includes aspects of the other two. The following will serve as a working definition of systematic theology for this study: "Systematic theology is the collecting, scientifically arranging, comparing, exhibiting, and defending of all facts from any and every source concerning God and his works."[2]

This book is intended for classroom use in Christian liberal arts and Bible colleges where surveys of doctrine are taught. It will also fill a need on the seminary level as a review of systematic theology. Busy pastors and other Christian workers will find this study helpful in brushing up on their theology. I want this book to whet the reader's appetite for further study in theology, the queen of the sciences. My goal has also been to encourage theological thinking. Too often doctrines are pigeonholed and the relationships between aspects of each doctrine and between all the doctrines themselves are overlooked. I have tried to highlight some of these relationships.

In each chapter I have included a historical perspective on the doctrine studied, a positive statement of the doctrine, the major difference among evangelicals over the doctrine, and practical suggestions and study questions for the application of the doctrine to life. Obviously, because of the size and nature of the study I have had to be selective in what I have included. The reader needs always to keep in mind that the volume is a survey and review,

---

1. Harold Lindsell, *The Bible in the Balance* (Grand Rapids: Zondervan, 1979), p. 306. Lindsell argues powerfully that those who deny total inerrancy of the Bible have no right to the courtesy of the term *evangelical*; see esp. pp. 308-11. James Barr, a critic who lumps together evangelicals, conservatives, conservative evangelicals, and fundamentalists, agrees that, for proponents of this position, biblical inerrancy is a major doctrinal belief. *Fundamentalism* (London: SCM, 1977), p. 287.

2. Lewis Sperry Chafer, *Systematic Theology* (Dallas: Dallas Seminary Press, 1950), 1:x.

not a systematic theology per se. The reader is also encouraged to take advantage of the suggestions for further study in the notes at the end of each chapter.

It is my sincere prayer that all who read and use this book will come to a better understanding of the triune God and his Word. The better we know these, the more effective and productive we can be in living the Christian life.

1

God's Word—The Bible

How are we to view the Bible? No more important question could occupy the human mind. It is impossible to ignore the query. An answer must be given. The title of this chapter reveals how I answer the question. The Bible in its entirety is the very Word of God. But not all who are pleased to be called evangelicals agree with this view, as we shall see.

Just why is the question so very important? Are not other questions about the doctrines of the Christian faith of equal importance? It cannot be denied that questions related to central doctrinal themes of the historic, orthodox Christian faith are of supreme importance, but they must follow, not precede, the question, "How are we to view the Bible?" This is true because we cannot know with absolute certainty anything about these other truths apart from the Bible. The Bible is the basis of the Christian faith. We get our knowledge upon which our faith is based from the Scriptures.

A Historical Perspective

The inspiration and therefore infallibility of the Bible was believed by the majority of Christians from the earliest days of the church. This belief dominated until the rise of materialistic rationalism and mysticism in the eighteenth and nineteenth centuries. Cecil Cadoux, who was not in sympathy with the belief in inspired Scripture, nevertheless wrote, "Scripture . . . was

5

accepted by Christendom with practical unanimity from the 2nd century to the 19th.''[1] Harold Lindsell, a contemporary historian and theologian who accepts a fully inerrant view of the Bible, makes the same claim: ''From the historical perspective it can be said that for two thousand years the Christian church has agreed that the Bible is completely trustworthy. It is infallible or inerrant.''[2] The International Council on Biblical Inerrancy, meeting in Chicago in 1978, concurred: ''We affirm that the doctrine of inerrancy has been integral to the Church's faith throughout its history. We deny that inerrancy is a doctrine invented by Scholastic Protestantism, or is a reactionary position postulated in response to negative higher criticism.''[3]

There is abundant evidence in the writings of the earliest church fathers and historians of their commitment to the infallibility of Scripture. Clement, Polycarp, Irenaeus, Tertullian, Cyprian, Origen, Athanasius, Chrysostom, Augustine, and a host of others believed the Bible to be the very Word of God in the whole and in the part.[4] The belief of the orthodox church for the first five centuries regarding the total infallibility of the Bible held true for the remaining centuries up to the nineteenth.

In recent years a major rift has developed within evangelicalism over the extent of the Bible's inspiration and infallibility. This will be discussed below when major differences among evangelicals are described.

The Old Liberal View[5]

From the day Satan denied what God said was true, God's Word has been rejected by many. The strongest and most formal rejection was set forth by what we now call classic, or old, liberal theology.

In a day when the rationalism and materialism of the Enlightenment were assailing historic Christianity, Friedrich

---

1. Cecil John Cadoux, *The Case for Evangelical Modernism* (London: Hodder & Stoughton, 1938), p. 64.
2. Harold Lindsell, *The Battle for the Bible* (Grand Rapids: Zondervan, 1976), p. 19.
3. R. C. Sproul, *Explaining Inerrancy* (Oakland, Calif.: International Council on Biblical Inerrancy, 1980), pp. 45-46.
4. See George Duncan Barry, *The Inspiration and Authority of Holy Scripture: A Study in the Literature of the First Five Centuries* (New York: Macmillan, 1919).
5. This section is taken in part from the author's *Neo-Liberalism* (Nutley, N.J.: The Craig Press, 1972), pp. 24-29.

Schleiermacher (1768-1834) introduced a new approach to the understanding of religion. He rejected the cold rationalism of the philosophers before him, but he did not embrace historic Christianity. For him, true Christianity was not revealed in a set of propositions and dogmas to which a believer must subscribe, but in an inner experience.

Scholars with interest in religion and with a strong confidence in reason addressed the Bible, especially the Gospels. These men sought to retain many of the features of historic Christianity and at the same time accept the findings of unbelieving philosophers. Men such as H. E. G. Paulus (1761-1851), Ferdinand Christian Baur (1792-1860), and David Friedrich Strauss (1808-1874) applied philosophical reasoning to the New Testament, and as a result ruled out the miraculous from the Gospels. The same attempt to restate the Word and make it conform to the findings of man was made with the Old Testament. Human reason became the determining factor as to what was and was not the Word of God. Therefore, rather than the Bible standing as judge over men, men stood over it as final judges.

Liberal theology was, and still is, diametrically opposed to the historic Christian faith. For liberals the Bible is composed mostly of myths and legends. The inspiration of the Bible was defined by classic liberals in terms of the one who wrote rather than what was written. The books of the Bible were rearranged and redated to fit the liberal presupposition denying supernatural predictions. It was believed that books and passages which claimed to tell the future had been written after the events had occurred. Even the existence of Jesus in history was doubted. What the New Testament recorded about him was considered to be a myth invented by the early church. These were some of the damaging results of higher criticism, which assumed a naturalistic and evolutionary world view. These assumptions, more than scientific discoveries, led to the denial of the Bible as a God-inspired book infallible in everything it declared.

The Neoorthodox View

The old liberal theology held sway until two world wars destroyed the optimism that had characterized its leaders. Believing in humanity's inherent goodness and inevitable progress toward utopia, liberals preached a social gospel rather than the gospel of God's saving grace in Christ. The wars dealt a death blow to this wishful thinking. A vacuum was created by the demise of the old liberal school of thought, and into the vacuum Karl Barth introduced what came to be known as neoorthodoxy. Barth reacted against the liberal view of God as immanent, man as morally good, and the kingdom of God a result of cultural evolution. His stress on God's transcendence, human sinfulness, revelation in Christ, and the need for a subjective, personal encounter with Christ seemed to be a return to orthodoxy. Crisis theology, however, failed to return to belief in the Bible as propositionally revealed and recorded truth.

Basic to the neoorthodox view of revelation, inspiration, and authority is its view of history, which sees two different kinds of history. There is historiographic history (*historie*), which deals with data observable by non-Christian reporters. Unhistoriographic history (*geschichte*) speaks of events known only to people of faith. Two other terms often used to explain these two realms are real history and primal history. Edward J. Young analyzed this view accurately when he said, "The Bible knows nothing about any region or realm which, in distinction from the historical, is to be labeled faith or redemption or supra-temporal, or supra-historical or *Urgeschichte*, or a realm where history and nature are inadequate. To put the matter boldly, it would seem that these are but new names for the old area of myth and legend.[6]

Neoorthodoxy does not view the revelation of God in the Bible as objectively valid, true propositions. None of the Bible is the Word of God in this sense. Neither does it become the Word of God in statements of fact. It may become the Word of God and convey the living Christ subjectively to the individual reader as he experiences an encounter, a crisis.

The Contemporary Liberal View

Though the world wars and neoorthodoxy devastated the old liberal concepts, a new variety of liberal theology arose to take its place. Neo- or new liberalism[7] attempts "to preserve the values of

---

6. Edward J. Young, *Thy Word Is Truth* (Grand Rapids: Eerdmans, 1957), p. 251.
7. See Lightner, *Neo-Liberalism*.

liberalism while reinterpreting them for a new age and new conditions."[8]

Like the neoorthodox, the contemporary liberal rejects objective, propositional revelation in Scripture. "There is no such thing as revealed truth. . . . There are truths of revelation, that is to say, propositions which express the results of correct thinking concerning revelation, but they are not themselves directly revealed."[9]

For the new liberal, Scripture is merely a witness to revelation. There is little difference between this postwar liberal view and the neoorthodox view of the Bible. The basic difference is that neoliberals such as Walter Marshall Horton and G. Bromley Oxnam allow for a limited sort of inspiration for parts of the Bible, even though they believe it contains both truth and error.

The Inspired Errant View

The adherents of the recently revived inspired errant view believe that the historic orthodox view of verbal, plenary inspiration must be reinvestigated. Their reinvestigation has brought them to believe the Bible is indeed infallible and trustworthy when it addresses itself to its major theme and purpose, faith in Christ and relational Christian living. However, when the Bible speaks about such "peripheral" issues as scientific, historic, chronological, and geographic matters, it is not only liable to error, but in fact does sometimes err. This view will be discussed later in more detail.

A Positive Statement of the Doctrine

There are a number of areas in the doctrine of Scripture where evangelicals are in full agreement.

Revelation

If God had not spoken, we could not know for sure that he exists. But he did speak. God's speaking, in both his world and

8. William Hordern, *A Layman's Guide to Protestant Theology* (New York: Macmillan, 1955), p. 100.
9. William Temple, *Nature, God, and Man* (London: Macmillan, 1954), p. 317.

his Word, is an evidence and illustration of his love. God willed that mankind, created in his image, know him, love him, and serve him. The term *revelation* may be defined as a divine act of communicating to man what otherwise man could not know but must learn to be rightly related to God.[10]

Although God's revelation in Scripture was given progressively, all that was given at any point in time was fully and equally inspired. Many different things contributed to the nature of the revelation God gave to man. It was God's will gradually to reveal himself and his plan over a long period of time, under varied circumstances and to meet a multitude of needs. Revelation has to do with the giving of the message. It is communication from God to man.

Revelation must be distinguished from reason. The two are often confused. Revelation is an activity of God, a means of communication, and of course also that which is communicated. Reason, on the other hand, is a human activity by which revelation is apprehended and understood.

John Gerstner explains: "The only way anything revealed is apprehended, grasped, or understood is by reason. There is no other way of communication but by revelation. There is no other way of apprehension but by reason. Without revelation there would be no knowledge. Without reason there would be no apprehension of knowledge."[11]

By his very nature God is estranged from fallen creatures. The fall of man broke man's contact with God. Before the fall God did indeed communicate with man. Of the content of that communication we know little, but we do know that man's sin separated him from God. After the fall Adam and Eve hid from God. No longer did God walk and talk with them in the cool of the day in the garden.

The need of a special revelation itself argues a supply. In nature provision is made to heal bruises and wounds in living organisms, to supply remedies for human ailments, and to supplement the failing energies of one member by the increased efficiency of another member. God does not break a bruised reed nor quench a

---

10. Robert P. Lightner, *The Saviour and the Scriptures* (Grand Rapids: Baker Book House, 1978), p. 38.

11. John H. Gerstner, "Jonathan Edwards and the Bible," *Tenth*, Oct., 1979, p. 3.

smoking flax. If God supplied such influences in nature in order that His purpose in creation be realized, there follows the strong probability that He will provide man's spiritual need in order to secure the highest development in the moral realm. God, infinitely and absolutely holy and perfectly good, will most assuredly do as much for man's spiritual life as He does for his physical life.[12]

It is customary for theologians to speak of two distinct kinds of revelation—referred to as natural and supernatural, original and soteriological, or general and special. The distinction between these kinds is based on the different ways by which God has communicated his message to man.

General Revelation. By general revelation is meant God's revelation in nature, human consciousness, providence, and preservation. Scripture testifies to this in several key passages (Ps. 19; Rom. 1-3; Acts 14:15-17; 17:22-37). A study of these passages makes a number of things very clear regarding general revelation.

> *First,* it is important to remember that all men everywhere do have some knowledge of God for which they are responsible. *Second,* . . . His revelation of Himself in nature makes men "without excuse" (Romans 1:20). *Third,* all men are lost even though God has made Himself known to all. *Fourth,* the knowledge of God from general or natural revelation is insufficient in itself for salvation, since it does not reveal man's lost condition and Christ's substitutionary atonement. However, God's revelation in nature corresponds perfectly with His revelation in the written word. The questions which natural revelation raises are answered in the Bible, God's special revelation. *Fifth,* man in his unregenerate state often distorts the revelation and fails to live up to the knowledge or light which he has (cf. Romans 1-3). *Sixth,* the reality of God's revelation in nature can be used as a beginning point in witnessing to the unsaved (cf. Acts 17:15-34 where Paul did just that).[13]

Special Revelation. Though incomplete, the revelation of God in nature is genuine and accurate because it is God's. But God has also revealed himself in words, not just works. He has not only done certain things, he has also said certain things. Special

---

12. S. J. Gamertsfelder, *Systematic Theology* (Grand Rapids: Eerdmans, 1968), p. 37.
13. Robert P. Lightner, *The God of the Bible* (Grand Rapids: Baker Book House, 1978), p. 48.

revelation designates God's revelation in Christ, his mighty acts in history, and his message to prophetic and apostolic spokesmen. Today its content is in Scripture. In the Bible we have the divine disclosure of propositional truth.

The Bible is not only *a* record of revelation, it is *the* divine record of revelation. Scripture is not simply a revelation from God, it is the only written revelation from him.

Inspiration

While special revelation communicates the redemptive message God wants sinners to know, inspiration was God's way of seeing to it that his special revelation in words was preserved from all error and omission. The human writers of Scripture were not inspired, but what they wrote under the Spirit's guidance was. He used their own personalities and styles and superintended them as they wrote the Word of God.

The term *inspiration* is from the Greek *theopneustos*. As used in 2 Timothy 3:16,[14] it means the Scripture was "breathed out" by God. This means the Holy Spirit of God superintended the human writers in the production of Scripture so that what they wrote was precisely what God wanted written.

The historic Christian view of the inspiration of Scripture included some important distinctions. Only the original documents of Scripture are inspired, not the copies and translations. The very words of Scripture are inspired, not just the divine concepts, though not all the words were inspired through a process of dictation.

Several other terms are related to inspiration.

Inerrancy. When applied to Scripture inerrancy means that the original documents were without error. If assertions are God-breathed, they must be without error, otherwise God would be guilty of asserting error. Until rather recently those who rejected Scripture's inspiration also rejected the inerrancy of its teaching.

To believe the Bible is inerrant is to believe that it does not lie in anything it affirms. An increasing number of those who classify themselves as evangelicals argue that the Bible is true in all it

---

14. An extended discussion of this passage may be found in Benjamin B. Warfield, *The Inspiration and Authority of the Bible* (Philadelphia: Presbyterian and Reformed Publishing Company, 1948); and Edward J. Young, *Thy Word Is Truth.*

affirms about salvation and the Christian life, but not necessarily in matters unrelated to these central themes. In other words, when the major purpose or central theme of the Bible is being addressed, it is without error, but not necessarily when so-called peripheral matters are presented.

Verbal, Plenary Inspiration. To describe inspiration as verbal and plenary is to explain not how Scripture was inspired but what resulted from that supernatural activity. Inspiration extended to the words (verbal inspiration), not just to the concepts or ideas. And it extended to all of Scripture (plenary inspiration), not just to parts of it. All the words of Scripture and all portions of it, as originally written, were God-breathed.

Infallibility. To say that Scripture is infallible is to say that it is incapable of teaching deception or of failing in its purpose. *Infallibility*, like *inerrancy*, is sometimes used as a synonym for *inspiration*.

Trustworthiness. The trustworthiness of Scripture means that it is credible and therefore deserves to be believed. One can rely on all its pronouncements.

The Dual Authorship of Scripture[15]

God's Word has come to us through humans. The Bible was not written by God and handed directly to man as a finished product. It came from God, to be sure, but he employed finite humans to write down his message and to recognize it as his Word. The Bible bears abundant testimony in both testaments to its dual authorship. The human writers God selected to pen his Word were not sinless humans, either. They were ordinary men who loved God and wished to serve him, but they had been affected by Adam's sin just like every other human. In fact, some of them had some rather dark marks on their lives evidencing their native depravity. David in his sin with Bathsheba and Peter in his denial of Christ serve as two glaring examples.

The Holy Spirit of God was the divine author of Scripture. Though he used erring humans as penmen, he supernaturally (miraculously) superintended them as they wrote, keeping them from all error and omission. The men who wrote God's Word

15. See Gordon R. Lewis's excellent contribution to this question in *Inerrancy*, ed. Norman L. Geisler (Grand Rapids: Zondervan, 1979), pp. 229-64.

were "moved by the Holy Spirit" (2 Peter 1:21), borne along as a vessel over water. While they used their individual personalities and skills, the Spirit of God so controlled and guarded the human authors that they wrote precisely what he wanted written. Although he did not dictate every word to them, the end product was just as inerrant as though he had. Those whom God used to record his Word used words that were theirs and God's at the same time.

Two extreme reactions have resulted from the dual authorship of Scripture. One has been to believe that because the human authors were indeed finite and fallen, God kept his Word pure by dictating it to them as an executive does to his secretary. The other extreme reaction to God's employment of humans has been to believe that his Word therefore contains errors.

Theories of Inspiration

Because finite members of Adam's sinful race were used by God to record his message, a number of theories of inspiration have been advanced. Some of the more important of these are described here.

Natural Inspiration. There have been a number of geniuses in history. Those who hold what has been called the natural inspiration theory believe the men who wrote the books of the Bible were geniuses. This view sees no supernaturalism involved in the production of the Bible. Evangelicals do not subscribe to this view.

Mystical Inspiration. Some see the writers of Scripture as having been divinely guided in much the same way as a believer may be guided today. This theory ascribes to the biblical writers a higher degree of inspiration than any other human writers have ever experienced, but it does not advocate that what they wrote was the Word of God. The theory of mystical inspiration is not held by evangelicals.

Partial Inspiration. This attempt to account for the human-divine involvement in the production of Scripture holds that certain parts of it were inspired by God and other parts were not. Inspired parts usually include such things as the accounts of creation and the prophetic portions. This view is not too dissimilar from the inspired-but-errant view described above.

Some who hold to partial inspiration believe the writers' thoughts were inspired by God, but not the words used to express those thoughts. Still others would argue that only the moral and spiritual teachings of the Bible are inspired; the problem is determining what constitutes moral and spiritual teaching.

Inspiration by Dictation. This view holds that the writers of Scripture were simply secretaries who wrote down only what God dictated to them. Some portions of Scripture were in fact dictated by God, but this does not mean that all of it was. The great variety of writing style evident throughout Scripture is hard to account for if all of it was dictated. Even though not all was dictated in a mechanical sort of way, nevertheless all the Bible is as accurate and inerrant as though it had been thus given. Some evangelicals have held to this view or variations of it.[16]

Inspiration by Personal Witness. This theory was advanced first by neoorthodoxy and is quite popular today. It believes that the Bible is a witness or a pointer to the Word of God, even though it was penned by erring humans whose errors naturally crept into their writings. Christ is seen as the Word in the primary sense. The Bible, despite its many errors, is the best witness to Christ. Those who hold this view can and do speak of the Bible as the Word of God. However, they do not mean that it is the Word of God in propositions of truth, but that it may become the Word of God to the individual as he experiences an encounter with God when he reads it. The Bible is not the revelation of God, but a pointer to where revelation occurred. Evangelicals do not subscribe to this view.

Inspiration According to the One Purpose of Scripture. In this theory the Bible, penned by fallible humans, contains factual errors. Despite this it is believed there is doctrinal integrity in Scripture. It does accomplish the salvific purpose God intended for it. Therefore, the human writers were kept from error in some of what they wrote, but not in all they wrote. This is a rather recent view advocated by some within neoevangelicalism and will be discussed later.

Authority

The authority of Scripture means that it is God's absolute standard of truth in all that it affirms. The Bible's teachings are his

---

16. A modern presentation and defense of this view is found in John R. Rice, *Our God-Breathed Book—the Bible* (Murfreesboro, Tenn.: Sword of the Lord, 1969).

criteria for all judgment and evaluation. The authority of God himself has been mediated to man in the Bible in propositions. Scripture doctrine is binding. Its predictions will all be fulfilled because it is God's Word.

When the questions of revelation and inspiration with regard to the Bible have been answered, the issue of authority will have been settled. In other words, how one views revelation and inspiration will determine how he views the Bible's authority.

Since the written revelation from God has been recorded under the Spirit's superintendence and is "the very breath of God," it is therefore authoritative—just as authoritative as the One who gave it. The Savior's own teaching concerning the Scriptures included not only its origination from God and its verbal inspiration but also, therefore, its absolute authority.

On one occasion Christ claimed to be God and the Jews were about to stone him. He defended himself and silenced his critics by appealing to a minute portion of the Old Testament. Two phrases in John 10:34-35 are very important to Christ's teaching on the authority of Scripture. In his question, "Is it not written in your law, 'I said ye are gods'?" Jesus ascribed his quotation from Psalm 82:6 to the law, but the psalms are not in that portion of the Jewish canon known as the law. Our Lord considered all of Scripture to be the law and therefore binding. (One should note also that Jesus based his entire argument on one word in Psalm 82:6, "gods.") The second important phrase is "the scripture cannot be broken." By this Christ meant that it is impossible for the Scripture to be annulled.[17] This passage provides clear and decisive evidence that even those passages concerning matters other than faith in Christ and relational Christian experience do possess absolute authority and therefore inviolability.

Canonicity

Each of the sixty-six books of the Bible has been recognized as inspired revelation from God, as teaching with normative authority, and therefore as canonical. Canonicity presupposes revelation, inspiration, and authority. The books of the Bible were

17. The ideas in this paragraph are taken in part from the author's *The Saviour and the Scriptures*, pp. 100-103.

inspired when they were written. When they were received as inspired, they became part of the canon, the collection of inspired writings.

The term *canon* is from the Greek *kanon*, which in turn is thought to be from the Hebrew *ganeh*, meaning a measuring rod or rule. It signifies that which measures or that which is measured by the rule or norm. In the fourth century the Greek Christians gave it a religious meaning and applied it to the Bible, especially to the Jewish books. The canon, then, is the list of biblical books regarded as inspired and accepted as authoritative for all Christians.

The Canonization of the Old Testament

The evidence clearly indicates that a fully developed canon existed in the second century B.C. That this canon was accepted and approved by Christ and the apostles in the New Testament is clear from the New Testament statements. There should be no difference of opinion among those who honor Christ and the Gospel as to what books belong in the Old Testament. There remains, however, the interesting and important question as to the principles used in antiquity, for placing certain books in the canon and excluding others.[18]

The Tests of Old Testament Canonicity. There were five tests usually applied to a book to determine whether or not it should be accepted in the canon. First, and most important, was the test of divine authorship. This is a question of inspiration. Books which were held to be inspired were revered and received, and were collected into a canon. When the question of inspiration was answered, so was the question of canonicity. The test of inspiration was wrapped up in the other tests.

Second was the test of human authorship. Here the question was, "Is the book written, edited, or endorsed by a prophet or a spokesman from God?" Prophetic authorship was the key criterion of canonicity.

Evidence is obviously not complete for all the OT books. But evidence is clear for the principles of their acceptance. Those

18. R. Laird Harris, *Inspiration and Canonicity of the Bible* (Grand Rapids: Zondervan, 1957), p. 154.

written by prophets were accepted, and kings and priests were also sometimes prophets. Any man to whom God revealed His Word was a prophet. Thus David and Solomon were prophets as truly as Joshua and Daniel. There are, of course, some books whose authorship is now not known. These were, however, classified by the Jews and by Christ as among the Prophets, and in the absence of the slightest evidence to the contrary, they may be thus accepted. God gave the Jews no test of an inspired book or list of canonical books. But He did give them very obvious and practical tests of a prophet, and it is clear that they accepted the writings of these prophets equally with their spoken words.[19]

Third, it was asked whether the book could be traced back to the time and writer from which it professed to come. Was it genuine? Fourth, the question was asked, "Is this a record of actual facts? Is it authentic?" This question related to the contents of the book and its own claims as being from God. A fifth test concerned the testimony of the Jews and later the early church councils and the ancient versions of the Bible. In other words, How was the book received?

The Threefold Division of the Old Testament Canon. The Jews of Christ's day viewed the Old Testament as divided into three parts—the Law, the Prophets, and the Writings—with a total of twenty-four books (identical to the thirty-nine books of our Old Testament). Precisely when the Jews first began to refer to their Scriptures in this way is uncertain, but Ecclesiasticus, a noncanonical book written probably in the second century B.C., so refers to them. Various reasons for these divisions have been offered to reflect degrees of inspiration, differences in content, or different stages or eras of inspiration.[20] None of these, however, agrees with Scripture itself. In keeping with the Bible's claims, evangelicals have believed that the threefold division of the Old Testament canon is related to the special position or status of the writers. But we do not know precisely why the threefold division exists or why each division contains the books it does.

19. R. Laird Harris, "Canon of Scripture—O.T.," *Wycliffe Bible Encyclopedia* (Chicago: Moody Press, 1975), p. 303.
20. See Merrill F. Unger, *Introductory Guide to the Old Testament* (Grand Rapids: Zondervan, 1951), p. 56-79, for an excellent presentation and defense of the conservative view.

The Old Testament Apocrypha. Between the time of the writing of Malachi and that of the first New Testament book, both revelation and therefore inspiration were inoperative. This period of some four hundred years is often called the four hundred silent years. It was a silent period because God did not speak as he had before. Though we do not believe any inspired documents were written during this time, other books were. A collection of a number of these came to be called the Apocrypha.

The word *apocrypha* denotes things hidden, and it was so used in classical language. The word came to mean obscure and still later was used in the sense of mysterious. Finally, the word was used of that which was spurious or not genuine. The Reformers used the term to describe the books that were not canonical.

Evangelical Protestantism acknowledges the value of the Apocryphal books from a political and literary point of view and for their reflection of the religious life of Israel between the testaments. But it rejects the Apocrypha from the canon. None of these books claims to be inspired. None is quoted in the New Testament. None was in the canon which Christ accepted. These books contain historical, geographical, and chronological errors, and they sometimes contradict the canonical books. Except for 1 and 2 Esdras and the Prayer of Manasseh, the Apocryphal books were officially acknowledged only by the Church of Rome at the Council of Trent, which was centuries after everyone else had agreed the canon was closed.

The Canonization of the New Testament

Twenty-seven books, written by eight to ten human authors over a period of about two generations, make up our New Testament. The churches and individuals to whom these books were addressed received them as the very Word of God and treasured them along with the Old Testament Scriptures. The books existed at the end of the first century A.D. throughout a territory spanning Babylon in the east and Rome in the west.

God did not see fit to preserve for us the original manuscripts, the autographs written by the New Testament writers. We may be sure that, had they been preserved, they would be worshiped by many. However, we have thousands of New Testament manuscripts and fragments dating back to within about fifty years of the originals. It is reasonable to believe that through the science of textual criticism we can determine what those autographs said.

The Collection of the Canonical Writings. Several factors gave rise to the collection of the New Testament books. The Old Testament canon paved the way for the collection of authoritative writings. People found the words of Christ and the apostles to be very precious and naturally wanted to collect and preserve them. At least one book, 1 Thessalonians, encouraged its recipients to read it during public worship (5:27). The development of canons by Marcion, the Gnostic of the second century, and others almost forced the early Christians to do the same. Finally, terrible persecutions under Roman emperors encouraged the collection.

The New Testament indicates that canonical writings were gathered. Paul encouraged it (Col. 4:16; 1 Thess. 5:27). The New Testament ascribes to its books an authority equal to that of the Old Testament. Peter placed Paul's writings on the same level as the Old Testament (2 Peter 3:15-16). Paul classified passages from both Deuteronomy and Luke as Scripture (1 Tim. 5:18).

There were three periods in the history of the canon. First was the period of separate circulation (A.D. 70-170). The early church had a concept of the canon based on the Old Testament. It also recognized Christ's authority and that of the apostles' teaching, which was first oral. The writings of the apostles were circulated and read in church gatherings. In principle, the New Testament canon was fixed during apostolic times. The extent of the canon took a bit longer, but even this was substantially complete by the end of this period.

The second period saw the complete separation between canonical and noncanonical writings (A.D. 170-303). This ended with a civil edict to burn the books of the Bible, which gave Christians added incentive to collect the canonical writings.

During the last period councils formally ratified or verified, not formulated, the canon. The Council of Laodicea (367) requested that only canonical books be read in the churches. The Third Council of Carthage (397) agreed on a list of canonical books identical to those in our Bible, a decision confirmed by the Council of Hippo (419).

The Tests of New Testament Canonicity. How did the early Christians determine whether or not a New Testament book was inspired? First, they looked at its content, and especially at its references to the person and work of Christ. Second, they considered the book's claim to inspiration and its concurrence with books already accepted. Third, they evaluated the book's moral and spiritual aspects, its ability to influence and even transform people's lives. Fourth, they asked what those closest to the writing of the book believed about it and how it was received by those to whom it was written. If the book was inspired, it passed this first group of tests.

The second matter concerned human authorship. Was the book written by an apostle or by someone closely associated with one? (Mark, for example, wrote his Gospel under the guidance of Peter; Luke was closely associated with Paul). Though not the final test, the question of apostolic authorship was very important. Apostles were those especially chosen representatives of the Lord Jesus Christ. To them he promised the Holy Spirit, who would cause them to remember and understand what Christ had taught them.

The Close of the Canon

The close of the canon is one of the most important matters regarding the Bible. There are four major reasons for believing the canon of Scripture is closed. The first reason is stated in two passages of Scripture. Jude 3 refers to "the faith which was once for all delivered to the saints," a body of truth more authoritative than one's personal belief. When Jude wrote his epistle, the only books not yet written were those of John. John then warned against adding to or taking from "the prophecy of this book" (Rev. 22:18-19). This warning applies to the Book of Revelation, the last book of the Bible and the culmination of God's recorded revelation. Therefore John's warning seems to apply to all Scripture and relates to the matter of canonicity.

As for the Old Testament canon, Christ accepted the same books received by the Jews of his day. He referred to the first and last books of the Jewish canon in one breath (Matt. 23:35; Luke 11:51), indicating his acceptance of its entirety. So this canon was clearly closed by Jesus' time.

The second reason is theological. If God desired to reveal himself completely, he would superintend the revelation's writing, preserve and collect the record, and see that it was recognized as such.

Third, the early Christians took great care in the selection of books for the canon. In some cases the final decision was not immediate, usually because of a question regarding human authorship. No serious effort has been made to add books already rejected except at the Council of Trent. Those closest to the actual writings agreed on the books in our canon, whose saving power has been attested time and again.

Fourth, there are no more prophetic or apostolic spokesmen for God. Those with these special gifts and abilities have passed from the scene.

Illumination

Illumination and interpretation are very closely related. They may be viewed as two ways, one divine and one human, to understand the recorded revelation from God. Illumination is the Holy Spirit's work by which he brings understanding and enables reception of the Scripture. It is his work of throwing light upon the Word of God so that the believer can assent to the meaning intended and act on it. Unbelievers do not experience the Spirit's illumination of Scripture. The things of the Spirit of God are spiritually discerned, and unbelievers do not have the Spirit of God (1 Cor. 2:14). True, unbelievers can and sometimes do study the Bible, even in the original languages. They often write commentaries on it. Yet apart from the Spirit's work of illumination there is no genuine assent to the Bible's true meaning or divine motivation, and no enablement to act upon it.

It is because of the spiritual depravity affecting intellect, emotion, and will caused by sin that the illumination of the Spirit is necessary. Habitual disbelief and disobedience make one insensitive to the Word of God, darkening the understanding of God's truth and creating a barrier for its reception. Paul told the believers in the church in Corinth that he could not speak to them as he would to spiritual Christians because they were acting carnally in their envy, strife, and divisions (1 Cor. 3:1-3). They were carnal in that they were not able to "accept" (2:14) and obey the plain teaching of God regarding divisiveness. By his Spirit God teaches (2:13) the unity of the body so that his own might walk in fellowship with him.

Before the Spirit began his new ministries after Christ's ascension, the Savior himself illuminated Scripture and opened the understanding and hearts of his own (Luke 24:13-35).

That the Holy Spirit of God continues the work of illumination begun by the Son is clear from Scripture. Christ himself promised the illuminating work of the Spirit. He had just reminded his own in his upper room discourse that apart from the Spirit's work of conviction, the unregenerate would never come to salvation (John 16:7-11). He then announced that the same Holy Spirit would reveal additional truth to them and enable them to remember that truth.

John assured the "little children" to whom he wrote that they were not bound to any human teacher for their understanding of God's truth. Each believer has the anointing and unction of the Holy One, the Spirit of God, to teach, lead, guide, comfort, and convict him (1 John 2:20, 27).

Interpretation

Illumination is a divine work enabling the child of God to understand and respond positively to Scripture. Interpretation is the human work of obtaining the meaning. More specifically, illumination has to do primarily with understanding the Bible while interpretation has to do with expounding it. The science of interpretation is called hermeneutics.

A number of different methods of biblical interpretation have been set forth in the history of the church.[21] Evangelicals generally agree on what it means to interpret the Bible though the question of contextualization raises some differences. They agree that each believer should be led by the Spirit of God as he interprets Scripture. However, evangelicals do not agree on a consistent method of interpretation. Generally speaking, evangelicals would define their view of hermeneutics as literal or normal, but there are differences among them regarding the extent to which that method is to be employed.

The Literal Method. "The literal interpretation as applied to any document is that view which adopts as the sense of the sentence the meaning of that sentence in usual or ordinary or normal conversation or writing."[22]

The literal meaning is best obtained by the grammatical-historical method. When the literal, normal, or plain method is employed in seeking to understand the Bible, the customary

---

21. See J. Dwight Pentecost, *Things to Come* (Findley, Ohio: Dunham Publishing Company, 1958), pp. 1-63, for an excellent survey of the interpretation of Scripture.
22. Bernard Ramm, *Protestant Biblical Interpretation* (Boston: W. A. Wilde, 1950), p. 53.

meanings of the words are understood. The literal or normal method of interpretation recognizes figures of speech, parables, etc., as figurative but looks for a literal, nonfigurative meaning.

> It is to be noted that all interpretation began with the literal interpretation of Ezra. The literal method became the basic method of rabbinism. It was the accepted method used by the New Testament in the interpretation of the Old, and it was so employed by the Lord and his apostles. This literal method was the method of the church fathers until the time of Origen when the allegorical method which had been devised to harmonize Platonic philosophy and Scripture was adopted. Augustine's influence brought this allegorizing method into the established church, and brought an end to all true exegesis. This system continued until the reformation. After the reformation the literal method of interpretation was solidly established and in spite of the attempts of the church to bring all interpretation into conformity to an adopted creed, the literal interpretation continued and became the basis on which all true exegesis rests.[23]

There are three major reasons given in support of a consistently literal hermeneutic—biblical, logical, philosophical. Of the biblical reason it has been said, "The prophecies of the Old Testament concerning the first coming of Christ—His birth, His rearing, His ministry, His death, His resurrection—were all fulfilled literally. There is no nonliteral fulfillment of these prophecies in the New Testament. This argues strongly for the literal method."[24] Concerning the logical reason, it has been argued, "if one does not use the plain, normal, or literal method of interpretation all objectivity is lost. What check would there be on the variety of interpretations which man's imagination could produce if there were not an objective standard which the literal principle provides?"[25] And, "philosophically the purpose of language itself seems to require a literal interpretation. Language was given by God for the purpose of being able to communicate with man."[26]

23. Pentecost, *Things to Come*, pp. 32-33.
24. J. P. Lange, *Commentary on the Holy Scripture: Revelation* (New York: Scribner's, 1872), p. 98.
25. Charles C. Ryrie, *Dispensationalism Today* (Chicago: Moody Press, 1965), p. 88.
26. Ibid., pp. 87-88.

Some of the more important advantages of the literal method over the spiritual or allegorical method are cited by Ramm: "(a) It guards interpretation. . . . (b) It exercises a control over interpretation that experimentation does for the scientific method. . . . (c) It has the greatest success in opening up the Word of God. Exegesis did not start in earnest until the church was a millennium and one-half old. With the literalism of Luther and Calvin the light of Scripture literally flamed up."[27]

The literal method of interpretation can be abused. Its most zealous advocates sometimes carry it to extremes and argue for ridiculous interpretations. They often overstate the case for a literal hermeneutic. All too often they stress the letter of Scripture to the point that the true meaning is lost. They frequently imply that those who do not use the literal method consistently throughout the Bible cannot possibly be evangelical, which simply is not true.

Those who do not believe the literal method is to be used consistently in interpreting the Bible sometimes misrepresent the view. The literal method is said to involve "crass literalism" if applied to all of Scripture. The critics of the literal method see it leading to ridiculous ends and sometimes accuse the literalists of not allowing for types, symbols, or even figures of speech in the Bible. This is a false charge.

The Spiritualizing or Allegorizing Method. "Allegorism is the method of interpreting a literary text that regards a literal sense as the vehicle for a secondary, more spiritual, and more profound sense."[28]

There are at least three serious dangers in the use of the allegorical method of interpretation. Pentecost has succinctly stated these: "(1) The first great danger of the allegorical method is that it does not interpret Scripture. . . . (2) The basic authority and interpretation ceases to be the Scriptures, but the mind of the interpreter. . . . (3) A third great danger in the allegorical method is that one is left without any means by which the conclusions of the interpreter may be tested."[29]

27. Ramm, *Protestant Biblical Interpretation,* pp. 62-63.
28. Ibid., p. 4.
29. Pentecost, *Things to Come,* pp. 5-6.

Evangelicals do not use the allegorical method in interpreting the Bible's teaching on the great essentials of the faith. Most generally it is used in some areas of the doctrine of last things.[30]

The Major Area of Difference Among Evangelicals

In the area of bibliology there is one major area of difference among those labeled evangelicals. It concerns the extent of the Bible's inspiration. Undoubtedly the theological battlefield today is the Bible. Strangely, the battle is not being fought, as it once was, by evangelicals who embrace all the essentials of the historic Christian faith, including its full inerrancy, on one side and nonevangelicals on the other, though some aspects of that old battle continue. Instead, today there is a conflict within the camp of those who lay claim to the label *evangelical*. Some believe the Bible in its original documents is free from all error and omission—the total inerrancy of Scripture. I heartily agree with this position. Others, who also view themselves as evangelical, believe there are errors in the Bible. They claim the errors are not in matters relating to the Bible's central theme, but only in the peripheral areas.[31]

An Inspired but Errant Bible

Today a number of evangelicals insist on distinguishing between the inspiration and the inerrancy of Scripture. They do not object to saying the Bible is inspired, but refuse to believe it is inerrant, at least not totally inerrant. They believe it is capable of error and in fact does err in some of its detail. They sometimes use the word *inerrant* but omit modifiers such as *totally* or *completely*. Instead they often use words that may be somewhat misleading because they are invested with new meanings.

Clark Pinnock, who argues for "modified inerrancy," asks seven questions of those who embrace total inerrancy:

---

30. See O. T. Allis, *Prophecy and the Church* (Philadelphia: Presbyterian and Reformed Publishing Company, 1945), pp. 17-18, for objections to a consistently literal approach.

31. For a discussion of this view by those who embrace it, see Jack Rogers, ed., *Biblical Authority* (Waco, Tex.: Word Books, 1977). For a critique from those who oppose it, see Geisler, ed., *Inerrancy*; Harold Lindsell, *The Battle for the Bible* and *The Bible in the Balance* (Grand Rapids: Zondervan, 1979).

Question One:	Is inerrancy scriptural?
Question Two:	Is inerrancy a logical corollary of inspiration?
Question Three:	Is inerrancy meaningful?
Question Four:	Is inerrancy an epistomological necessity?
Question Five:	Is inerrancy theologically decisive?
Question Six:	Is inerrancy critically honest?
Question Seven:	Ought inerrancy to be the test of evangelical authenticity?[32]

To all seven of these questions Pinnock's answer is "no."

Adherents to the inspired but errant view refer to peripheral matters in Scripture in contrast to matters related to faith and life that are believed central to the Bible's major theme. So-called peripheral matters are not considered inerrant, while the matters of faith and life are. Errors in history, geography, or physical science are present in the Bible, it is claimed. These are called "inconsequential errors." A distinction is made between revelational and nonrevelational matters in Scripture as well.

Those who believe in total inerrancy are said to be guilty of "an excessive veneration and overbelief about the Bible." Emphasis must be placed on the saving truth of the Bible, not the minor details, Christians are told. The Bible is to be viewed as a source of spiritual strength, not a battlefield over details. In this view the Bible contains some truth and some error. This means it cannot always be relied on. To be sure, there is more truth than error in the Bible, we are told, but error is present nevertheless.

Why do some who still wish to be called evangelicals believe the original autographs of the Bible contained errors? Pinnock gives this answer:

> It has happened as a result of the *collision* between the traditional belief in the infallibility of the Bible and the critical perspective on the Scriptures nurtured in the enlightenment which saw in it only a record of man's imperfect spiritual and moral evolution. . . . The result has been an unsettling ferment in which Christians have been forced to ask after the sense in which the Bible is the Word of God.[33]

32. Clark Pinnock, "Three Views of the Bible in Contemporary Theology," in *Biblical Authority*, ed. Jack Rogers, pp. 63-68.
33. Ibid., p. 49.

The same writer joins with others who seek to explain the reasons for the current debate when he stresses that we must give as much attention to the human side of the Bible as to the divine. Allowing for and admitting to some errors in the Bible does justice to the human side, the argument goes.

The inspired but errant view of the Bible among evangelicals is the result of looking at the difficult problem areas in Scripture, which are seen as evidences that the Bible cannot be totally inerrant. Even the claims of the Bible for itself and our Lord's view of it are adjusted to fit the view that is based on looking at the problems. To the contrary, those who hold to a totally inerrant Bible begin theologically by basing their conclusions on the claims the Bible makes for itself and then seek honestly to wrestle with the problems and find solutions in harmony with this testimony.[34]

Why Believe in a Totally Inerrant Bible?

God cannot lie. For him to do so would be a flagrant violation of his holy and sinless character. God has spoken in his Word about his Word. Many, many times he claims it as his own. One's view of the Bible ought surely to be harmonious with what the One who has given it has said about it. To reject what he has said about his Word seems to accuse him of falsehood. Does not rejection of what he says in his Word about his Word impugn his character? God's own veracity is at stake. A book with errors in it could hardly be God's revelation, be God-breathed. Such a book cannot be divinely authoritative and fully trustworthy.

The belief in an errant but inspired Bible is difficult to defend. An errant yet God-breathed Bible is a meaningless designation. How can a book which claims to be the Word of God be divine and erroneous at the same time? An errant Bible which claims to be God's Word is philosophically indefensible. To deny total inerrancy is to show sympathy for and surrender to the philosophy of relativism, which says absolute truth cannot be communicated in the phenomenal world.

---

34. For an example of how those who believe in the total inerrancy of Scripture handle problems, see Gleason Archer's excellent article in *Inerrancy*, ed. Geisler, pp. 57-82.

Biblical Reasons for Total Inerrancy[35]

In a very real sense every scriptural argument for inspiration is at the same time an argument for its inerrancy. Literally hundreds of times the Bible claims to come from God. Also, nowhere in the Bible does one portion criticize another portion or accuse another portion of being in error.

Two familiar texts which claim inspiration for the Bible are 2 Timothy 3:16-17 and 2 Peter 1:19, 21. These and many other passages (e.g., Matt. 5:17-18; John 10:33-36; 1 Tim. 5:18; 2 Peter 3:16) have often been ably expounded.[36]

The Teaching of Christ Concerning the Old Testament.[37] Christ accepted and taught a high view of the Word of God in existence in his day. His very use of the Word and his firm conviction that behind the human writers God was the ultimate author reveal his estimate of it. Though some question Christ's knowledge and some even his integrity, it is a generally accepted fact that he had the highest esteem for the Scriptures, including their historical detail.

Christ said, "Think not that I am come to destroy the law, or the prophets. I am not come to destroy, but to fulfill" (Matt. 5:17). The Savior could not have employed stronger words to declare his view; the law and the prophets was one way of referring to the entire Old Testament in his day. That Christ accepted the inspiration of the whole Old Testament is proven also by his reference to the threefold division of his day. He declared that all things must be fulfilled which are written of him "in the law of Moses, and the prophets and the psalms" (Luke 24:44).

Christ's references to the threefold division of the Old Testament not only reveal his attitude toward the entire body of Scripture but also make clear his confidence in the inspiration of each of the parts. For him the law, the prophets, and the psalms or writings were all inspired. He referred to the laws of the

---

35. An excellent evaluation of this line of argument is in John H. Gerstner, *A Bible Inerrancy Primer* (Grand Rapids: Baker, 1965).

36. See e.g., Warfield, *The Inspiration and Authority of the Bible*; Harris, *Inspiration and Canonicity of the Bible*; Young, *Thy Word Is Truth*; Rene Pache, *The Inspiration and Authority of Scripture* (Chicago: Moody Press, 1969).

37. This section taken in part from *The Saviour and the Scriptures*, pp. 60-69. I recommend also John W. Wenham's article in *Inerrancy*, ed. Geisler, pp. 3-8.

Pentateuch as commandments of God as opposed to the traditions of men (Mark 7:8-9). The "it is written" of Matthew 4:4, 7, 10, certainly placed Christ's unshakable confidence in the portion of Deuteronomy he quoted. Every reference of Christ to the Scripture as that which must be fulfilled is evidence of the fact that he believed in the complete truth of the passages referred to.

Christ not only accepted the entire Old Testament as that which was breathed out by God, but he also insisted on the very words of Scripture. Frequently the weight of his argument rested on one or two words quoted from the Old Testament. If that word or those words did not have the authority which he claimed for them, his arguments would have been fruitless and would certainly have been recognized as such by his critics who knew the Scriptures so well (see Matt. 22:23-33, 43, 45).

The Savior went one step further by teaching the inspiration of the letters and smallest details of the words. Evidence for this appears clearly in two carefully worded statements of the Lord. Just prior to his sermon on the mount he said, "For verily I say unto you, till heaven and earth pass, one jot or one tittle shall in no wise pass from the law, till all be fulfilled" (Matt. 5:18; cf. Luke 16:17). The determining words of these passages are *jot* and *tittle*. The jot, it is believed, was a reference to the Hebrew yodh ('), which is the smallest letter of the Hebrew alphabet—taking up about as much space as an apostrophe.

The tittle is not as easily identified. It most likely means the little lines or projections that differentiate certain Hebrew letters which in other respects are similar. It is not an entire letter, only a portion of a letter. To alter one small jot, one small point or tittle, might change the meaning of the word. It is thus abundantly clear from Christ's teaching that the minutest part of the law as originally written must be accomplished. He affirmed the inerrancy of the specific historical points taught.

If the Savior was teaching anything at all by the words *jot* and *tittle*, he was teaching that the most minute portions of the Old Testament as originally written, the very markings that gave meaning to words of Scripture, would not fail of fulfillment because they came from God and were thus without error. This exalted view of Scripture is the Bible's testimony to itself (e.g., 1 Cor. 2:13; Gal. 3:16).

In summary, Christ not only accepted the whole Old Testament as the inspired Word of God, but he also viewed the individual parts and words as the very words of God and therefore free from error, bearing the authority of the God who gave them. Dozens of times Christ referred to historical narratives in the Old Testament and always treated them as records of fact.

In his *The Authority of the Bible*, John R. W. Stott bases his view of Scripture's authority and therefore trustworthiness primarily on Christ's teaching regarding Scripture. As far as Stott is concerned, Jesus believed and taught that what Scripture said, God said. One's view of the Bible depends on his loyalty to Christ, Stott insists. He raises a most important question in this regard, and provides the only possible answers:

> How then can we, the disciples of Jesus, possibly have a lower view of Scripture than our Teacher himself had? . . .
>
> There are only two possible escape routes from this obligation. The first is to say that Jesus did not know what he was talking about, that the incarnation imprisoned him in the limited mentality of a first-century Palestinian Jew, and that consequently he believed the Old Testament as they did, but that he, like them, was mistaken. The second is to say that Jesus did know what he was talking about, that he actually knew Scripture to be unreliable, but that he still affirmed its reliability because his contemporaries did and he did not want to upset them. According to the first explanation, Jesus' erroneous teaching was involuntary (he could not help it); according to the second it was deliberate. These theories portray Jesus as either deceived or a deceiver. They discredit the incarnate Son of God. They are incompatible both with his claims to speak what he knew (Jn. 3:11), to bear witness to the truth and to be the truth (Jn. 18:37; 14:6), and with his known hatred of all hypocrisy and deceit. They are totally unacceptable to anybody who has been led by the Holy Spirit to say "Jesus is Lord" (I Cor. 12:3). Over against these slanderous speculations we must continue to affirm that Jesus knew what he was teaching, that he meant it, and that what he taught and meant is true.[38]

The Teaching of Christ Concerning the New Testament.[39] Christ stands between the Old and New Testaments. He placed his divine approval upon every jot and tittle of the Old Testament. Likewise, in anticipation, he guaranteed the same inspiration for

---

38. John R. W. Stott, *The Authority of the Bible* (Downers Grove, Ill.: Inter-Varsity Press, 1976), pp. 16-17.
39. This section taken in part from *The Saviour and the Scriptures*, pp. 70-73.

the New Testament by his promise of the Holy Spirit. He looked back upon that which was already written as the inspired Word of God. He looked ahead and assured the writers of the New Testament of that same divine superintendence of the Holy Spirit, thus guaranteeing inerrancy to the Scripture they would write (John 14:26; 15:26-27).

Ample evidence for the teaching and guiding work of the Holy Spirit as promised by Christ is given by the New Testament writers themselves (1 Cor. 2:9-12; Rev. 1:1-2). Not only did the writers of the New Testament claim the authority of God for their own writings, they also claimed the authority for the writings of their peers (1 Tim. 5:18; 2 Tim. 3:16).

The Bible and the Believer

To believe the Bible is God's Word is one thing. To live according to its precepts is another. If we are consistent, the moment we confess that we believe the Bible to be God's inerrant revelation to us, we have placed ourselves under its divine authority and are therefore obligated to obey its normative commandments. Since the authority of Scripture is based on the authority of the God who gave it, we have also confessed our allegiance to him. How should we then live?

Just as we base our beliefs on what the Bible teaches, so we should shape our behavior according to what it teaches for our times. That is how we should live as the people of God according to Scripture.

Acceptance of the Bible as God's Word, and even a thorough knowledge of it, does not automatically mean a godly life will follow. God's Word must be appropriated personally as the Spirit illuminates it for the believer. Its precepts must be obeyed and its truth lived before it will have its intended effect in our lives. To live according to Scripture one must know what it teaches. But knowing what it teaches is not the same as living in harmony with, or yielding to, the Holy Spirit's teaching in it.

Questions for Discussion

1. What is the primary reason for believing the Bible is God's Word?
2. How would you distinguish between revelation, inspiration, authority, canonicity, illumination, and interpretation?
3. Why do evangelical Protestants not accept the Old Testament Apocrypha as God's Word?
4. How do illumination and interpretation relate to each other?
5. Why should the literal method of interpretation be followed?

Suggestions for Further Reading

Geisler, Norman L., ed. *Inerrancy*. Grand Rapids: Zondervan, 1979.

Haley, John W. *An Examination of Alleged Discrepancies of the Bible*. Nashville: Gospel Advocate Company, 1967.

Lightner, Robert P. *The Saviour and the Scriptures*. Grand Rapids: Baker Book House, 1978.

Lindsell, Harold. *The Battle for the Bible*. Grand Rapids: Zondervan, 1976.

_____. *The Bible in the Balance*. Grand Rapids: Zondervan, 1979.

Pache, Rene. *The Inspiration and Authority of Scripture*. Chicago: Moody Press, 1969.

Packer, J. I. *Fundamentalism and the Word of God*. Grand Rapids: Eerdmans, 1960.

Rogers, Jack, ed. *Biblical Authority*. Waco, Tex.: Word Books, 1977.

Sproul, R. C. *Explaining Inerrancy: A Commentary*. Oakland, Calif.: International Council on Biblical Inerrancy, 1980.

Warfield, Benjamin B. *The Inspiration and Authority of the Bible*. Philadelphia: Presbyterian and Reformed Publishing Company, 1948.

Young, Edward J. *Thy Word Is Truth*. Grand Rapids: Eerdmans, 1957.

2

God the Father

By beginning our study with God's Word, we have recognized the true source of evangelical theology. Next, in harmony with the theocentric nature of evangelical theology, we proceed to the doctrines of God the Father, God the Son, and God the Holy Spirit.

There is no greater or more important knowledge than that of God himself. Every Christian doctrine has its foundation in the doctrine of God—his reality and his work. All the other great truths of Scripture can be understood properly only as they are seen in relation to the person and work of the God of the Bible.

Knowledge of God is most practical and relevant to life. Truly it is a self-imposed cruelty to try to live this life without knowing God. "Disregard the study of God, and you sentence yourself to stumble and blunder through life blindfolded, as it were, with no sense of direction and no understanding of what surrounds you."[1]

Only through a knowledge of God can a person enter into eternal life, according to Christ's own statement (John 17:3). Knowing God enables man to know himself (Isa. 6:5). When we know God, we have a better knowledge of the world itself. Knowledge of God is also absolutely essential to personal holiness (Jer. 9:23-24). Only through a knowledge of God can the people of God be strong (Dan. 11:32).[2]

1. J. I. Packer, *Knowing God* (Downers Grove, Ill.: Inter-Varsity Press, 1973), pp. 14-15.
2. James Montgomery Boice, *The Sovereign God* (Downers Grove, Ill.: Inter-Varsity Press, 1978), pp. 21-24.

Knowledge of facts about God and knowing God himself are, of course, two different things. It is possible to be thoroughly familiar with facts and yet have little or no personal relationship with God.

Separate discussion of each member of the Godhead will be given in this volume because of the wealth of information the Bible provides on each. While it is common to find individual studies of the second and third members from the conservative viewpoint, rarely is the first person given separate consideration. The present approach is taken with the hope that the reader will know God the Father better.

A Historical Perspective

For the first two or three centuries after the death of the apostles Christian literature was mostly of a devotional nature. Prior to Augustine (354-430), one of the earliest and greatest postapostolic theologians, most attention was given to encouraging believers in their faith and stimulating their growth in Christ. Actually, it was not until doctrinal error and heresy arose that the need for theological formulations was seen. Systematic theology arose and developed in response to deviations and departures from the plain statements of Scripture. With the continuing opposition to God's truth its importance has been obvious ever since. At first there were few attempts to harmonize portions of Scripture that appeared to be in conflict. A striking exception was in the trinitarian controversy (170-325), when the need for theological specifics and formulations was forced upon the fathers.

A brief overview of major contributions to the doctrine of God the Father made by key figures in important periods of the church's history follows. Though these writers did not always specify God the Father as the subject of their discussion, yet it is apparent they often had the first member of the Godhead in mind.

The Postapostolic Fathers

The postapostolic fathers were early Christian writers who were the immediate successors of the apostles. They labored in the years 90 to 140. Some of these men may well have been students of the apostles.

The literature of this early period gives overwhelming evidence of belief in one God (monotheism), as opposed to the heathen belief in many gods (polytheism). The Shepherd of Hermas, for example, begins with a clear statement of the singularity of God who created all things and who is able to comprehend all things even though he himself is incomprehensible.

These writers also give evidence of belief in a trinitarian relationship in the Godhead. To be sure, they did not elaborate on the relation each member sustained to the other members. Yet Clement of Rome in his First Letter does speak of God, the Lord Jesus Christ, and the Holy Spirit as being distinct persons.

The Second-Century Apologists

In the second century writers placed special emphasis on defending the Christian faith against the inroads of Judaism, Gnosticism, and heathenism in general. Some outstanding men among them were Aristides, Justin Martyr, Tatian, and Athenagoras. Without doubt, Justin Martyr is the most famous. The apologies these men wrote were addressed primarily to the rulers but also to the intelligent public. They were indeed apologies and not doctrinal treatises.

The apologists emphasized that God is one. They viewed him as self-existent, unchangeable, and eternal in his being. He was the creator and preserver of the world, entirely unique in his person. They spoke of God as "invisible," "unbegotten," and "incomprehensible."[3]

The Anti-Gnostic Fathers

Most of what we know about Gnosticism we have learned from the church fathers who wrote to oppose this second-century development. Gnosticism sought to form an alliance between the pagan religions and Christianity. Its primary teaching centered in

3. Justin, *Apology* 1. 10, 13, 25, 49, 53; 2. 6; *Dialogue* 127.

philosophical dualism, claiming that there were two original gods
or principles which opposed each other.

Berkhof gives this excellent summary of the Gnostic teaching,
especially with reference to God:

> The supreme or good God is an unfathomable abyss. He
> interposes between himself and finite creatures a long chain of
> aeons or middle beings, emanations from the divine, which
> together constitute the Pleroma or fullness of the divine essence. It
> is only through these intermediate beings that the highest God can
> enter into various relations with created beings. The world is not
> created by the good God, but is the result of, probably, a fall in the
> Pleroma, and is the work of a subordinate, possibly a hostile, deity.
> This subordinate god is called the Demiurge, is identified with the
> God of the Old Testament, and is described as an inferior, limited,
> passionate, and vengeful being. He is contrasted with the supreme
> God, the source of goodness, virtue, and truth, who revealed
> himself in Christ.[4]

To the anti-Gnostic fathers the Gnostic separation between the
true God and the Creator, or the Spirit God and the God of the
Old Testament, was unthinkable. The view was blasphemous and
arose in the devil himself, they believed. In contrast, the anti-
Gnostic fathers believed in one God who was not only the Creator
but also the Redeemer. The law was given by him, and so was the
gospel. This God was one in essence but three in subsistence.

Two of the most outstanding anti-Gnostic fathers were Irenaeus
(ca. 130-202) and Tertullian (ca. 160-220). The latter was the first to
write of the tripersonality of God and to use the term *trinity* with
reference to God.

Irenaeus in his *Against Heresies* presented this clear statement
about God the Father:

> He only is God who made all things. He alone is omnipotent. He
> only is Father who made and created all things, visible and
> invisible, objects of sense and objects of understanding, things in
> heaven and things in earth by the Word of His Power. He adapted
> and arranged all things by His wisdom. He contains all things and
> is contained of none. He is Creator, Maker, and Fashioner. He is
> the Moulder and Lord of all. And neither is there anything above

4. Louis Berkhof, *The History of Christian Doctrines* (Grand Rapids: Baker, 1959), p. 52.

or beside Him . . . But there is only one God, the Creator. He is above every principality and power and dominion and virtue. He is Father, He is God, He is Founder and Maker and Builder. He made all these things by Himself, that is, by His Word and His Wisdom. He formed men, He planted Paradise. He made the world, He sent the flood, He saved Noah. He is the God of the living, whom the Law proclaims, the prophets preach, and Christ reveals; whom the Apostles announce, and in whom the Church believes. He is the Father of our Lord Jesus Christ, through His Word who is His Son.[5]

In a similar work, entitled *The Prescriptions Against Heretics,* Tertullian wrote:

The Rule of Faith [apostolic tradition; creed]—to state here and now what we maintain—is of course that by which we believe that there is but one God, who is none other than the Creator of the world, who produced everything from nothing through his Word, sent forth before all things; that this Word is called his Son, and in the Name of God was seen in divers ways by the patriarchs, was ever heard in the prophets and finally was brought down by the Spirit and Power of God the Father into the Virgin Mary, was made flesh in her womb, was born of her and lived as Jesus Christ.[6]

The Alexandrian Fathers

The Alexandrian fathers, especially Clement of Alexandria (ca. 150-213) and Origen (ca. 185-254), sought to glean the good from Gnostic teaching in their formulation of the church's faith. They represented the speculative theology of the East. The contrast between them and such writers as Irenaeus and Tertullian was largely due to their allegorical interpretation of the Bible.

Clement's *Stromata* has a revealing section on his view of God the Father:

This discourse respecting God is most difficult to handle. For since the first principle of everything is difficult to find out, the absolute

5. Cited by Hugh T. Kerr, ed., *Readings in Christian Thought* (Nashville: Abingdon Press, 1966), p. 32.
6. Cited ibid., p. 40.

first and oldest principle, which is the cause of all other things being and having been, is difficult to exhibit. For how can that be expressed which is neither genus, nor difference, nor species, nor individual, nor number; nay more, is neither an event, nor that to which an event happens? No one can rightly express him wholly. For on account of his greatness he is ranked as the All, and is the Father of the universe. Nor are there any parts to be predicated of him. For the One is indivisible; wherefore also it is infinite, not considered with reference to inscrutability, but with reference to its being without dimensions, and not having a limit. And therefore it is without form and name. And if we name it, we do not do so properly, terming it either the One, or the Good, or Mind, or Absolute Being, or Father, or God, or Creator, or Lord. We speak not as supplying his name; but for want, we use good names, in order that the mind may have these as points of support, so as not to err in other respects. For each one by itself does not express God; but all together are indicative of the power of the Omnipotent.[7]

Origen believed God is primarily the personal Father who has revealed himself and his works through the Logos. Berkhof said of Origen:

Like the Apologetes, Origen speaks of God in absolute terms, as the incomprehensible, inestimable, and impossible One, who is beyond want of anything; and like the Anti-Gnostic Fathers, he rejects the Gnostic distinction between the good God and the Demiurge or Creator of the world. God is One, the same in the Old and in the New Testaments. He ascribes absolute causality to God, and since he can conceive of such attributes as omnipotence and justice only as eternally in action, he teaches the doctrine of eternal creation.[8]

Monarchianism

As Gnosticism was the heresy of the second century, so monarchianism was the heresy of the third. The doctrine of Christ the Logos as a separate, fully divine person distinct from the

---

7. Cited by Robert L. Ferm, *Readings in the History of Christian Thought* (New York: Holt, Rinehart, and Winston, 1964), pp.15-16.
8. Berkhof, *History of Christian Doctrines*, pp. 75-76

Father and the Spirit was viewed as endangering the unity of God by some. On the other hand, viewing the Logos as in some sense subordinate to the Father compromised his deity. The attempt was made to maintain the sole government of God and at the same time retain belief in the full deity of Christ. Two different schools of thought arose to which Tertullian applied the name monarchianism. Dynamic monarchianism was concerned primarily with stressing God's unity and oneness; Paul of Samosata, bishop of Antioch, was its most noted representative. Modalistic monarchianism was more influential; it laid more stress on the christological side of the issue, though the unity of God was still a point of interest. The three persons of the Godhead were conceived as three different modes of existence in which God manifested himself. Sabellius was the chief spokesman for modalistic monarchianism.

The Trinitarian Controversy

The background of the trinitarian controversy lies in the monarchian debate and its aftermath.

Arius, a presbyter of Alexandria, set forth antitrinitarian views. He believed Christ was of another substance from the Father. The Logos had a beginning at a point in time, having been created out of nothing before the world came into being.

Athanasius, archdeacon of Alexandria, opposed Arius and Arianism. He championed the unity of God and insisted on the basis of Scripture that the Son was of the same divine essence as the Father.

In 325 the Council of Nicaea convened to settle the dispute. Finally, after considerable discussion from both sides and the presentation of a compromise position by Eusebius of Caesarea, Emperor Constantine threw his weight on the side of Athanasius. The final statement regarding the Father and the Son was: "We believe in one God, the Father Almighty, Maker of things visible and invisible. And in one Lord Jesus Christ, begotten not made, being of one substance [*homoousios*] with the Father." As might be expected, the council's decision did not end the controversy. In point of fact, it still rages today.

In his *De Trinitate* Augustine spoke for the Western branch of the church. He stressed the unity of essence and, at the same time, the trinity of persons. Each person, he said, possesses the entire essence. Other Latin theologians, such as Roscelinus and Gilbert of Poiters, erred either on the side of God's unity or of his tripersonality.

In his *Institutes* Calvin discussed the doctrine of the Trinity at some length. In essence he defended the view set forth at Nicaea and held by the early church. At first he avoided using the terms *person* and *trinity*; later he not only employed them but was critical of those who did not.

The Socinians of the sixteenth century rejected the doctrine of the Trinity because it was contrary to reason. Their views paved the way for Unitarianism and liberal theology, both of which reject the biblical doctrine of the Trinity.

A Positive Statement of the Doctrine

The Reality of God: Philosophical Arguments

Thomas Aquinas (1225-1274) was perhaps the first to set forth what has come to be known as the theistic arguments from nature for God's existence. They start with observable evidence and infer that an adequate cause must exist and must be wise, good, and powerful.

Not all agree on the value of these arguments. For some they provide strong evidence of God's existence. Others within evangelicalism do not place as much confidence in them. Certainly it must be acknowledged that these arguments for the existence of God fall short of logical proof. Yet they do demonstrate the reasonableness of the reality of God. They do raise questions for the skeptic and the denier which demand an answer.

Evidence from the World's Existence. The Greek word for world is *kosmos*, and so this line of reasoning has been called the cosmological argument. Behind it is the basic rule that every effect must have an adequate cause. Viewed as an effect, the world, so the argument goes, must have a cause sufficient to have produced it.

The argument raises questions of where and how and why. Where did the world itself come from, and all the creatures in it? This is the question of ultimate origins. How did the world and its inhabitants come to be? Can existence come from nonexistence?

The cosmological argument insists that the world we live in demands a first cause, a first mover that was great enough to have brought it into existence. The example of the watch and the watchmaker is often used to illustrate the point. The world is here, and reason insists there must have been a world-maker.

The evidence from the world demands a verdict. Evangelical theists believe the only satisfactory explanation is that the God of the Bible brought the world into existence by the word of his power. They believe this because they do not believe in the eternality of matter or the evolutionary hypothesis.

Evidence from the World's Order. This evidence builds upon that presented above and has been referred to as the teleological argument from the Greek *telos*, meaning end or goal. It looks at the purpose in the world and infers that the first cause demanded by the cosmological argument must have been an intelligent being. There is so much order and design in our world. How can this be accounted for apart from a wise and purposeful Creator? The world is filled with evidence of design and order, of complexity and precision. This observed order requires an adequate cause. Therefore, the world was brought into existence by a first cause who was wise beyond description.

Evidence from Personal Existence. The very ones who deny the existence of the personal God of the Bible are the first to admit that man has the ability to think, to determine, to make judgments, and to feel. These are evidences of personality, of intellect and emotion, and form the evidence for the anthropological argument. How can personal existence arise from some lifeless, impersonal source? Evangelicals argue from man as a personal intelligent being to an adequate cause, a first cause who is personal.

Evidence from Man's Idea of a Supreme Being. This causal argument observes that all men everywhere hold the idea of a most perfect Being. Such an idea requires an adequate cause. If this Being does not exist, it is asked, where has this idea come from? The idea could not have arisen with man himself, since he normally does not lay claim to perfection. The universe also contains many imperfections and therefore could not have produced this idea of a perfect Being. Only a perfect Being could have originated such an idea of perfection, and that Being is God.

The Reality of God: Biblical Arguments

God's Revelation of Himself in His Word. The existence of God is usually assumed in Scripture. Nowhere in the Bible are there set forth deductive arguments for God's existence, though he is presented to unbelievers as the only living and true God. Holy Writ begins with the great, grand assertion that he is (Gen. 1:1). In the New Testament the message is similar; those who would come to God "must believe that he is" (Heb. 11:6).

However, when it comes to believing in God, to exercising faith in him, we are not called upon to disregard reason. It is by means of reason that we understand the revelation of himself God has given us in the Bible. Reason is indeed a gift from God, but faith must be distinguished from presumption here. We do not simply presume God is. Instead, we accept as true what he has said about himself in his Word. Faith in God is exercised when we receive as true the scriptural testimony he has given us.

Warfield's pointed statement about the concept of God in the Old Testament applies equally to the New Testament:

> The Old Testament did not occupy itself with how Israel thought of God. Its concern is with how Israel ought to think of God. To it, the existence of God is not an open question; nor his nature, nor the accessibility of knowledge of him. God himself has taken care of that. He has made himself known to his people, and their business is not to feel after him if haply they may fumblingly find him, but to hearken to him as he declares to them what and who he is. The fundamental note of the Old Testament in other words is revelation. Its seers and prophets are not men of philosophic minds who have risen from the seen to the unseen and, by dint of much reflection, have gradually attained to elevated conceptions of him who is the author of all that is. They are men of God whom God has chosen, that he might speak to them and through them to his people. Israel has not in and by them created for itself a God. God has through them created himself a people.[9]

Much, perhaps most, of the Bible was addressed to believers, who normally need no defense of Christianity's truth claims. But because there are times when the faith of even the faithful is

9. Benjamin B. Warfield, *Selected Shorter Writings of Benjamin B. Warfield*—I, ed. John E. Meeter (Nutley, N.J.: Presbyterian and Reformed Publishing Company, 1970), pp. 69-70.

shaken, Scripture sometimes supports with evidence what it usually assumes: God does exist. When addressing unbelievers, Scripture also may provide evidence. One example was Moses' encounter with Pharaoh.

> In response to Moses' plea to release the Jews from Egyptian slavery, Pharaoh said, "I do not know the Lord" (Ex. 5:2). The ruler was not asked to assume God's existence, but was given the "signs" of the plagues. Their intensity increased until the oldest son in each family died. After letting the Israelites go, Pharaoh changed his mind and pursued them. Fleeing in the wilderness the Israelites complained against Moses in unbelief. Then God promised deliverance through the Red Sea. The purpose of that additional sign was that "the Egyptians shall know that I am the Lord, when I am honored through Pharaoh, through his chariots and his horsemen" (Ex. 14:18). After that remarkable deliverance, not only the surviving Egyptians were convinced, but so were the Israelites. When they "saw the great power which the Lord had used against the Egyptians, the people feared the Lord; and they believed in the Lord and in his servant Moses" (Ex. 14:31).[10]

God's Revelation of Himself in His World. Evangelicals are not in total agreement on how to interpret God's revelation in the world, which they often refer to as natural or general revelation. But all acknowledge that in several clear scriptural statements God has spoken of the revelation of Himself in nature (Ps. 19; Rom. 1; Acts 14:15-17; 17:22-34). In his Word, God has told us about the revelation of himself in his world.

God's revelation in the world extends to all, even though all do not receive it as the Giver intended. Some distort it and worship the creature rather than the Creator (see Rom. 1-2). Some of God's people, such as David, saw in it much more (Ps. 19).

The apostle Paul also believed in the universal scope of God's revelation of himself in the things he had made (Acts 14:15-17). He argued that God's eternal power and Godhead were understood by the things that he made and that this revelation of himself in nature made all men without excuse before him (Rom. 1:20). This was true, he insisted, even for those "who hold the truth in unrighteousness" and do not glorify God as God (Rom. 1:18, 21).

10. Gordon R. Lewis, *Testing Christianity's Truth Claims* (Chicago: Moody Press, 1976), pp. 27-28.

David saw in God's world his glory and handiwork (Ps. 19:1). In describing what he saw, he used the name *Elohim* for God, the same name Moses used the first time God is spoken of in the Bible (Gen. 1:1). The name speaks of God's eternal power and might. Both day and night spoke to David about God as did the orderliness of the stars and the moon in their courses (Ps. 19:3-4). These gave forth a continuous message throughout the whole world.

> Several facts stand out with prominence concerning man and God's revelation in the world. *First,* it is important to remember that all men everywhere do have some knowledge of God for which they are responsible. *Second,* as has already been pointed out, God declares in the Written Word that His revelation of Himself in nature makes man "without excuse" (Rom. 1:20). *Third,* all men are lost, even though God has made Himself known to all. *Fourth,* the knowledge of God from general or natural revelation is insufficient in itself for salvation since it does not reveal man's lost condition and Christ's substitutionary atonement. However, God's revelation in nature corresponds perfectly with His revelation in the Written Word, and the questions which natural revelation raises are answered in the Bible, God's special revelation. *Fifth,* man in his unregenerate state often distorts the revelation and fails to live up to the knowledge or light which he has (cf. Rom. 1-3). *Sixth,* the reality of God's revelation in nature can be used as a beginning point in witnessing to the unsaved (cf. Acts 17:15-34 where Paul did just that).[11]

God's Revelation of Himself in His Son. The supreme and final revelation of God to man was in the person of his Son. Before Christ came into the world, no one had ever seen God in all his fullness. Christ the only begotten Son was both the revelation and the revealer of God (John 1:18).

> Christ revealed the *Person* of God as He had never been made known before. He declared the Father to man (cf. John 1:18; 14:8, 9; I Tim. 3:16). The *glory* of God was made known by Christ (John 1:14; II Cor. 4:6; Isa. 40:5). God's *power* was revealed by God's Son. He did this many times and in many different ways (John 3:2;

---

11. Robert P. Lightner, *The God of the Bible* (Grand Rapids: Baker Book House, 1978), p. 23.

I Cor. 1:24). The *wisdom* of God was made known in the Person of Christ (John 7:42; I Cor. 1:24). The *life* of God was also declared by Him (I John 1:1-3). To be sure, God's boundless *love* was revealed and demonstrated by the Saviour (John 3:16; Rom. 5:8; I John 3:16). The *grace* of God, the undeserved favor which He bestowed upon mankind, was also revealed by the Lord Jesus (Luke 2:40; John 1:17; II Thess. 1:12).[12]

The Trinity

Another basic doctrine of the historic Christian faith is that of the Trinity. Augustine, the celebrated church father of the fifth century, is reputed to have said of the Trinity, "In no other subject is error more dangerous or inquiry more laborious, or discovery of the truth more profitable." Truly, herein lies the greatest mystery of all revealed truth.

Evangelical theology embraces the doctrine of the triune God because of the teaching of Scripture as a whole. Three persons, each possessing full and equal deity, are presented. Equally as emphatically the Bible knows of but one God. When all that Scripture has to say is put together, there is a stress on unity and diversity in unity within God. He is seen as one in three and as three in one. Early Christian writers described the God of the Bible as of one essence or substance and existing in three subsistences or persons.

Christianity is monotheistic, not tritheistic. It believes in one God, not three. Father, Son, and Holy Spirit are each fully God. Each exists as a separate person with individual responsibilities within the Godhead.

Old Testament Implications.[13] Throughout the Old Testament there are hints of the Trinity but God's unity is stressed. The revelation is much clearer and more complete in the New Testament. We need the teaching from both testaments for the full picture.

Plurality Implied. The plural name for God, *Elohim*, is used of him many times in the Old Testament (e.g., Deut. 6:4). Other plural titles are used of God as well (Eccles. 12:1; Isa. 54:5). The

---

12. Ibid., p. 55.
13. For Old and New Testament teaching I have drawn upon my earlier presentation in *The God of the Bible*, pp. 70-74.

plural personal pronouns are also used of God (eg., Gen. 1:26; 3:22; 11:7; Isa. 6:8).

Clearly, Jehovah-God is distinguished from the angel of Jehovah (Gen. 16:7-13; 22:11-18; Zech. 1:12-13). The "Lord" and "his anointed" are two separate persons in Psalm 2:2, 6. The fact that the Holy Spirit is spoken of as distinct from the Father and the Son and yet just as truly God argues for a plurality in the Godhead as well (Ps. 139:7; Job 26:13).

Trinity Implied. In addition to the clear implications of plurality in the Godhead there are also implications of trinity in the Old Testament.

Three separate persons are implied in Isaiah's vision of the angelic response, "Holy, holy, holy" (Isa. 6:3). This seems to be more than the customary Hebrew mode of emphasis, especially since the plural "us" is in the immediate context. It seems clear enough that the Father is the one addressed. When John 12:40-41 is studied along with Isaiah 6:10, it becomes apparent that the Son's glory was beheld by the prophet. Also, Acts 28:25-26 and Isaiah 6:9, when taken together, provide further evidence of the presence of the Holy Spirit in the passage.

Even clearer presentations of three persons in the Godhead are to be seen in Isaiah 48:16 and 63:7-10. Three distinct persons are in the passages. The preincarnate Christ speaks (48:16), and the Lord, the angel of his presence, and the Holy Spirit are specifically mentioned (63:7-10).

New Testament Revelation. Though the word *trinity* does not appear in either the Old or New Testament, the revelation of the doctrine is certainly clear in the New.

Three persons are spoken of as God. The Father is called God (John 6:27; Rom. 1:7), as is the Son (John 1:1, 14; Heb. 1:8) and the Spirit (Acts 5:3-9). Each of these divine persons is seen to be associated with the work of the others. In the great commission Christ gave to the church, the going, teaching, and baptizing are to be "in the name of the Father, and of the Son, and of the Holy Spirit" (Matt. 28:19). The divine equality of each, and yet the personal distinction between each, is also explicit in Paul's benediction to the Corinthian Christians (2 Cor. 13:14).

Attributes peculiar to deity are possessed by each member of the Godhead. Each possesses omnipotence—the Father (1 Peter 1:5), the Son (Matt. 28:18), and the Holy Spirit (Rom. 15:19). Each also possesses omniscience—the Father (Rom. 11:33), the Son (Rev. 2:33), and the Holy Spirit (1 Cor. 2:11). Omnipresence is likewise true of each—the Father (Matt. 19:26), the Son (Matt. 18:20), and the Holy Spirit (Ps. 139:7).

While evangelical theology insists that each member of the Godhead is fully and equally divine, it also maintains there is nevertheless an order of priority and subordination among these persons. That is, there is a difference in the office, function, and work of each. To acknowledge this in no way denies or diminishes the divine equality of the three persons. In essence they are one and possess all the divine attributes. In role or function there are distinctions. Through the Son, by means of the Spirit, the child of God has access to the Father (Eph. 2:18). The Father is the one who sent the Son into the world to be the Savior (Gal. 4:4). The Son sent the Holy Spirit into the world to continue his work (John 15:26).

> Perhaps the clearest and strongest [evidence] for the doctrine of the Trinity from the New Testament is to be found in Christ's teaching. The Saviour's upper room discourse (John 14:1-16:33) is filled with evidence for the Trinity. He was certainly distinct from the Father to whom He prayed and from the Holy Spirit whom He promised would come to continue His own work. Though all three were separate Persons, they were all one in essence (John 17:1-26). No doubt this clearest and most concise statement from Christ regarding the existence of three members in the Godhead is found in John 14:16: "And I [Christ] will pray the Father, and he shall give you another Comforter [the Spirit], that he may abide with you for ever."[14]

The Person of God the Father

God the Father possesses all the essential elements of personality. He is rich with both wisdom and knowledge. His judgments are, in fact, past finding out (Rom. 11:33). He is love (1 John 4:8) and is not willing that any should perish but that all should come to repentance (2 Peter 3:9). The God and Father of

14. Ibid., p. 74.

our Lord Jesus Christ is a person, not a mere force or power. With all their limitations, the theistic arguments for God's existence support his personality, wisdom, and power.

The attributes, or characteristics, of God the Father also argue for his personality. The ability to know all things and do all things, for example, requires personality. Throughout Scripture personal pronouns are used in referring to God. These also imply his personality.

Man is said to be made in God's image (Gen. 1:26-27). Surely this does not mean man has the physical appearance of God. Whatever else it may include, it must mean there is a spiritual similarity of some sort between God and man. There is in the immaterial part of man's makeup a correspondence with God. This was still true even after the fall and the flood (Gen. 9:1-6). God and man are both persons. That is part of what it means to be made in God's image and after his likeness.

Perfections

God's perfections are usually designated his attributes, a word that is better avoided. (Some people think of a being's attributes as adding something to that being.) The qualities or characteristics of God the Father that describe him and set him off from all his creatures and creation are truly perfections of his being. They reveal to us his nature. God cannot be thought of apart from these, and yet he is more than the sum total of them all. When we have exhausted the list of perfections which Scripture gives us, we still have not fully defined God. From eternity these perfections were his and belonged to the divine essence. He always possessed all of them in their fullness.

The major perfections of God are as follows.[15]

Self-existence. God is the Uncaused One. He alone possesses the ground of existence in himself. He does not depend on anyone or anything outside himself for his life. God is the source of life, and the life principle comes from him.

The life of the self-existent God is taught clearly in Scripture. He is the "living God and everlasting king" (Jer. 10:10), the "living and true God" (1 Thess. 1:9). God is not dependent on anyone else or anything else for his thoughts (Rom. 11:33-34), his will

---

15. This section has been taken in part from ibid., pp. 90-106.

(Rom. 9:19), his power (Ps. 115:3), or even his counsel (Ps. 33:10-11).

Infinity. The infinity of God means he has no limitations; he is restricted only by his own nature. When this perfection is related to time, we say God is eternal. He is indeed the author of time and yet is not conditioned or confined by it (Ps. 90:2). Neither is God restricted by space. To describe this truth older theologians referred to the immensity of God, by which they meant he transcends all spatial limitations and yet remains present in every point of space. As we will see, this is synonymous with his omnipresence.

Spirituality. That God is Spirit means that he is without material substance and free from all temporal limitations (John 4:24). He is incorporeal. On the positive side this perfection includes God's life and personality. He is a self-conscious and self-determining Being. In Scripture physical terms are sometimes ascribed to God as though he were a man, with arms (Deut. 33:27), hand (John 10:29), and mouth (Isa. 58:14). These are anthropomorphic expressions and are not to be understood as though God possesses such physical properties but rather that he experiences precisely the functions that are performed by these in man.

Immutability. This perfection emphasizes the fact that God never alters his purposes or changes his nature. God never changes either in his being, or essence, or in his character and nature (Exod. 3:14; Ps. 102:26-28; Mal. 3:6; James 1:17).

Some Scripture seems to teach that God does change. For example, he is said to repent (Gen. 6:6; Jonah 3:10). Such statements may be understood as examples of anthropomorphic expressions. God does speak in terms that man can understand. The change in most cases is really a change in man, not in God, since many of the threats made by God were conditional in the first place (e.g., Jonah 3:4, 10).

Holiness. When Scripture affirms that God is holy, it means he possesses absolute perfection in every detail and that he is completely separate from evil in his person and in his dealings with his creatures (Lev. 19:2; Ps. 99:9; 1 John 1:5). God has always been holy. He did not arrive at the state of perfection, nor does he struggle to maintain it. His holiness is always the same even though he deals with Satan, sin, and sinners.

To say God is righteous and just is to speak of his holiness in

relation to mankind. Righteousness implies a rule or law to which
there has been conformity. God's holy person is his own
standard. God never violates his holiness; neither does he allow
his creatures to violate it without full payment and satisfaction for
their sins. Thus, God is just (Zeph. 3:5; Rom. 3:26). He also carries
out his righteous standards justly and with equity. There is never
any partiality or unfairness in God's dealing with men. God
carried out the just demands of his absolute but offended
righteousness on Christ. Therefore, all who are in him are
forgiven and accepted in the Beloved.

Love. God is the very personification of love, and he never
existed apart from it (1 John 4:8). Even before he created any
creature to whom he could display his love, he was love. Since he
is perfect and holy, his love is also.

Humans love because of qualities and virtues they see in each
other. Not so with God. He loved the world of sinners, and still
does, and he sent his Son to be their Savior (John 3:16; 1 Tim. 2:3-
4). Because of the believer's family relationship to God he is said
to be under God's special care. He is the special object of the
Father's unfathomable, immeasurable love. God the Father also
loves his Son (John 17:24).

Closely related to God's love is his mercy and grace. His mercy
is seen in his withholding deserved judgment and results in his
patience and long-suffering. It explains his disposition toward
sinners and those in need (Ps. 103:8). God's mercy is shown to
them that fear him (Exod. 20:2; Luke 1:50) and even to those who
do not (Ezek. 18:23, 32).

The grace of God, on the other hand, is more positive. It is his
undeserved favor shown to man. Mercy and grace function
harmoniously in God and are expressions of his love. God's
mercy allows him to withhold merited punishment, and his grace
allows him to freely bestow unmerited favor. Grace opened the
way of redemption (Rom. 3:24). Because of God's grace sinners
are justified freely (Rom. 4:16; Titus 3:7) and blessed abundantly
(2 Cor. 8:9).

Omniscience. This perfection in God means he comprehends all
things—past, present, and future, things actual and things
possible. God has universal and complete knowledge which he
did not acquire by discovering facts (Isa. 40:13-14; Rom. 11:34-36).
The outworking of his eternal plan takes place in time, yet the

things of the past and future are as real as the here and now with him.

God's knowledge is complete. He knows all things completely and perfectly. Nothing surprises him. What often appears to be a complete reversal or contradiction of God's plan comes as no shock to God. He knew, for example, the first Adam would sin and plunge the entire human race in sin and guilt. He knew also that man would crucify his Son, the last Adam.

The omniscience, or complete knowledge, of God is also all-inclusive. The God and Father of our Lord Christ knows perfectly the past, present, and future; he knows not only the actual—that which has or will come to pass—but also the possible—that which could have taken place but never did or will. God knows, for example, what will happen if and when the unregenerate turn to him in faith, and he knows as well what will happen if they do not (Matt. 11:21-23).

It is through his wisdom that God applies his knowledge to the fulfillment of his purpose in ways that will bring the most glory to himself. He is the "only wise" God (1 Tim. 1:17).

Omnipresence. Perhaps the clearest passage in the Bible to define and describe God's omnipresence is Psalm 139:7-16. The psalmist stressed how God is infinite, transcending all spatial limitations. This does not mean he is somehow diffused through space, with parts of him everywhere. Neither does it teach he is present everywhere in the same sense or that he is everything or that everything is God. God is immanent, within the world, acting within and through his creation. He is also transcendent, over and beyond his creation.

Omnipotence. God possesses infinite power; he is all-powerful (Matt. 19:26; Rev. 19:6). He has the ability to do anything that does not contradict his nature. His power is potential as well as actual. No tiring effort is involved in his activity (Ps. 33:9). Evidences of God's mighty power are everywhere.

Sovereignty[16]

To confess God's sovereignty is to view him as the absolute and sole ruler in all the universe. True, he uses human and even

16. A useful discussion of God's sovereignty, especially as it relates to evangelism, is J. I. Packer, *Evangelism and the Sovereignty of God* (Downers Grove, Ill.: Inter-Varsity Press, 1961).

angelic means to accomplish his ends, yet he remains in complete control of his world and everything in it. Absolutely nothing escapes his notice, and nothing takes place that is not under his jurisdiction.

We have already seen that God possesses absolute power and complete knowledge. But sovereignty goes beyond these. The sovereignty of God includes his omnipotence and omniscience, yet it involves more. He is in control; he is working out his plan.

That God is sovereign does not mean he deals arbitrarily with his creatures. Neither does it mean he is carrying out his eternal plan after some sort of trial-and-error method.

God's sovereignty includes his freedom to do whatever he wills. He has no limitations or restrictions except his own self, and he never violates his own holy character. He never wills or performs anything contrary to himself and his purposes. There is no inner conflict with God. He is always consistent with himself.

The Father's sovereignty is supported by his work in creation and by his providence. All of his perfections discussed above also argue for his exalted position as Supreme Ruler. In addition to these lines of evidence, there are a host of scriptural passages that teach specifically the Father's sovereignty. Only a few of these will be included here:

Hannah, mother of the prophet Samuel, acknowledged God's sovereignty. Her testimony was that Jehovah-God was beyond comparison. He raised up and brought down as he pleased. All the pillars of the earth belong to him, who set the world upon them.

David, the human king, gladly bowed before the sovereign lordship of God. His response to God's sovereignty was simply to praise and exalt him for it (1 Chron. 29:11-12).

God the Son said the believing sinner is in the hand of God the Father, who is "greater than all" (John 10:29; cf. John 6:37-44). Interestingly, in the same context Christ said he and the Father were one (John 10:30).

God works all things together for good to them that love him and are called according to his purpose. Those he foreknew he will ultimately glorify. That being true, it certainly follows that he is in control (Rom. 8:28-30).

An extended passage supportive of the sovereignty of God appears in Romans 9-11. Here the apostle uses the people of Israel to demonstrate the righteousness of God in his sovereign dealings. God is presented as the potter who has a right to mold and shape the vessel as he chooses. And he does so! The outworking of God's sovereignty is to the praise of his own glory (Eph. 1:1-11). He works all things according to the council of his own will.

J. I. Packer summarized the controversy over divine sovereignty and at the same time sounded a needed warning:

> What is true is that all Christians believe in divine sovereignty, but some are not aware that they do, and mistakenly imagine and insist that they reject it. . . . People see that the Bible teaches man's responsibility for his actions; they do not see . . . how this is consistent with the sovereign Lordship of God over those actions. They are not content to let the two truths live side by side, as they do in the Scriptures, but jump to the conclusion that, in order to uphold the biblical truth of human responsibility, they are bound to reject the equally biblical and equally true doctrine of divine sovereignty, and to explain away the great number of texts that teach it . . . . The irony of the situation, however, is that when we ask how the two sides pray, it becomes apparent that those who profess to deny God's sovereignty really believe in it just as strongly as those who affirm it.[17]

Names[18]

As we have seen, the perfections of God reveal his person and his relations with man. His names do the same; they are not meaningless titles but revelations of himself. As he dealt with man, God made himself known by assigning to himself descriptive titles, character-revealing names.

The three names for God in the Old Testament are Elohim, translated *God*; Yahweh, translated *Jehovah* (appearing in the Authorized Version as God and LORD); and Adonai, translated *Lord*. The first two of these are used frequently in combination with other words forming compound names.

God (Elohim). This most common name is first used of the Creator in Genesis 1:1. From this usage and the many others it is

17. Ibid, pp. 16-17.
18. See Herbert F. Stevenson's excellent *Titles of the Triune God* (Westwood, N.J.: Fleming H. Revell, 1956).

clear that eternal power and might are to be understood. The name refers to God as the source of all things.

Not long after creation the worship of the one Creator God became corrupted. The nations scattered and the people intermarried. They carried with them the name of Elohim but no longer used it only of the one true God. They applied the name to parts of God's creation and to gods of their own making (Gen. 35:1, 2, 4). The name was retained, but its true meaning was lost.

Elohim is an anglicized Hebrew word which is plural in form. The Hebrews often used the plural as a means of assigning special meaning that could not be expressed in the singular. Also, this plural name for the one true God is consistent with the fact that he is one in three and three in one.

LORD *(Yahweh).* The Jews refused to pronounce this name for God because it was filled with such respect and honor. It is generally believed the name comes from the verb "to be." This means it speaks of God as the self-existing one. It is used over six thousand times of God. He explained its meaning as "I *AM*" (Exod. 3:14). The title speaks also of God as the unchangeable one (Exod. 3:15ff.) who maintains a relationship with his people. He is the covenant-keeping, faithful God.

Lord *(Adonai).* Like the name Elohim, Adonai occurs most frequently in the plural form. When the same term in the singular is used of men, it is always clear from the context. When so used it speaks of an intimate personal relationship. It refers to the master of a slave and the husband of a wife and connotes the idea of authority as well as love and faithfulness. From this we learn what the name means when used of God.

> There are many instances where no specific name of God is employed, but *the name* of God is used. Abraham called on *the name* of the Lord (Gen. 12:8; 13:4). The Lord proclaimed His own *name* before Moses (Ex. 33:19; 34:5). Israel was warned against profaning the *name* of the Lord (Lev. 13:21; 22:2, 32). The *name* of the Lord God was not to be taken in vain (Ex. 20:7; Deut. 5:11). The priests of Israel were to minister in *the name* of the Lord (Deut. 18:5; 21:5).[19]

---

19. Lightner, *The God of the Bible*, p. 108.

The Work of God the Father

Since God is sovereign, it follows that he has a sovereign plan for the universe and mankind which he is bringing to fulfillment. When viewed from the perspective of Scripture, history is more than the recording of the events of the past. Rather, what has happened in the past, what is happening now, and what will happen in the future is all evidence of the unfolding of a purposeful plan devised by the personal God of the Bible. All the circumstances of life—past, present, and future—fit into the sovereign plan like pieces of a puzzle.

The decree or plan of God is one. To be sure, there are many aspects to it, many facets or steps, yet there is one master plan (Acts 15:18) which harmoniously includes all things (Eph. 1:11).

According to Scripture the Father's sovereign plan was designed before the foundation of the world (1 Peter 1:20). Formed in eternity, the plan is being manifested in time. The whole plan was conceived and determined by God at once and is not subject to change or alteration. The Father may be viewed as the master architect who knew the end from the beginning, even before his plan was adopted.

Because it is God's plan, it is a wise plan (Rom. 11:33-36). He needed no counsel in determining it. He alone is responsible for the plan (Isa. 40:13-14). And since it is God's sovereign plan, we can be sure it is the best possible way to bring the most possible glory to his name.

As to the scope of the Father's sovereign plan,

> the apostle Paul's declaration that God works "all things after the counsel of his own will" (Eph. 1:11) makes it abundantly clear that the decree or plan of God includes all things. There are no areas over which He is not the supreme Ruler. All His creation is subject to Him (Isa. 46:10,11). Though it is all-inclusive, the plan of God does not apply to His own person. We must never think that He decreed His own existence nor the mode of it in three persons. He did not decree to be holy and just. These things, and all others which concern the being of God, were not optional with Him; they were necessary by virtue of the fact that He is God . . . . There are some aspects of His plan which God carries out directly through various means and for which He acknowledges responsibility (Job

28:26; Phil. 2:13). Other parts, such as the sinful acts of men, He permits; and He always places the responsibility for the results with man (Acts 14:16; Ps. 78:29). This does not make those things less certain nor outside the plan of God, but it does remove from God any blame for man's sin, even though that sin is permitted by Him and thereby constitutes a part of His plan (Acts 2:23; 4:27, 28). The entrance of sin into the universe was made certain by God's sovereign plan. God did not create sin, but in His infinite wisdom He allowed its entrance into the universe. Satan and sin did not catch God off guard.[20]

God's sovereign plan includes not only the end to be achieved but also the means to accomplish it. This distinguishes it from fatalism. The fact is, human responsibility is a part of God's sovereignty. The purpose of God's sovereign plan, of course, is to bring glory, praise, and honor to himself. True, benefits do come to man as God achieves his purpose, but these are secondary to the chief end of glorifying God (Eph. 1:12).

Major Areas of Difference Among Evangelicals

In the doctrine of God the Father there are several points on which evangelicals are not agreed. There are differences, for example, over how the attributes of God are to be classified. Several variations have been suggested to distinguish between those which belong to God alone and those which he shares at least to some degree with man.

In answer to the question of how God may be known there is not a united voice. Some insist that God cannot be known at all through his revelation in nature. Others argue that not only can God be known through nature but that such knowledge of him has redemptive merit. Still others believe the unregenerate person's lost condition keeps him from knowing God in any true sense through the things God has made. Most evangelicals, however, insist that God has indeed made himself known through nature and has also enabled all men to know of his existence and power.

---

20. Ibid., pp. 82-83.

Differences exist, too, over whether or not God has an individual will for the believer or simply a sovereign and moral will. There are differences among evangelicals, but without doubt the single most important one relates to what has come to be known as the Calvinist-Arminian debate over God's purposes before the foundation of the world. It cannot be stressed too strongly that both Calvinism and Arminianism involve more than what is included in the famous five points that characterize each. Calvinism and Arminianism should be viewed as systems of theology. Their five points, which will be presented later, revolve around the doctrine of man's sin, God's sovereignty, and the work of Christ and the Holy Spirit in salvation. The two points of view differ greatly over these matters. In addition, Calvinism is also characterized by a distinct doctrine of the church and of last things.

The difference between Calvinism and Arminianism over the doctrine of God the Father centers in the areas of the Father's sovereignty and his pretemporal election of individuals to salvation. I classify myself as a moderate Calvinist embracing only those doctrines which I believe can be clearly and emphatically defended in Scripture.

Arminianism is the term used to designate those who subscribe to the teaching of James Arminius (1560-1609), a noted professor of theology at the University of Leyden in Holland. His writings show a moderate Calvinism, and he became a central figure in the theological controversy of his day within the Dutch Reformed Church. Followers of Arminius have often misrepresented his view. A good deal of what passes today as Arminianism would hardly be compatible with Arminius' Declaration of Sentiments delivered to the States General of Holland in 1608.[21]

A year after Arminius' death some of his loyal supporters drew up five articles of faith in the form of a protest, called a "Remonstrance." All five of its points were in opposition to statements in the Belgic Confession of Faith and the Heidelberg Catechism, which stress what later came to be called the five points of Calvinism. Even though our concern here is with the first of the five Arminian points, all of them should be set forth.

21. See *The Works of James Arminius, D. D.*, Vol. I, trans. James Nichols (Buffalo: Derby, Miller, and Orton, 1853).

I. God elects or reproves on the basis of foreseen faith or unbelief. II. Christ died for all men and for every man, although only believers are saved. III. Man is so depraved that divine grace is necessary unto faith or any good deed. IV. This grace may be resisted. V. Whether all who are truly regenerate will certainly persevere in the faith is a point which needs further investigation.[22]

Evangelicals who follow the Arminian teaching on the first of these five points view the biblical teaching on the Father's sovereignty, his election, and predestination to salvation differently. Generally, however, they embrace an election that is conditioned on man's choice and God's foreknowledge of it:

The biblical doctrine of election, then, definitely includes the conditional election of individuals to salvation. Through his foreknowledge God sees who will believe upon Christ Jesus as Savior and Lord, and become united with him in Christian baptism; then even before the creation of the world he predestines these believers to share the glory of the risen Christ.[23]

Other evangelicals holding the Arminian view of the Father's sovereignty and election see the Bible as teaching an election not of individuals but of the church, or of all who are in the Son.[24]

Meeting in Dort, Holland, from November, 1618 to May, 1619, an international synod rejected as heretical the views of the Arminians set forth in the Remonstrance of 1610. In addition to rejecting the Arminian five points, the synod set forth what they viewed as the true Calvinistic teaching on the matters in question. This was presented in what has come to be known as the five points of Calvinism: 1) total depravity; 2) unconditional election; 3) limited atonement, or particular redemption; 4) irresistible grace, or the efficacious call of the Spirit; and 5) perseverance of the saints, or eternal security.[25]

22. Roger Nicole, "Arminianism," *Baker's Dictionary of Theology*, ed. Everett F. Harrison (Grand Rapids: Baker Book House, 1960), p. 64.

23. Jack W. Cottrell, "Conditional Election," in *Grace Unlimited*, ed. Clark H. Pinnock (Minneapolis: Bethany Fellowship, 1975), p. 62. The chapters "Predestination in the Old Testament," by David J. A. Clines, and "Predestination in the New Testament," by I. Howard Marshall, are also written from a moderate Arminian point of view.

24. See Robert Shank, *Elect in the Son* (Springfield, Mo.: Westcott Publishers, 1978).

25. These five points are discussed at length and contrasted with the Arminian five points in David N. Steele and Curtis C. Thomas, *The Five Points of Calvinism Defined,*

Evangelicals who differ with the Arminian interpretation of the
biblical teaching on election, predestination, and related doctrines
generally subscribe to a Calvinistic interpretation. This view has
been well stated as follows:

> God's choice of certain individuals unto salvation before the
> foundation of the world rested solely in his own sovereign will. His
> choice of particular sinners was not based on any unforeseen
> response or obedience on their part, such as faith, repentance, etc.
> On the contrary, God gives faith and repentance to each individual
> whom he selected. These acts are the result, not the cause of God's
> choice. Election, therefore, was not determined by or conditioned
> upon any virtuous quality or act foreseen in man. Those whom
> God sovereignly elected he brings through the power of the Spirit
> to a willing acceptance of Christ. Thus, God's choice of the sinner,
> not the sinner's choice of Christ, is the ultimate cause of
> salvation.[26]

God the Father and the Child of God

The first and most important need for the child of God in his
relation to his heavenly Father is to know him with *both* mind and
heart. Knowing about God and knowing God are not necessarily
the same, but both are crucial. A theologically and biblically
accurate statement about him leads us away from idols to the
living God with whom we have a father-child relationship, a
relationship which brings responsibility, dependency, obedience,
and great blessing.

In his first epistle, the apostle John stressed the important
characteristics of the true child of God who walks with his
heavenly Father. God the Father is light and has no darkness in
him at all (1 John 1:5). This was John's way of saying God is holy.

Defended, Documented (Philadelphia: Presbyterian and Reformed Publishing Company,
1963). Other books advancing the Calvinistic point of view, especially on the matters
under discussion here, are Loraine Boettner, *The Reformed Doctrine of Predestination*
(Philadelphia: Presbyterian and Reformed Publishing Company, 1963); Arthur W. Pink,
The Sovereignty of God (London: The Banner of Truth Trust, 1961).

26. Steele and Thomas, *Five Points of Calvinism*, pp. 16-17.

Those who claim this absolutely pure God as their own are challenged therefore to walk in the light (1:6-7). John also wrote that God is love (4:8). He not only loves, he is the personification of love. Because this is true, the believer is to love others (4:11). God is not only light, or holiness, and love; he is also life (5:20), and his children are exhorted to keep themelves from lifeless idols (5:21).

Those who are truly children of God will evidence a family relationship; there will be a family resemblance. No one can be a partaker of the divine nature (2 Peter 1:4) and remain the same. All the great perfections of God the Father ought to make a difference in the behavior of the child of God. Through Moses, Jehovah-God told his people, "For I am the LORD your God; ye shall therefore sanctify yourselves, and ye shall be holy; for I am holy" (Lev. 11:44). Peter reminded the believers to whom he wrote of the same exhortation (1 Peter 1:15).

Questions for Discussion

1. What has God revealed about himself in nature?
2. How would you define the doctrine of the Trinity?
3. How would you defend the doctrine of the Trinity before one who does not accept it?
4. What differences should the holiness, love, mercy, and grace of God the Father make in the believer's life?
5. Is it possible to relate man's responsibilities to God the Father's sovereignty? How?

Suggestions for Further Reading

Bavinck, Herman. *The Doctrine of God*, trans., ed., and outlined by William Hendriksen. Grand Rapids: Baker Book House, 1977.

Bickersteth, Edward. *The Trinity*. Grand Rapids: Sovereign Grace Publishers, 1971.

Lightner, Robert P. *The God of the Bible*. Grand Rapids: Baker Book House, 1978.

Packer, J. I. *Knowing God*. Downers Grove, Ill.: Inter-Varsity Press, 1973.

Schaeffer, Francis. *The God Who Is There*. Downers Grove, Ill.: Inter-Varsity Press, 1968.

3

God the Son

Christianity is Christ! He is the center and the circumference of the historic Christian faith. Orthodox Christians have always embraced him as fully God and assert his virgin birth, his substitutionary atonement, bodily resurrection, and literal second coming. Skeptic and saint alike are attracted to him, if for different reasons. Jesus Christ has been the subject of both ridicule and worship from the very beginning of the Christian era to the present hour.

Jesus Christ and his work on the cross are absolutely central and essential to Christianity. One's view of Christ will determine in large part his views of other cardinal doctrines of the Christian faith. It is generally true, for example, that one's view of Christ, the Living Word, will correspond with his view of the Bible, the written Word. The reverse is also true; one's view of the written Word in large measure reveals his view of the Living Word. If consistency be maintained, the two Words from God stand or fall together, since both claim to come from God, and yet both were touched by erring humanity.

There can be no escaping it: Jesus of Nazareth, the Son of the living God, is without doubt unique among all persons who ever lived. The Bible presents him as both fully God and fully man. The Son of God's birth of Mary did not mark the beginning of his existence. Before he was born he lived eternally. On earth he lived a totally sinless life. No evil thought, word, or deed ever came from him. Jesus made claims and demands unlike those made by any other.

The emphasis in this chapter is on the person of Christ. Those areas of his work discussed in chapter 7 will not be included here.

A Historical Perspective

From the earliest times there has been much discussion on the person of Christ, but the purpose and nature of our study allows us to touch only the high points.

Postapostolic Age

The Postapostolic Fathers. Some of the most familiar church leaders who were the immediate successors of the apostles are Clement of Alexandria, Ignatius of Antioch, and Polycarp of Smyrna.

The postapostolic fathers were not theologians, nor did they pretend to be. Their chief concern was to promote a close personal walk with Christ. These men wrote devotional literature, not theological treatises. In their writings Christ stands out as both divine and human. No attempt was made to explain how one person could be both Son of man and Son of God at the same time. Only as controversy arose over this belief was any attempt made to explain it.

The Christian writers of this period reveal their belief in Christ's sinlessness as well. To all of them he was indeed a proper object of worship and adoration. There is also evidence that these fathers believed in the preexistence of Christ the Son of God.

The Second-Century Apologists. The apologists, including Aristides, Tatian, and Justin Martyr, sought to contend for Christianity, combat heathenism, and construct doctrinal belief. They had as their chief concern to make Christianity acceptable, to present it as a live option. However, in seeking to accomplish their goal the apologists watered down the biblical teaching of Christ to such an extent that he was not really proclaimed. They presented a philosophical concept of Christ not at all in harmony with the teaching of the New Testament. To them the Logos, or Word, of John 1:1 was not the eternally existing person of God the Son. They insisted rather that the Logos existed eternally in God only as divine reason, not as a person.

Ebionism. The Ebionites were heretical Jews, a continuation of the Judaizers of Paul's day. As Jews they naturally felt constrained to deny the deity of Christ. They held such belief to be in conflict with monotheism. Christ's virgin birth was also denied by the Ebionites. To them he was a mere man on whom the Holy Spirit descended at his baptism, qualifying him to be the Messiah. Some Ebionites said Christ was the incarnation of the ideal man, and they called him the highest archangel.

Gnosticism. A second-century perversion of Christianity, Gnosticism derived its name from the Greek word meaning "to know," or "knowledge." The Gnostics claimed a superior knowledge and even taught that man's salvation was through knowledge. They were heavily influenced by the dualistic philosophy of the Greeks, who viewed matter and spirit as two opposing principles, the former evil and the latter good.[1]

The Gnostics viewed Christ as the highest aeon who emanated from the spirit, or good God. They emphasized the life of Christ, not his death. The incarnation of Christ was rejected since it involved a contact of spirit with matter. Christ, according to the Gnostics, did not have a real physical body and they denied his true humanity. According to some of them, Christ, "descended upon the man Jesus at the time of his baptism, but left him again before his crucifixion; while according to others he assumed a merely phantasmal body."[2] The Gnostics were docetic (from the Greek *dokeo*—"seeming") with respect to Christ, believing that he only appeared to be human.

Monarchianism. Near the close of the second century there arose an early form of unitarianism which became known as monarchianism. Its proponents sought to defend the sole government of God. The modalistic monarchians denied the humanity of Christ and thus were also docetic. Christ was to them a mere mode or manifestation of the one God and not a separate person within the Godhead.

Marcionism. The Marcionites, followers of Marcion, denied the genuine humanity of Christ, embracing some of the Gnostic teaching. Marcion believed the Demiurge, or Gnostic God of the Old Testament, had promised a world-conquering Messiah who

---

1. Louis Berkhof, *Systematic Theology* (Grand Rapids: Eerdmans, 1968), pp. 50-51.
2. Ibid., p. 306.

would judge the heathen. The spirit of God, or the good God, would not allow this. Instead he descended to Capernaum in an unreal body and called himself Messiah. He disregarded the laws instituted by the Demiurge, and as a result the Demiurge had him crucified. But since the self-acclaimed Messiah did not have a genuinely human body, the Demiurge was defeated and his power destroyed. The Messiah then compelled the Demiurge to acknowledge him.

Pre-Nicaean Period

The Teachers. The outstanding teachers of this period included Irenaeus, Clement of Rome, Origen, and Tertullian. They rejected doceticism and accepted the full humanity and absolute deity of Christ as well as his personal preexistence and coeternality with the Father. Origen coined the phrase "the eternal generation of the Son." For the fathers of this period the God of the Old Testament was the one and only true God and Father of the Lord Jesus Christ. The Son of God was subordinate to the Father not in essence but in function or office.

The Tensions. While some unscriptural concepts about Christ surfaced in the writings of the church fathers of this period, nevertheless they reacted strongly to Gnosticism and other heresies.

At this time the church was searching for a conception of Christ that would maintain 1) his true and full humanity, 2) his absolute deity, 3) the union of deity and humanity in one person, and 4) the necessary distinction between his deity and humanity in his person. All the christological controversies from the earliest centuries to the present stem from a failure to include all of these truths in regard to Christ.

Arianism was another attempt to explain the person of Christ. Arius, a presbyter in Alexandria, taught that Christ was not eternal but the first and highest creature of God, superior to man but not equal with God. Christ was of a different substance, Arius insisted. The battle raged for some time before it culminated in the Council of Nicaea in 325.

Arius' greatest opponent was Athanasius, who had been educated in the Catechetical School in Alexandria. He argued that Christ was of the same substance with the Father. A middle party led by Eusebius of Caesarea said Christ was of similar substance. With deep concern for the unity of the church, Constantine called the Council of Nicaea to resolve the issue. The emperor threw his weight in favor of Athanasius, and the Nicene Creed resulted.[3] But this by no means meant that all the opposing parties agreed with the decision or embraced orthodox views.

Post-Nicaean Period

Several serious errors regarding the person of Christ were promoted and subsequently exposed and condemned in this period. The fact that these views were classified as errors did not mean they were no longer embraced by supporters. The significance of the statements at the various ecumenical councils is that when they were made, those who held to the errors condemned were considered unorthodox.

Otto Heick has well summarized the conciliar decisions concerning Christ in this period. "Christ is divine—Nicaea (325); Christ is human—Constantinople (381); Christ is one in person—Ephesus (431); Christ is two in nature—Chalcedon (451); although not possessing 'two faces'—Constantinople (553); yet possessing two wills—Constantinople (680)."[4]

The Apollinarian Error. Apollinaris, bishop of Laodicea, believed that at the incarnation God the Son took up residence in the human body of Jesus. In his view Christ did not possess a full and genuine human nature. Opposed by orthodox leaders, Apollinaris and Apollinarianism were condemned in a succession of synods and councils from 362 to 691.

The Nestorian Error. Nestorius was made Patriarch of Constantinople in 428. Concerned to preserve the full humanity of Christ, he separated the two natures in Christ and failed to unite them in

---

3. *"We believe in one God, Father Almighty, Maker of all things visible and invisible. And in one Lord Jesus Christ, the Son of God, begotten of the Father; only-begotten, that is, of the substance of the Father, God of God, Light of Light, Very God of Very God, begotten not made, being of one substance with the Father: by Whom all things were made both in heaven and on earth: Who for us men, and for our salvation, came down from heaven, and was incarnate, and was made man; He suffered, and rose again the third day; He ascended into heaven, and is coming to judge both quick and dead."* (Cited from Robert L. Ferm, *Readings in the History of Christian Thought* [New York: Holt, Rinehart, and Winston, 1964] p. 138).

4. Otto W. Heick, *A History of Christian Thought* (Philadelphia: Fortress Press, 1965), 1:187.

one person. The man and the error were condemned at the Council of Ephesus in 431.

The Eutychian Error. Eutyches, an opponent of Nestorianism, sought to teach the unity of Christ's person. He claimed there were two natures in Christ before the incarnation but only one afterward. In reality this made Christ a third sort of being who was neither truly human or divine. The error was condemned by a synod at Constantinople in 448, after which Eutyches was reinstated, with final condemnation coming in 451 at Chalcedon.

A continuation of the Eutychian error, monophysitism, stemmed from those who were not pleased with the Chalcedon decision of the two natures in the one person of Christ. The monophysite error, as the name implies, held to one nature in Christ. After considerable debate the final settlement came in 553 at the Council of Constantinople, which condemned monophysitism.

The Middle Ages

Up until the medieval period discussions about the person of Christ were approached from the side of theology proper, the doctrine of God. The chief concern was the relation of the Son of God to the Father. In the Middle Ages there was little development in the doctrines related to the person of Christ, which received scant attention. The contributions that were made concerned Christ's work and were therefore from the side of soteriology. Most of the so-called theories of the atonement were advanced during this time (see Table 1). Christian writers of the Middle Ages were heavily influenced by unbiblical philosophies which distracted from theological pursuits.

During the Middle Ages a monophysite sect called monothelitism arose. Embracing the unity of Christ's person, monothelites went on to say he possessed only one divine-human will. This was another attempt to change the decision of Chalcedon. This error was condemned at the Sixth Council at Constantinople in 680, which declared that Christ had both a human and a divine will, with the former always subordinate to the latter and the two always in complete harmony.

TABLE 1 Theories of the Atonement

Theories	Original Exponents	Major Teaching
Recapitulation	Irenaeus (*ca.* 130-202)	Christ recapitulated in himself all the stages of human life that related to sin. In this way he reversed the course on which Adam, by his sin, started humanity.
Ransom to Satan	Origen (*ca.* 185-254)	Christ's death was a ransom paid to Satan for claims he had on man.
Satisfaction	Anselm (1033-1109)	Christ's death rendered satisfaction to God's honor.
Moral influence	Abelard (1079-1142)	Christ's death was a manifestation of God's love. The suffering love of Christ awakens a responsive love in sinners.
Example	Socinus (1539-1604)	Christ's death did not atone for sin. By his teaching in life and example in death, Christ brought salvation to man.
Governmental	Hugo Grotius (1583-1645)	Sin disrupted God's government. By his death Christ demonstrated the high estimate God placed on his law and government.
Mystical	Friedrich Schleiermacher (1768-1834)	Christ's death exercises some influence to change man. Christ's unbroken unity with God enabled him to bring a potential mystical influence for good to man through his death.
Vicarious repentance	McLeod Campbell (1800-1872)	By his death Christ offered to God a perfect and vicarious repentance which man could not perform but from which he benefits.

Reformation Developments

Lutheran Christology. In regard to the person of Christ, Luther and his followers embraced the Christology of the ancient church with one major exception. In his teaching on the inseparable union of the two natures Luther set forth the idea that there was a communion and transference of the properties or attributes of the divine nature to those of the human. This view will be discussed in greater detail in the section on differences.

Reformed Christology. The Reformed position is most clearly stated in the Second Helvetic Confession of 1566:

> Therefore the Son of God is co-equal and consubstantial with the Father, as touching his divinity; true God, and not by name only, or by adoption, or by special favor, but in substance and nature. . . . We therefore do abhor the blasphemous doctrine of Arius, uttered against the Son of God. . . . We also teach and believe that the eternal Son of the eternal God was made the Son of Man, of the seed of Abraham and David; not by means of any man, as Ebion affirmed, but that he was most purely conceived by the Holy Spirit, and born of the virgin Mary. . . . Moreover, our Lord Jesus Christ had not a soul without sense or reason, as Apollinaris thought; nor flesh without a soul, as Eunomius did teach; but a soul with its reason, and flesh with its senses. . . . We acknowledge, therefore, that there be in one and the same Jesus Christ our Lord two natures—the divine and the human nature; and we say that these two are so cojoined or united that they are not swallowed up, confounded, or mingled together, but rather united or joined together in one person (the properties of each nature being safe and remaining still), so that we do worship one Christ, our Lord, and not two. . . . As, therefore, we detest the heresy of Nestorius, which makes two Christs of one and dissolved the union of the person, so do we abominate the madness of Eutichus and of the Monothelites and Monophysites, who overthrow the propriety of the human nature. Therefore we do not teach that the divine nature in Christ did suffer, or that Christ according to his human nature, is yet in the world, and so in every place. For we do neither think nor teach that the body of Christ ceased to be a true body after his glorying, or that it was deified and so deified that it put off the properties, as touching body and soul, and became altogether a divine nature and began to be one substance alone; therefore we do not allow or receive the unwitty

subtleties, and the intricate, obscure, and inconsistent disputations of Schwenkfeldt, and such other vain janglers, about this matter; neither are we Schwenkfeldians.[5]

Post-Reformation Developments

During the first sixteen hundred years of the church's history, discussion concerning the person of Christ generally began with Christ as the Logos (John 1:1), the second person of the Godhead. The incarnation was then interpreted in such a way as to harmonize with the unity of Christ's person and the duality of his natures as set forth in Scripture. These studies began with the deity of Christ and then attempted to explain his humanity and the precise relation between his deity and humanity.

There was a noticeable change in this procedure during the eighteenth century that is still observable today. The new approach begins with the humanity of Christ, as represented in the so-called historical Jesus in contrast to the Christ of faith.[6] While there was the danger of neglecting the humanity of Christ in the earlier approach, much of the contemporary approach not only neglects the deity of the Savior but flatly denies it.[7]

Berkhof has rightly evaluated the new approach in these words:

Not what the Bible teaches us concerning Christ, but our own discoveries in investigating the phenomena of his life and our experience of him, was made the determining factor in forming a proper conception of Jesus. A far-reaching and pernicious

5. Cited from Louis Berkhof, *The History of Christian Doctrines* (Grand Rapids: Baker, 1959), pp. 116-17.

6. See Charles C. Anderson, *Critical Quests of Jesus* (Grand Rapids: Eerdmans, 1969) for a survey of the quests for the Jesus of history.

7. The seventeenth-century Westminster Confession of Faith and evangelical Christologies based on it stand in striking contrast to the denials and departure which began soon after the Reformation and continue today. The Presbyterian creedal statement on the person of Christ reads: "The Son of God, the second person in the Trinity, being very and eternal God, of one substance, and equal with the Father, did, when the fullness of time was come, take upon him man's nature, and all the essential properties and common infirmities thereof, yet without sin: being conceived by the power of the Holy Ghost, in the womb of the Virgin Mary, of her substance. So that two whole, perfect, and distinct natures, the Godhead and the Manhood, were inseparably joined together in one person, without conversion, composition, or confusion. Which person is very God and very man, yet one Christ, the only Mediator between God and man."

distinction was made between the historical Jesus, delineated by the writers of the Gospels, and the theological Christ, the fruit of the fertile imagination of theological thinkers from the days of Paul on, whose image is now reflected in the Creeds of the Church. The Lord of Glory was shorn of all that is supernatural—or nearly so—and the doctrine of (concerning) Christ gave way for the teachings of Jesus. He who had always been regarded by the Church as an object of divine worship now become a mere teacher of morality.[8]

Several of the significant personalities and developments that paved the way for contemporary Christology should be observed.

Socinianism, named after Faustus Socinus, denied the biblical doctrine of the Trinity. Christ was seen as only a man in whom God revealed himself. During Christ's mission on earth he was taken to heaven, where he was taught by God before he began his public ministry. Though worshiped as God, he is not God.

During the eighteenth century antibiblical views gained a foothold in the church. Immanuel Kant, for example, spoke and wrote of Christ as the only human who represented an ideal perfect man.

Friedrich Schleiermacher was the father of liberal theology. He taught that Christ was not God but was created as the ideal and perfect man whose sinlessness constituted his divinity.

The Greek word for the self-emptying of Christ is *kenosis*. In an attempt to do full justice to the humanity of Christ the theories of Christ's emptying (*kenosis*, Phil. 2:7) arose. These appeared first in Lutheranism soon after the Reformation. Later, in the nineteenth century, German Reformed theologians revived the controversy. The kenotic theories sought to explain the relation of the human to the divine in Christ by saying Christ divested himself of his divine attributes during his earthly life.[9]

Along with Kant, Schleiermacher, and Hegel, Albrecht Ritschl paved the way for theological liberalism and neoorthodoxy. Ritschl taught that God had revealed himself in Christ, who reflected the attributes of deity but was not preexistent. We know Christ is the Son of God, Ritschl insisted, because he had the

---

8. Berkhof, *History of Christian Doctrines*, p. 118.

9. For an excellent summary of the major theories see John F. Walvoord, *Jesus Christ Our Lord* (Chicago: Moody Press, 1969), pp. 138-45.

worth or value of God for us. We know this because he
accomplished a religious and ethical work in us which only God
could have done.

The theologies of Karl Barth and Rudolf Bultmann are also
important to a historical perspective of Christology. While trying
to overcome the deficiencies and failures of liberal theology, each
of these failed to embrace the Christ of Scripture.[10]

In 1977 a group of British churchmen and theologians produced
a book entitled *The Myth of God Incarnate*, edited by John Hick. As
is clear from the title the authors categorically reject the ontological
or literal incarnation of Christ and regard all talk of the same as
myth. This volume was a veritable bombshell in the theological
world. What the authors proposed in this book was by no means
new; they were simply bold enough to join together and say in
print what much of contemporary theology has been saying in a
fragmented fashion for a long time. *The Myth of God Incarnate*
repudiates the orthodox and biblical doctrine of Christ.[11]

An excellent summary of the confusing contemporary picture
regarding the person of Christ is given by Donald Bloesch:

A confusing picture of the person of Christ emerges as we turn to
the contemporary scene. Docetism and ebionitism are both very
much present, but the latter is dominant. Pannenberg, in
jettisoning the doctrine of the two natures, maintains that Jesus
was a real man who lived completely in and for the future, that is,
in and for God. He begins not with the incarnation of our Lord but
with his resurrection and avers that this event gives us the clue to
the status of Jesus—as the One who anticipates and embodies the
future of world-history. J. A. T. Robinson affirms the full humanity
of Jesus but not his deity except in a functional sense. Jesus
represents God to man. He is but the parable or sign by which it is
possible to recognize the Christ in others. Ellen Flessman, a Dutch
theologian, in her book *Believing Today* has a similar view: "The
Son Jesus Christ is not God, but a man who was so one with God
that in him I meet God." Thomas O'Meara regards Jesus as "the

10. For discussion of these see ibid., pp. 11-21.

11. The following works have appeared from evangelicals in response to *The Myth of
God Incarnate:* Michael Green, ed., *The Truth of God Incarnate* (Grand Rapids: Eerdmans,
1977); Jon A. Buell and O. Quentin-Hyden, *Jesus: God, Ghost or Guru?* (Grand Rapids:
Zondervan, 1978); George Carey, *God Incarnate* (Downers Grove, Ill.: Inter-Varsity Press,
1977); Norman Anderson, *The Mystery of the Incarnation* (Inter-Varsity Press, 1978).

climax of man," the culminating point in human evolution. He is "not the creator of salvation but its prophet." For Ernst Fuchs Jesus should be considered "a man who dares to act in God's stead." In Schoonenberg's Christology Jesus is basically a human person who embodies and reveals the presence of God rather than a divine person who assumes human nature. Hans Küng depicts Jesus as "God's advocate and deputy," the man who by his words and deeds attests God's love for us. The impact of positivistic historicism is clearly evident in his attempt to show what can be believed and what can be discarded in the life of Jesus. John Cobb rejects the traditional idea of Jesus Christ as a supernatural being in human form and contends instead that he was an extraordinary prophetic figure who fully realized the divine creative urge to fulfillment within him.[12]

A Positive Statement of the Doctrine

There is a large measure of agreement among evangelicals on what the Bible teaches regarding Christ's person and work. Both in his person and his work the Lord Jesus Christ is unique. Though one in person he is presented in Scripture as the God-man, possessing ontologically both a real divine nature and a perfect human nature. With these two natures in one person, he is unlike any other who ever lived. Jesus' life on earth and death on the cross were equally unique. He entertained no evil thought and committed no evil act. The sacrifice he provided for sin was himself. He gave himself as the substitute for sin, dying in the stead of sinners.

The Person of Christ

Christ's Preexistence and Eternality

Only of the Son of God can it be said that his birth did not signal his beginning. He existed as God's Son before he was born of Mary. He always existed, being as eternal as God himself. When

12. Donald G. Bloesch, *Essentials of Evangelical Theology* (New York: Harper & Row, 1978), 1:138-39.

evangelicals refer to the preexistence of Christ, more is meant than that he existed prior to his incarnation. They mean he existed eternally as the second person of the Godhead.

Evangelicals base their claim for Christ's preexistence on ample biblical support. First, every valid support for the Savior's deity is, of course, also support for his eternal preexistence. Second, the doctrine of the Trinity provides a defense for the timeless existence of Christ. The two doctrines stand or fall together. Third, names and titles of Christ used in the Old Testament lend strong support for his eternal preexistence.[13] He of necessity is as eternal as the God whose names were assigned to him in his preincarnate state. For example, Christ is called, "Jehovah our righteousness" (Jer. 23:5-6; 1 Cor. 1:30). Both the divine names Jehovah and Elohim are used, of Christ (Isa. 40:3; Luke 3:4). Micah the prophet wrote of the Son of God as "from of old" (Mic. 5:2). This same expression is used by Habakkuk to refer to God's eternal nature (Hab. 1:12). Therefore, the Son is as eternal as God himself. Hundreds of years before Mary conceived by the Holy Spirit, Isaiah called the Son yet unborn "the mighty God, the everlasting Father" (Isa. 9:6).

If the angel of Jehovah is identified as Christ in his preincarnate state, further support is gained for his preexistence.[14] The identification usually follows along these lines: The angel of Jehovah is identified as Jehovah in Genesis 16:7-13; 22:15-18. In other Scripture the angel is seen as an altogether distinct person from Jehovah (Zech. 1:12-13). Only the second person of the Trinity is seen in bodily, visible form in the New Testament. It would seem to follow, therefore, that the second person of the Trinity was the one who appeared bodily in the Old Testament. After the incarnation the angel of Jehovah no longer appears. Both the angel in the Old Testament and the Son in the New were sent by the Father. This provides additional identification of the two as the same and thus supports Christ's eternal preexistence.

13. See James A. Borland, *Christ in the Old Testament* (Chicago: Moody Press, 1978) for the contribution of the Old Testament to Christology.

14. See Walvoord, *Jesus Christ Our Lord,* pp. 44-46 for a good treatment of the standard arguments.

Christ's Virgin Birth

Evangelical theology has always included belief in the miraculous conception of Jesus Christ by the Virgin Mary.[15] At the turn of the twentieth century the virgin birth was numbered among the five fundamentals of orthodoxy by the great stalwarts of the faith. Those who denied any one of the cardinal doctrines of the faith—the inspiration and authority of the Bible, the virgin birth of Christ, the deity of Christ, the substitutionary atonement of Christ, and the bodily resurrection and second coming of Christ—were not considered orthodox in faith.

Nonevangelical theologians have just as consistently rejected the virgin birth of Christ. The rejection is in accord with the liberal refusal to accept the supernatural in biblical inspiration and all other areas of the historic Christian faith. In reality liberal theology assumes a closed system of natural laws by its denial of supernaturalism. It is not coincidental that the same persons who deny the biblical teaching of the virgin birth also deny all other biblical teaching that involves the supernatural.

The Meaning of the Virgin Birth. The evangelical belief in the virgin birth of Christ is not the same as the Roman Catholic belief in the immaculate conception of Mary. The Bible does not teach that the mother of Jesus was herself without sin, that from the very beginning of her existence she was free from original sin.[16]

On the positive side evangelicals believe the Holy Spirit was the efficient cause—that is, he supernaturally produced the effect or result of Mary's conception. The Holy Spirit brought about conception in Mary's womb in a unique way. It was the Spirit who through the miraculous conception sanctified the human nature of Christ at its very inception, thus keeping it free from the pollution of sin.

Walvoord explains from the evangelical perspective:

> The whole tenor of Scripture as presented in both the Old Testament prophecies that he was to be God and Man and the New Testament fulfillment makes the virgin birth a divine explanation, insofar as it can be explained, of an otherwise

---

15. See Robert Glenn Gromacki, *The Virgin Birth of Christ Doctrine of Deity* (Nashville: Thomas Nelson, 1974) for presentation of the doctrine from an evangelical perspective.

16. For the original statement of the doctrine issued by Pope Pius IX on December 8, 1858, and a scriptural refutation, see Loraine Boettner, *Roman Catholicism* (Philadelphia: Presbyterian and Reformed Publishing Company, 1962), pp. 158-62.

insuperable problem. How could One who was both God and Man have perfectly human parents? The account of the virgin birth therefore, instead of being an unreasonable invention, becomes a fitting explanation of how in the supernatural power of God the incarnation was made a reality.[17]

The Importance of the Virgin Birth. Evangelicals believe the virgin birth is vitally important for a number of reasons: First, it is a teaching of Scripture; and since Scripture is authoritative, all its teachings are to be believed. Second, the virgin birth determines whether we have a naturalistic or supernaturalistic Christ. Only when his unique person is divorced from the discussion does the virgin birth create difficulties. Third, by means of the virgin birth God kept his Son from receiving a sin nature from either Joseph or Mary, and therefore he was qualified to be man's redeemer. Fourth, historically the virgin birth of Christ has been an essential doctrine of the faith.

Scriptural Support. Several lines of biblical evidence are used to substantiate Christ's virgin birth.

Early in the Old Testament the virgin birth was implied in God's word to the serpent after the fall of man (Gen. 3:15). The reference to "her seed" is unparalleled. Normally reference is to the seed of the male.

Matthew's quotation (1:23) of Isaiah 7:14 makes very clear that virgin is the intended meaning of *almah*, which was used by the prophet. Also, Matthew's use of the feminine relative singular pronoun "of whom" (Matt. 1:16) provides strong support because Matthew thereby associated Christ's birth with Mary only. Joseph was completely eliminated. This is especially significant in contrast to the associations of male and female ancestors in the immediate context. Mary was with child "before" she and Joseph "came together" (Matt. 1:18). Joseph "knew her not till she had brought forth her firstborn son" (Matt. 1:25).

Luke, the physician, records the angel's explanation to Mary of her pregnancy. The Holy Spirit of God had come upon her to generate the child within her womb (Luke 1:34-35).

Consistently throughout John 8:19-48 the beloved disciple assigns God as the Father of the Lord Jesus Christ. This was his way of affirming the virgin birth.

---

17. Walvoord, *Jesus Christ Our Lord*, p. 104.

Why did not Paul and other writers of Scripture refer directly to the virgin birth? Perhaps it is because they were not concerned with the process involved in the incarnation as much as with the product that resulted from the incarnation. Matthew and Luke did deal with the process, as is evidenced by their careful genealogies.

Christ's Perfect Humanity

Through the incarnation and means of the virgin birth, the eternal Son of God took on humanity. He was fully and truly man, though unlike any other human since he did not have the capacity to sin and therefore never sinned. According to the New Testament the Son of God became incarnate so that he might reveal God to man (John 1:18), give himself as a sacrifice for sin (Heb. 10:1-10), and eventually sit on the earthly throne of David forever (Luke 1:31-33). In his coming Christ fulfilled both soteriological and eschatological purposes.

Christ possessed a true human body. He was born of a woman just as any other human. The conception was supernatural, not the birth. Christ also had a human soul (Matt. 26:38) and a human spirit (Luke 23:46). Luke said the Christ child grew in wisdom and stature as a man (Luke 2:52). Characteristics of humanity such as hunger, thirst, and sorrow were experienced by him. He was seen and touched as a man.

Human titles such as Son of man, the man, the man Christ Jesus, the Son of David, and man of sorrows were assigned to Christ and accepted by him. The human body he possessed was made up of flesh, bone, and blood (Heb. 2:14).

Christ's Undiminished Deity

Throughout the history of the church the Savior's deity has been denied by what would now be called liberal theology. Evangelicals, on the other hand, while not denying Christ's humanity have tended to neglect it. This has been true because one group wants to make certain he is seen as fully human while the other group wishes to present him as altogether God. The truth is, he is both. He is the God-man. Both Christ's perfect humanity and his undiminished deity are absolutely essential to the scriptural portrait of him.

By ascribing undiminished deity to Christ, evangelicals affirm that he is absolutely and truly God. Contemporary liberals speak of him as Godlike and nearer to God than anyone else. While liberals fail to do justice to biblical language concerning Christ's deity, evangelicals continue to affirm the historic, orthodox view that Christ, the Son of God, is as much God as the Father is God.

At least six lines of evidence of Christ's deity are delineated in Scripture. 1) Christ was called God (Isa. 9:6; John 1:1, 14; Heb. 1:8). 2) Christ possesses attributes of God. He is eternal (John 17:5), omnipresent (John 3:13), omniscient (John 2:25), omnipotent (Heb. 1:3), immutable (Heb. 13:8). 3) Christ performed works of God: creation (Col. 1:16), preservation (Col. 1:17), providence (Heb. 1:2), forgiveness of sins (Luke 5:20-24), judgment (John 5:22). 4) Christ demanded honor and worship due only to God (Matt. 14:33; John 5:23). 5) Christ himself made divine claims: to hold authority over the laws and institutions of God (Matt. 12:6), to be the object of saving faith (John 17:3), to have met in himself all the spiritual and eternal needs of humanity (John 7:37; 14:6). 6) Christ affirmed unequivocally that he was equal with God (John 8:24, 58; 10:30).

The Union of Humanity and Deity in Christ

"We confess that He is Very God and Very Man; Very God by His power to conquer death and Very man that He might die for us" (Belgic Confession, 1562). "He continueth to be God and man, in two distinct natures and one person forever" (Westminster Shorter Catechism, 1647). To deny either the undiminished deity or the perfect humanity of Christ is to put oneself outside the pale of orthodoxy. Equally as essential to orthodox theology is the belief that these two are inseparable and will remain eternally united in the person of Christ. The hypostatic union is the theological description of this and refers to the two hypostases, or natures, forming the one person in Christ.

Apart from this union Christ could not have been mediator between God and man. If he had only been man, his death could not have atoned for man's sin. If he had been only God, he could not have died, since God cannot die. If he had not been man, he would not have had a genuine link with humanity and would not have had perfect sympathy with man.

A Description of the Union. First, it is important that the meaning of *nature* and *person* be understood.

The English word "nature" is derived from the Latin *natura* and is the equivalent of the Greek *physis* (cf. Rom. 2:14; Gal. 2:15; 4:8;

Eph. 2:3; 2 Pet. 1:4). In the history of Christian doctrine the usage of the term "nature" has varied, but the word is now commonly used to designate the divine or human elements in the person of Christ. In theology the expression "substance" from the Latin *substantia* is also used, corresponding to the Greek *ousia*. All of these terms are used to define the real essence, the inward properties which underlie all outward manifestation. As this refers to the person Christ, nature is seen to be the sum of all the attributes and their relationship to each other. . . . Nature as used of the humanity of Christ includes all that belongs to his humanity. As applied to the deity of Christ it includes all that belongs to his deity.[18]

Nature and person are not synonymous. Persons have natures, yet personhood involves more than a nature. Person includes nature plus independent subsistence or reality embracing intellect, emotion, and will. The Son of God, who was one in person and nature (divine), became two in nature (divine and human) while remaining one in person through his incarnation. The eternal Son of God did not join himself with a human person, it must be remembered, but with a human nature.

In the union of the human and divine in Christ each of the natures retained its own attributes. Deity did not permeate humanity, nor did humanity become absorbed into deity. The two natures retain their complete identity even though they have been joined together in a personal union. Christ is thus theanthropic (God-man) in person. Embracing perfect humanity made him no less God, and retaining his undiminished deity did not make him less human.

The Reality of the Union. Scriptural evidence for the unipersonality of Christ abounds. He always spoke of himself as one. The Savior never distinguished himself as a divine person from himself as a human person (John 8:18, 23, 58; 16:7). Both of the natures in Christ are seen in Scripture to be united in one person. Of the many instances where Scripture teaches this, three central passages are especially helpful. Christ is said to be "of the seed of David," which stresses his humanity, and at the same time "declared to be the Son of God" (Rom. 1:2-5). To the Galatian Christians, Paul declared Christ as God's Son who was also "made of woman" (Gal. 4:4-5). In the great kenosis passage

18. Ibid., p. 114.

Christ is seen as "equal with God" and at the same time in the "form of a servant" (Phil. 2:5-11).

The Mystery of the Union. The apostle, under the guidance of the Spirit, said of the person of Christ, who possessed two natures, "Without controversy, great is the mystery of godliness; God was manifest in the flesh" (1 Tim. 3:16). Again, the same writer wrote of the "mystery of God" as he referred to the incarnation of Christ (Col. 2:2). Truly the relation of the human and divine in Christ will remain inscrutable to us. We do not have any analogies to it in our own natures or experiences. But the fact of this mystery must not deter us from accepting by faith the consistent biblical teaching.

Warfield wrote of this great mystery and warned of the dangers in attempting to solve the mystery completely: "We can never hope to comprehend how the infinite God and finite humanity can be united in one single person; and it is very easy to go fatally astray in attempting to explain the interactions in the unitary person of natures so diverse from one another."[19]

The Duration of the Union. Evangelical theology holds the incarnation of Christ is in perpetuity. That is, the act of incarnation was not an arrangement just for the time of his life on earth. The fact is, his human nature continues forever. This is supported in several ways: Christ's resurrected body was glorified and suited for heaven. Presently he is seated at the right hand of the Father and will return to earth as the Son of man (Matt. 26:64). The fact that he appeared in a visible body after his resurrection and was worshiped (John 20:17) also supports the contention. Christ ascended bodily to heaven (Mark 16:19; Acts 1:1-11; 7:56). At the present time he is the "one mediator between God and men, the man Christ Jesus" (1 Tim. 2:5).

The Earthly Life of Christ

The Kenosis of Christ. This Kenosis comes from the verb *kenoo* used in Philippians 2:7 and refers to the self-emptying of Christ. Evangelicals and liberals have been sharply divided over the meaning of this doctrine.[20] The question is: Of what did Christ "empty" himself and how?

---

19. Benjamin B. Warfield, *The Person and Work of Christ* (Philadelphia: Presbyterian and Reformed Publishing Company, 1970), p. 69.
20. See Walvoord, *Jesus Christ Our Lord*, pp. 138-45, for an extended discussion of the kenotic theories as well as a statement of the proper doctrine of kenosis from an evangelical perspective.

Obviously, if Christ emptied himself of any of his divine attributes when he became man, he was less than God. Those who believe Christ did surrender some of his attributes of deity usually cite omniscience, omnipotence, and omnipresence. Yet it is clear from the Gospels that Christ did not surrender these for his time on earth, though he certainly did not always employ them (Matt. 18:20; 28:18; Mark 2:8).

The humiliation or self-emptying of Christ means that his preincarnate glory was veiled (John 17:5). According to Philippians 2:1-11 he surrendered his appearance as God in order to take on the form and appearance of man. The Son of God condescended to take to himself human flesh (Rom. 8:3). Voluntarily he chose not to use some of his divine attributes during his earthly pilgrimage (Matt. 24:36).

The classic statement of A. H. Strong summarizes the evangelical view of the kenosis:

> Our doctrine of Christ's humiliation will be better understood if we put it midway between two pairs of erroneous views, making it the third of five. The list would be as follows: (1) Gess: The Logos gave up all divine attributes; (2) Thomasius: The Logos gave up relative attributes only; (3) True View: The Logos gave up the independent exercise of divine attributes; (4) Old Orthodoxy: Christ gave up the use of divine attributes; (5) Anselm: Christ acted as if he did not possess divine attributes.[21]

The Spheres in Which Christ Lived. One thing that makes the Gospels difficult to interpret is that Christ's life and ministry touched the law of Moses; the kingdom promised to Israel; and the church, which was to be composed of Jew and Gentile.

The law of Moses—indeed, the entire Levitical system—was still operative throughout Christ's life on earth. He lived under its jurisdiction (Gal. 3:23-25; 4:5). The law was, in fact, often interpreted by him (Matt. 5:17-19). The Savior kept the law perfectly (2 Cor. 5:21) and was "the end of the law for righteousness to every one that believeth" (Rom. 10:4).

Christ's forerunner, John the Baptist, preached, "Repent, for the kingdom of heaven is at hand" (Matt. 3:2). The same message

---

21. A. H. Strong, *Systematic Theology* (Philadelphia: American Baptist Publication Society, 1907), 2: 704.

was proclaimed by Christ himself (Matt. 4:17), the twelve he chose to be his disciples (Matt. 10:7), and the seventy he sent out to preach (Luke 10:11).

The day of Pentecost, bringing the formation of the church, was still future during Christ's life and ministry on earth. But he promised both to build the church and that it would withstand even the gates of hell (Matt. 16:18).

It can be said, therefore, that the life of the Son of God on earth touched each of these spheres. All three were not operative during his life, yet it touched all three. His death also may be seen to relate to each of them.

The Offices of Christ. Prophet, priest, and king: Christ was all three at the same time.

As prophet he proclaimed God's message (Matt. 5-7; 24-25; John 14-16) and predicted future events (John 13:26; 14:2-3).

Christ fulfilled all the qualifications of the Old Testament priesthood. He qualified fully for the office (Heb. 31*b*), was appointed by God (Heb. 5:1-10), was of the right order (Heb. 5:6, 10), was able to offer sacrifice and make intercession (Heb. 7:23-28), and was eternal in his priesthood (Heb. 7:25).

It is clear from the Old Testament that God promised his people a king who would fulfill the promise of God to David (2 Sam. 7:16; Ps. 2). Many, but by no means all, evangelicals believe that Christ came not only as man's Savior from sin but also as Israel's Messiah. These same evangelicals also believe that since the earthly kingdom Christ preached was not established, he will come again to do so. According to this view, the full revelation of the Savior's work as king is reserved for the future.

The Baptism of Christ. G. Campbell Morgan called John's baptism of Christ in the Jordan a crisis in the Savior's life because he saw it as both a dividing and uniting point between the thirty years of silence and the three years of service in Christ's earthly life.

Three Gospel writers describe Christ's baptism (Matt. 3:13-17; Mark 1:9-11; Luke 3:21-22), each saying clearly that the God-man was baptized at the hands of John. This was most unusual because in proselyte baptism, the apparent historical antecedent to Christ's baptism, the proselyte, seeking to experience Jewish blessing, was required to baptize himself.

Did John sprinkle Jesus or immerse him? Some believe he was sprinkled, as in Old Testament washings. Others believe he was immersed, as in proselyte baptism. Most say that the mode of Christ's baptism was the same as that for believer's baptism, whether sprinkling or immersing.

John's baptism of the Israelites was "unto repentance." Christ the Messiah had no need of repentance. Therefore, while he was indeed baptized at the hands of John, his baptism meant something very different from what baptism by John meant to the repentant Jews.

Christ's baptism is significant because by it he publicly identified himself with his forerunner, the forerunner's message, and with Israel whose Messiah he was. Also, in this way he was introduced to his public ministry. It is significant that at his baptism he received a public display of divine approval.

Support for the doctrine of the Trinity may be gleaned from the account of Christ's baptism. God the Son was the one baptized. God the Father spoke through the opened heavens. God the Spirit descended upon the Son in the form of a dove. The opened heavens spoke of the perfection of Christ's thirty years of life on earth. The descending dove, symbol of the Spirit, was a reminder of his gentle character and disposition. The voice from heaven was a recognition and declaration of his office, divine approval, and divine pleasure.

The Temptation of Christ. There is a consensus among evangelicals that Christ was tempted by Satan soon after his baptism by John. What is not agreed among them is whether he was peccable or impeccable. This question will be discussed later in the section dealing with differences among evangelicals. Here only the realities of his temptation will be set forth.

The scriptural record of the Son of God's confrontation with Satan is found in three major passages (Matt. 4:1-11; Mark 1:12-13; Luke 4:1-13). It is important to note several specifics with regard to the event.

Immediately after the divine approval was given at his baptism, Christ was confronted by the devil with what must have been the fiercest of all his temptations. Significantly, Jesus was in the wilderness, where he had been led by the Spirit of God (Matt. 4:1). He was there, in other words, by divine appointment. The instrument the third person of the Godhead allowed to bring the temptations was the devil himself.

Two purposes—Satan's and God's—must be distinguished in the temptation of Christ. Satan was bent on keeping Christ from the cross. This may be traced all through the Old Testament, where he sought continually to destroy the godly line through which Christ was to be born. At the birth of Christ, Herod, inspired by Satan, tried to have him killed. If Christ had sinned at any time, he would have disqualified himself as the substitute for sin. That, it seems clear, was the major intent of Satan in tempting Christ—to disqualify him.

God the Father's intent was very different, of course. The Father demonstrated the sinlessness of his Son and set him forth as the rightful King of Israel and Savior of the world through allowing him to be tempted of the devil.

The Work of Christ

Some of the major areas of Christ's work on the cross are included in chapter 7 under the doctrine of soteriology, and in chapter 9 extensive discussion is given to the return of Christ. Those aspects of the Savior's work not covered there will be outlined here.

Christ's Suffering and Death

Life Sufferings. That Christ endured suffering before his death on the cross is beyond dispute. The purpose and accomplishments of those sufferings are viewed differently by believers, and alternate views will be presented in the section on differences.

Whatever one's view of the relation of Christ's sufferings in life to his sufferings at death, the reality of those sufferings cannot be denied. Christ suffered because he embraced humanity. Having taken on humanity the Savior naturally experienced many of the physical properties common to man. Suffering also came to Christ through Satan. The archenemy of God was allowed to tempt Christ often. At the hands of those who rejected him and what he offered, Christ certainly endured suffering. He even suffered at the hands of his friends, who often deserted him when he needed them most. Though perfect in his humanity Christ was not exempted from hardships common to humanity. What was accomplished by these sufferings will be discussed later in this chapter.

Death Sufferings. Christ's accomplishments by his death on the cross are many. Four major ones that encompass them all are discussed in chapter 7—substitution for sin, redemption, propitiation, and reconciliation. Lewis Sperry Chafer describes fourteen.[22]

Without doubt the most important of all Christ's accomplishments on the cross was his substitution for sin and sinners. The Savior did not die that he might demonstrate great bravery in the hour of death. His death, according to Scripture, was not simply for man's benefit. And he was certainly not a victim of circumstances or of his persecutors. Rather, the Son of God died in the place of sinners. On the cross he was the sinless vicar intervening for man. His death was truly a vicarious transaction once-for-all in the sinner's place and stead. Both the objectivity and the finality of the substitution he provided hold true, whether or not anyone ever appropriates the benefits. The reality and value do not depend on the application to the individual sinner.

On the cross Christ was both the sacrifice and the sacrificer. Willingly he gave himself to satisfy the demands of God's offended righteousness. The primary evidence that his substitutionary death on the cross completely satisfied every demand of God is seen in his resurrection from the grave.

Christ's Resurrection from the Dead[23]

The Evidence. Those who accept the Bible's historical reliability find conclusive evidence to support the historic orthodox Christian belief in the bodily resurrection of Christ from the dead. After all, people witnessed to Christ's resurrection, and sinners came to believe it before the New Testament was written. The resurrection as historic fact is usually buttressed by the following lines of support:

1) The tomb in which Jesus Christ was placed was empty on the third day.
2) Jesus Christ appeared to a large number of people after his death, most of whom had access to the empty tomb: Mary Magdalene (John 20:14-17), other women (Matt. 28:9-10),

---

22. Lewis Sperry Chafer, *Systematic Theology* (Dallas: Dallas Seminary Press, 1948), 3:55-115.

23. Two excellent volumes are Merrill C. Tenney, *The Reality of the Resurrection* (New York: Harper & Row, 1963); and William Lane Craig, *The Son Rises: The Historical Evidence for the Resurrection of Jesus* (Chicago: Moody Press, 1981).

Peter (Luke 24:34), two on the road to Emmaus (Luke 24:13-35), ten disciples (John 20:19-23; Luke 24:36-43), eleven disciples (John 20:26-29), seven disciples by the sea (John 21:1-23), five hundred brethren (1 Cor. 15:6), James, the Lord's half brother (1 Cor. 15:7), eleven on the mountain in Galilee (Matt. 28:16-20), disciples at the time of the ascension (Acts 1:3-9), Stephen (Acts 7:55-56), Paul (Acts 9:3-6, 26-30; 20:24; 23:11), the apostle John (Rev. 1:12-20).

3) There was a definite change in the disciples after the resurrection, especially noticeable in Peter.

4) After the resurrection of Christ the first day of the week rather than the seventh day became the special day of worship.

5) On the day of Pentecost, fifty days after the resurrection, Peter preached to thousands who had access to the tomb owned by Joseph of Arimethea. If his message about the resurrected Christ was false, why did not someone disprove him?

The Importance. Christ's resurrection is highly significant for several reasons. First, it began a series of events which culminate in his present and future exaltation. Evangelicals who hold a postmillennial or amillennial view list these events: Christ's resurrection, ascension, position at the right hand of the Father, return in power and great glory. Premillennialists add Christ's position on the throne of David and his exaltation in the new heaven and earth.

Second, the resurrection of Christ is essential to the validity of the Christian faith. This was the apostle Paul's emphasis to the Christians in Corinth (1 Cor. 15:1-20). Apart from the resurrection, he wrote, the believer's faith and the preaching of the gospel are vain; those who proclaim the resurrection are liars, and there is no hope for future resurrection if Christ was not raised.

Third, the Father's acceptance of the Son's finished work on the cross is verified by the resurrection. Without it there is no basis for believing that what Christ did in his death was accepted by the Father as payment for the debt incurred by man's sin.

The Character. The Son of God arose bodily from the grave. The body placed in the tomb was the one that came out of it on the third day. The nail prints and wounds were still recognizable, and Christ ate food (Luke 24:39, 42-43).

There were several new qualities of Christ's resurrected body, however. It was not subject to the normal limitations of our bodies. Christ could pass through closed doors (John 20:19). He could appear suddenly and disappear just as suddenly. Distance was no restriction to him. His resurrected body was not sustained by blood and did not require rest. The most distinctive feature of Christ's resurrected body is that it will never again be subjected to death (Rom. 6:9).

The Agents. Each member of the Godhead was involved in raising Christ from the dead. Clearly the Father's part is seen in such passages as Psalm 16, Acts 2:24, and Ephesians 1:19-20. The Son's promise that he would raise himself from the dead is also clear (John 2:19; 10:17-18). The role of the Holy Spirit is less clear in Scripture. The passages usually cited in support of the Spirit's part in raising Christ from the dead are Romans 1:4; 8:11, and 1 Peter 3:18. There are questions about the correct interpretation of each of these, however.[24]

Though it may be difficult to be dogmatic from Scripture that the Holy Spirit raised Christ from the dead, there is little doubt that the third person was in fact involved in that great event. The members of the Godhead always work in conjunction with each other; and since the roles of the Father and Son are clear, it is reasonable to assume the Spirit was active also.

Christ's Present Ministry

By the present ministry of Christ is meant his activity since his ascension and until his return for his own.

The historic event of the ascension of Christ is recorded three times in Scripture: Mark 16:19-20; Luke 24:50-53; Acts 1:6-11 (the Markan reference is often questioned on textual grounds). As a climax of his life and resurrection from the dead, Christ returned to his Father.[25] The other appearances of the resurrected Savior demonstrated beyond doubt that he had indeed conquered death

---

24. See Charles C. Ryrie, *The Holy Spirit* (Chicago: Moody Press, 1965) pp. 49-51, for a discussion of these passages.

25. Some evangelicals believe Christ ascended to heaven prior to the event recorded in Acts 1. For a discussion of this view see John F. Walvoord, *The Holy Spirit* (Findlay, Ohio: Dunham Publishing Company, 1958), pp. 220-21.

and hell, but his appearance and departure at the time of the ascension was different. The transition period was past; a new era was to begin. That little band of believers gathered at Bethany knew they were not to expect the Son of God to appear again until he came to gather them to be with him forever. Until that time theirs was the responsibility of being witnesses to him in the power of the Holy Spirit (Acts 1:8, 11).

At least seven figures are used in the New Testament to describe the present ministry of Christ to believers.[26] These along with important facts concerning them are set forth in Table 2.

TABLE 2   **Figures of Christ's Present Relationship with Believers**

Figure	Scripture	Meaning	Application
Shepherd and sheep	John 10:1-21	Provision and protection	Sheep need to follow shepherd
Vine and branches	John 15:1-14	Sustenance, strength, relationship	Abide in Christ
Cornerstone and stones of building	Eph. 2:19-22	Support, unity in body, dependence	Dwell in unity
High priest and kingdom of priests	Heb. 5:1-10; 1 Peter 2:5, 9	Intercession and advocacy	Believer-priests need to reflect his grace
Head and body	1 Cor. 12:12-31	Direction, control, guidance	Follow his guidance
Last Adam and new creation	1 Cor. 15:20-50	Resurrected and eternal life	Live in power of resurrection
Bridegroom and bride	Eph. 5:25-27	Relationship with him	Show our relationship with him to others

Major Areas of Difference Among Evangelicals

The Meaning of Christ's Life Sufferings

There are two basic views regarding the meaning of Christ's life sufferings. Evangelicals who embrace dispensational theology usually hold to one view and nondispensational evangelicals to the other. It appears that one's view of the value of Christ's life

26. These are given extensive treatment in Walvoord, *Jesus Christ Our Lord*, pp. 226-53.

sufferings and obedience to the law of Moses is directly related to one's acceptance or rejection of covenant theology. The view normally held by covenant, or Reformed, theology will here be designated the vicarious atoning view, and that held by dispensational theology the non-atoning view.[27] I view the latter as the most scripturally defensible.

Very closely associated with the vicarious atoning view is the classification of Christ's obedience into active and passive obedience. While some distinction is made between these two by making the active refer to Christ's obedience in life and the passive to his obedience in death, yet it is often conceded that the two cannot be separated. "The two accompany each other at every point in the Savior's life."[28]

Berkhof explains his view of the vicarious nature of Christ's life sufferings by seeking to show the relation of the first Adam to Christ, the Last Adam:

> The first Adam was by nature under the law of God, and the keeping of it as such gave him no claim to a reward. It was only when God graciously entered into a covenant with him and promised him life in the way of obedience that the keeping of the law was made the condition of obtaining eternal life for himself and his descendants. And when Christ voluntarily entered into the federal relationship of the Last Adam, the keeping of the law naturally acquired the same significance for him and for those whom the Father had given him.[29]

Charles Hodge explains the meaning of Christ's being under the law: "This subjection to the law was not only voluntary, but vicarious."[30]

John Murray, a more contemporary adherent to the view, also presents the idea that what Christ suffered in life was as vicarious and substitutionary as what he endured on the cross: "Christ's obedience was vicarious in the bearing of the full judgment of God upon sin, and it was vicarious in the bearing of the full discharge

27. The following section regarding these two views is taken from the author's "The Savior's Sufferings in Life," *Bibliotheca Sacra*, Jan., 1970.
28. Berkhof, *Systematic Theology*, p. 379.
29. Ibid, pp. 380-81.
30. Charles Hodge, *Systematic Theology* (Grand Rapids: Eerdmans, 1968), 2:613.

of the demands of righteousness. His obedience becomes the ground of the remission of sin and of actual justification."[31]

Those who subscribe to this interpretation of the sufferings of Christ and his obedience to the law of Moses relate what he did in life to what he did in death. Boettner states:

> A moment's reflection should convince us that the suffering and death of Christ, although fully effective in paying the debt which his people owed to divine justice, was in a sense only a negative service. Being of the nature of a penalty, it could relieve his people from the liability under which they labored, but it could not provide them a positive reward. Its effect was to bring them back up to the zero point, back to the position in which Adam stood before the fall. It provided for their rescue from sin and its consequences, but it did not provide for their establishment in heaven. By his passive obedience they have been rescued from hell, and by his active obedience they are given entrance into heaven.[32]

Berkhof's view is the same: "And finally, if Christ had suffered only the penalty imposed on man, those who shared in the fruits of his work would have been left exactly where Adam was before he fell. . . . By his active obedience, however, he carried his people beyond that point and gave them a claim to everlasting life."[33]

The non-atoning view, without in any way detracting from the reality or intensity of Christ's sufferings in life, or from the sinlessness of his person and his absolute obedience to the law of God, denies that the active obedience of the Savior was in any way vicarious or atoning. Those who subscribe to this view reserve the substitutionary work of Christ to his death on the cross and to that alone. Only as he became a curse as he hung on the accursed tree and cried, "It is finished," did he become the full and final sacrifice for sin as he took the sinner's place. All the opposition and ridicule of sinners which the Savior endured in life were real and cannot be viewed lightly. Though genuine and

31. John Murray, *Redemption Accomplished and Applied* (Grand Rapids: Eerdmans, 1955), p. 28.
32. Loraine Boettner, *The Atonement* (Grand Rapids: Eerdmans, 1941), p. 59.
33. Berkhof, *Systematic Theology*, pp. 380-81.

without comparison, they were not vicarious according to this view.

Two basic things were accomplished by the Savior's suffering in life, according to the non-atoning view: He gave evidence of his sinless character, and he prepared for his sacrificial death.

To determine that the Paschal lamb was without blemish, it was confined from the tenth day of the month until the fourteenth (Exod. 12:3, 6). During this time the lamb was not a sacrifice for sin, but this time was needed to demonstrate its qualifications as a sacrifice to be offered. Christ was the antitype of that Paschal lamb. His life of suffering served to exhibit his eligibility both as an offerer and as the offering for sin. His sufferings in life did not provide a sacrifice, or even make him eligible to offer one, but they did demonstrate his right to be the sacrifice. They indicated his eligibility to offer the one eternal sacrifice for sin. Though tested often and "in all points," he remained the sinless, spotless Savior. Thus his sinless life of suffering was a natural and necessary part of his person and his work on the cross.

One minute infraction of the law would have disqualified Christ as the sin-bearer. His death would then not have availed as a sacrifice. Like the priest under the Levitical system, he would have had to provide a sacrifice for himself before he could offer one for sinners. Furthermore, he would have had to repeat the sacrifice continually, as those priests did. In fact, his sacrifice would have been no different from theirs. In contrast to the repeated sacrifices of the old economy and in contradiction of the view that his life sufferings were vicarious, Peter declares: "Christ also hath once suffered for sins, the just for the unjust, that he might bring us to God, being put to death in the flesh, but quickened by the Spirit" (1 Peter 3:18).

True to the prophecy of Isaiah, the Savior was "despised and rejected of men: a man of sorrows, and acquainted with grief: and we hid as it were our faces from him; he was despised, and we esteemed him not. Surely he hath borne our griefs, and carried our sorrows" (Isa. 53:3-4*a*; cf. Matt. 8:17). However, it was only when he was "stricken, smitten of God and afflicted" that he was "wounded for our transgressions," and was "bruised for our iniquities." It was only in death that the Lord "laid on him the iniquity of us all" (Isa. 53:4*b*-6).

Could Christ Have Sinned?

Evangelicals are in agreement on several important matters regarding the relation between Christ and sin. They agree he was indeed tempted, he had no sin nature, the temptation came because he possessed a human nature, and he did not sin.

What they are not united on is the answer to the question: Could Christ have sinned? The theological issue is whether he was merely able not to sin or manifestly not able to sin. Was he peccable or impeccable? The debate is not new. In recent days the issue has been brought to the attention of the Christian laity through the Radio Bible Class broadcasts and the publication of a booklet entitled *Could Jesus Sin?* by Richard W. DeHaan. DeHaan answered the question in the affirmative. In a direct response David Boyd Long wrote a booklet, *Could God Incarnate Sin?* His answer was a resounding "no."[34]

The question is not merely an academic one, as might at first appear. The person of Christ is at issue: Was he fully God and therefore equal with the Father or was he not? If he was capable of sinning in his incarnate state is he capable of sinning now? Which is temptable, natures or persons, and which sins? On the other hand, if he was impeccable, was Christ's temptation real? Was he truly and fully human? Can he really sympathize with his people?

Whether Christ was peccable or impeccable must be settled primarily on theological rather than exegetical ground. The problem also raises the question as to why he was tempted. If one believes Christ was tempted to determine whether or not he would sin, one will believe he was peccable and thank God he didn't sin. On the other hand, if one believes the Savior was tempted to demonstrate his sinlessness, one will embrace an impeccable Christ, as I do. Both sides of this issue have been ably defended.[35]

---

34. The DeHaan booklet was published by the Radio Bible Class, Grand Rapids. The Long rebuttal was published by Everyday Publications, Toronto, Canada.

35. See Hodge, *Systematic Theology* 2:456-59 and the DeHaan booklet for statements on peccability. For presentations of both sides from those who embrace impeccability, see Walvoord, *Jesus Christ Our Lord*, pp. 145-52 and W. G. T. Shedd, *Dogmatic Theology* (New York: Scribner's, 1889), 2:330-49.

The Relation Between the Human and
Divine Attributes in Christ

Early in the history of the church, as we have seen, discussion
arose as to how two incompatible natures could unite in one
person in Christ without either one losing its attributes or
individual identity. It was concluded that Scripture teaches this to
be precisely the case. A. H. Strong summarized well the historic
orthodox position in these words:

> Distinctly as the Scriptures represent Jesus Christ to have
> been possessed of a divine nature and of a human nature,
> each unaltered in essence and undivested of its normal
> attributes and powers, they with equal distinctness represent
> Jesus Christ as a single undivided personality in whom these
> two natures are vitally and inseparably united, so that he is
> properly, not God and man, but the God-man.[36]

Evangelicals all agree that Christ is two in nature and one in
person. What they do not concur on is the relation of the two
natures to each other. Has there been a transfer of attributes from
one nature to the other?

Lutheran theology teaches there has been a real communication
between the attributes or properties of the two natures.
Traditionally Lutheran teaching embraces the ubiquity of the
human body of Christ. This means the body of Christ is present
everywhere, including in the elements used in observing the
Lord's Table.

Luther and his early followers believed the attributes of each
nature were transferred to the other—divine to human and human
to divine. Later and in more recent times the transfer is viewed as
only from the divine to the human.[37]

In contrast Calvinistic or Reformed theology has insisted the two
natures are united in the person of Christ without any transfer of
attributes whatsoever.

> Just as an essence is composed of the sum of its attributes and their
> relationship, a change of any attribute would necessarily involve a

36. Strong, *Systematic Theology* 2:683-84.
37. For a complete discussion of this issue see Hodge, *Systematic Theology* 2:405-18, and
Walvoord, *Jesus Christ Our Lord*, pp. 114-17.

change in essence. For instance, infinity cannot be transferred to finity; mind cannot be transferred to matter; God cannot be transferred to man, or vice versa. To rob the divine nature of God of a single attribute would result in destruction of true humanity. It is for this reason that the two natures of Christ cannot lose or transfer a single attribute.[38]

The Meaning of Christ's Present Ministry

Depending upon whether or not they believe there will be a literal kingdom on earth in the future, evangelicals understand Christ's present position at the Father's right hand differently.

Generally postmillennialists and amillennialists[39] advocate that what Christ is now doing as sovereign Lord with power and authority is the fulfillment of the promises to David concerning the throne and kingdom. In other words, they believe the throne Christ is presently occupying is the throne of David.[40] This view is the result of a less than literal approach to the promises given to David, especially those in 2 Samuel 7:12-16. Also it is held that the natural fulfillment of the promises in the Davidic covenant were realized in the reign of Solomon. The eternal aspects, it is believed, include Christ of the seed of David in his present session in heaven, as seen from Acts 2:31.[41]

On the other hand, premillennialists distinguish carefully between the present universal lordship of Christ and the throne of David from which they believe Christ will rule over the earth in the future.[42] Premillennialists insist the Davidic covenant, upon which the belief in the future millennial reign of Christ on earth rests, has not been and is not now being fulfilled by Christ's present session. I along with other premillennialists hold this view because we interpret the covenant literally. Peters, a defender of the classic premillennial view, lists the best reasons for interpreting the Davidic covenant literally.[43]

---

38. Walvoord, *Jesus Christ Our Lord*, p. 115.

39. Millennial views are defined and explained in chapter 9.

40. For the amillennial perspective see Berkhof, *Systematic Theology*, pp. 351-53; for the postmillennial perspective see Hodge, *Systematic Theology* 2:596-609.

41. George Murray, *Millennial Studies* (Grand Rapids: Baker, 1948), p. 44.

42. See Walvoord, *Jesus Christ Our Lord*, pp. 224-25, and Charles C. Ryrie, *The Basis of the Premillennial Faith* (New York: Loizeaux Brothers, 1953), pp. 78-84.

43. George N. H. Peters, *The Theocratic Kingdom* (Grand Rapids: Kregel Publications, 1957), 1:343-44.

The Son of God and the Child of God

The Son of God longs to be Lord of the life of every child of God. Christians think of him chiefly as Savior and Redeemer and so he is, but he is also Lord. The apostle Paul's burden for the Roman Christians was that they would take self off the throne of their lives and reserve that position for Christ (Rom. 6:11-23). That needs to be the burden and practice of every believer.

The New Testament presents each child of God as "in Christ," and Christ is said to be in each believer. This means that positionally the child of God and the Son of God are united. Each believer is joined to him and he to each one in spiritual union. This divine transaction was accomplished at the time of salvation. The work is finished and cannot be improved. It is the result of the work of the Holy Spirit of God giving life to those without it.

Positional truth is one thing; the practical daily application of that truth is another. For Christ the Son of God to be Lord of the life of the child of God there must be surrender and obedience to his lordship. But how is this done? If Christ's lordship is to be a reality, obedience to the inscripturated Word of God is indispensable. No amount of church attendance, Christian stewardship, prayer, Bible reading, or any other Christian responsibilities of themselves will accomplish the goal. Only as the child of God knows, loves, and obeys the written Word of God will the Son of God be Lord of life.

Questions for Discussion

1. In the historical development of the doctrine of the person of Christ, which specific issues were discussed first?
2. Why are such things as the deity of Christ, his virgin conception, substitutionary atonement, and bodily resurrection denied?
3. What relationship do you see between the life sufferings and the death sufferings of Christ?

4. For whom, do you believe, did Christ die?
5. How do you view the present ministry of Christ in relation to any future reign of Christ? Why?

Suggestions for Further Reading

Anderson, Norman. *The Mystery of the Incarnation*. Downers Grove, Ill.: Inter-Varsity Press, 1978.

Borland, James A. *Christ in the Old Testament*. Chicago: Moody Press, 1978.

Gunn, James. *Christ the Fullness of the Godhead*. Neptune, N. J.: Loizeaux Brothers, 1983.

Henry, Carl F. H. *Jesus of Nazareth*. Grand Rapids: Eerdmans, 1966.

Warfield, Benjamin B. *The Person and Work of Christ*. Philadelphia: Presbyterian and Reformed Publishing Company, 1950.

Walvoord, John F. *Jesus Christ Our Lord*. Chicago: Moody Press, 1969.

4

God the
Holy Spirit

The person and work of the Holy Spirit have suffered from both abuse and neglect throughout the history of the church. The natural question is, Why? Certainly there is no scarcity of scriptural teaching on either the Spirit's person or his work. Both Old and New Testaments abound with references to the third person of the Godhead and to his role in the plan of God and the affairs of the world.

The abuse and neglect can be accounted for in several ways. Perhaps the most important reason relates to man's response to his experiences. Abuse of the doctrine in many cases is the result of constructing one's faith around how one feels. Neglect comes about because some persons react so strongly to emotionalism that they avoid thinking and studying about the Spirit out of fear.

Evangelical theology is at great variance with liberal theology when it comes to God the Holy Spirit. This is true of both the person and the work of the Spirit. The basic reason, of course, is because of opposing views regarding the authority of Scripture. Differences among evangelicals center largely in the Spirit's work. They all agree that the Holy Spirit is the third person of the Godhead and is just as much God as the Father and the Son.

Discussion of the historical development in pneumatology will touch only the high points. The positive statement does not include the Spirit's work in initiating and consummating salvation, since these matters are treated in chapter 7.

A Historical Perspective

A survey of developments in pneumatology will serve as preparation for the positive evangelical statements.[1] It will also provide assistance in understanding some of the major differences among evangelicals in areas of pneumatology.

Before Nicaea

Not until the orthodox acceptance of biblical statements regarding the Holy Spirit were challenged was there any formulation of the doctrine. However, from the brief statements in the baptismal formula, the Apostles' Creed, and early hymns and liturgies, belief in the personality and full deity of the Holy Spirit is apparent. In the second and third centuries views opposing these simple statements drew attention to the doctrine. Exactly how the Spirit related to the other members of the Trinity became a matter for debate.

Three movements in opposition to the orthodox beliefs regarding the Holy Spirit were of special importance. These movements were related to each other and also to the development of Christology.

Montanism (ca. 170). Montanus claimed to be possessed with the spirit of prophecy. He boldly announced that the age of the Paraclete had come, and that the Paraclete, or Spirit, spoke in Montanus.

His two women companions—Prisca and Maximilla—also claimed the gift of prophecy. Together the three proclaimed the restoration of the primitive gifts of the Spirit. They also announced the descent of the heavenly Jerusalem as near at hand. Asceticism and celibacy were strictly enforced in order to prepare for the imminent kingdom.

Montanism is generally viewed as a reactionary movement against the secularization of the church and the eschatological climate of the day. In contrast to Gnosticism, it was an orthodox movement, though an extreme overreaction to existing problems in the church.

---

1. The history of the doctrine of the Holy Spirit has been well summarized by H. B. Swete, *The Holy Spirit in the Ancient Church*, George Smeaton, *The Doctrine of the Holy Spirit* (London: The Banner of Truth Trust, 1958), and George P. Fisher, *History of Christian Doctrine*. I am indebted to these sources.

Near the close of the second century Montanism was driven from the church. Its insistence on additional revelation beyond Scripture was one of the major reasons. With its rejection the church established that the canon of Scripture was closed. Stress was then placed on the Spirit's work in illumination of the existing revelation rather than appealing to extrabiblical messages.

Sabellianism (ca. 215). Sabellianism was a form of monarchianism. Tertullian used the term *monarchian* to designate those seeking to defend the sole government or monarchy of God. The movement sought sincerely to escape making the Son and the Spirit subordinate to the Father while at the same time maintaining monotheism.

Sabellius was the most influential leader of modalistic monarchianism. He said that in the Father, God revealed himself as Creator, in the Son as Redeemer, and in the Spirit as Sanctifier. Father, Son, and Spirit were therefore not three distinct persons but roles played by one person. In other words, Sabellianism rejected the teaching that God is one in three and three in one. It insisted rather that Father, Son, and Holy Spirit were simply different modes of revelation or manifestations of the one true God. It is usually acknowledged that Sabellianism was the first major false teaching related to the Godhead that gained a large following in the church.

Arianism (ca. 325). Arius did not deny the personality of the Son or the Spirit but said they were both created beings. The Son, he said, was generated by the Father and was of another substance from him. Arius believed further that the Spirit of God was created by the Son.

The Arian controversy eventually led to the Council of Nicaea (325), where Arianism was designated as error and condemned. The creed which resulted from the council stressed that Christ was of the same substance with the Father but stated only belief in the Holy Spirit. It was after Nicaea that turmoil developed over the person of the Spirit.

After Nicaea

From Nicaea to the Council of Constantinople (381). Soon after the Nicene Council, the Macedonian sect arose, named after Macedonius, who believed the Holy Spirit was a creature and thus not God. He was opposed by defenders of the Spirit's deity, including Athanasius, Basil, Gregory of Nazianzus, and Greogory of Nyssa. These defended the Spirit as fully God by appealing to the attributes of omniscience, omnipotence, and omnipresence assigned to him in Scripture. They also called attention to the baptismal formula, which certainly implied the Spirit's equality with the Father and the Son.

In 381 the second council that met at Constantinople added to the Nicene Council's brief reference to the Holy Spirit. The enlargement referred to the Spirit as "the Lord and Giver of Life, who proceedeth from the Father, who, with the Father and Son together, is worshiped and glorified, who spoke by the prophets." Though we might wish for a clearer and more specific statement, this enlargement did address the Macedonian heresy.

From Constantinople to the Council of Chalcedon (451). In the years between the two councils discussion continued over the deity of the Spirit. The issue of his procession also arose. The Council of Chalcedon was widespread in its representation, which included the sees of Rome, Jerusalem, Constantinople, and Antioch. It agreed with and reinforced the decisions of previous councils in their statements about the Holy Spirit.

The Council of Constantinople did not state that the Holy Spirit proceeded from the Son but said he proceeded from the Father. The matter of the procession of the Spirit was an attempt to describe the Spirit's precise relation to the other persons in the Godhead. That the Holy Spirit was fully divine was settled by the Constantinopolitan Creed, but a clearer statement regarding his relation to the Father was still lacking. The Western branch of the church added the *filioque* ("and the Son") phrase at the Synod of Toledo (589) to the Constantinopolitan statement. Thus the West stated that it believed the Spirit of God proceeded from, and therefore was identical to, the Father and the Son in essence.

Discussion of the development of the doctrine of the Holy Spirit in the period after Nicaea would not be complete without a word about Augustine's contribution. His *On the Trinity* represents the Western church's concept of the Trinity. Augustine's emphasis on man's total inability to merit favor with God and therefore his need of God's grace necessarily drew attention to the sovereign work of God the Spirit.

Augustine's debate with Pelagius continued until the Council of Ephesus in 431, where Pelagianism was condemned. Semi-Pelagianism, which arose and continued after 431, was condemned at the Synod of Orange in 529. The whole Pelagian-

Augustinian controversy brought into prominence the work of the Holy Spirit in man's salvation.

The Middle Ages

Augustine's biblical views of man's sin and God's grace, and therefore the need for the work of the Spirit, became widespread and were considered representative of the church's views.

The Roman Church, however, soon reinterpreted these views and misused them to enhance its own system. Rome brought to Augustinianism its view of the church as authoritative in doctrine and in the administration of the sacraments, which it viewed as the means of grace. This meant that grace was viewed as bestowed on man through partaking in the sacraments and to some degree through hearing the Word proclaimed by the church. As a result practically no attention was paid to the work of the Holy Spirit or the need for it. Earthly priests were substituted for the Holy Spirit.

In his history of the doctrine of the Holy Spirit, Walvoord has given an accurate summary of the doctrine in the Middle Ages:

> Few grasped the need for personal conversion and the work of the Spirit in regeneration. Practically no attention was given to such subjects as the indwelling Spirit, the baptism of the Spirit, and the filling of the Spirit. It was expressly denied that the Spirit could teach all Christians through the Word of God. Earthly priests were substituted for the Holy Spirit. The "things of the Spirit of God" were lost in the wilderness of sacramentarianism, ignorance of the Word, superstition, humanism, and scholasticism.[2]

The Reformation

The Reformation turned attention to the work of the Holy Spirit. The two clarion calls were *sola fide* (faith alone for salvation) and *sola scriptura* (Scripture alone as divinely authoritative); both of these naturally drew attention to God the Spirit's work.

There was a new emphasis on the need for the Spirit's work in regeneration in recognition of man's total inability to do anything to merit favor with God. Since the Bible alone was viewed as authoritative, it must be read and understood, and this required

2. John F. Walvoord, *The Holy Spirit* (Findlay, Ohio: Dunham Publishing Company, 1958).

the illuminating work of the Spirit. Through its emphasis on the sacraments and its view of the power of the Word of God by itself to bestow grace, the Roman Church had drawn attention away from the work of the Holy Spirit. The result was that while pneumatology was not a prominent doctrine of the Reformers, doctrinal formulations concerning it soon developed.

In general the Protestant Reformation revived and propagated the earlier Augustinian doctrines of total depravity and man's need, and therefore of the efficacious work of the Holy Spirit. While differences developed later as to how the Spirit worked and what he used to do the work, the Reformers were united on the necessity of the Spirit's work to make saving faith possible.

The confessional statements that developed out of the Reformation bear testimony to the doctrine of the Holy Spirit which developed at the time. Smeaton quotes from the Augsburg Confession, the Formula of Concord, the Helvetic Confessions, the Scots Confession, the Westminster Confession, and others to illustrate this point.[3]

Not long after the Reformation two major theological problems arose which greatly affected the doctrine of God the Spirit. Under the leadership of Melanchthon, who changed his mind shortly after Luther's death about man's will and natural powers, synergistic views arose. The synergism was that God and man cooperated in salvation, thus implying man was not totally incapable of contributing to his salvation. Naturally this view detracted from the work of the Spirit in salvation.

Arminianism did the same. Arminius argued that the human will, not the work of the Holy Spirit, was decisive in man's salvation. Whereas the human priest had replaced the Holy Spirit in the Middle Ages, the human will did much the same in Arminian theology. At the Synod of Dort (1618-19) the Reformed position was reaffirmed, and Arminianism received a serious blow.

The Modern Period

In England the Puritan movement, under the able leadership of such men as John Owen (1616-83), served to champion God's grace through the Spirit's work.[4]

---

3. George Smeaton, *The Doctrine of the Holy Spirit*, pp. 311-14.

Another great contribution to pneumatology was made by Abraham Kuyper (1837-1920).[5] His work was especially significant at the time when the detrimental effects of such men as Schleiermacher and Ritschl were being felt.

To the Plymouth Brethren, under the early leadership of J. N. Darby and William Kelly, evangelicals owe the emphasis on the baptism of the Spirit in forming the New Testament church as distinct from Israel.

Liberal theology, both classic and contemporary, denies the personality and deity of the Holy Spirit. In fact, it was in the denial of the doctrine of the Trinity that liberal theology made one of its first departures from evangelical theology. That denial, of course, came because of a rejection of the Bible as God's Word.

The doctrine of the Holy Spirit in neoorthodox theology has been well summarized by Charles Ryrie:

> Although neoorthodoxy has about as many exponents as there are neoorthodox theologians it may be said that in general its view of the Holy Spirit leaves much to be desired. Most neoorthodox writers deny the distinct personality of the Spirit and affirm his deity only in that he is represented as a divine manifestation of God. The Holy Spirit is regarded as more of an activity of God than a person of the Godhead.[6]

This historical perspective would not be complete without a word about the developments in pneumatology within the Pentecostal wing of evangelicalism.

Classic or historic Pentecostalism began in 1901 with students in Charles F. Parham's Bethel Bible School of Topeka, Kansas, who claimed a Pentecostal experience. It received impetus in 1906 from similar happenings at the Azusa Street Mission in Los Angeles. Early Pentecostalism held strongly to the baptism of the Spirit as an experience distinct from salvation and to speaking in tongues as evidence of the experience.

By 1960 Pentecostalism was beginning to spread into mainline

4. John Owen's *A Discourse Concerning the Holy Spirit* is recognized by many evangelicals as unsurpassed in excellence. See *The Works of John Owen* (Philadelphia: Protestant Episcopal Book Society, 1862).

5. Abraham Kuyper, *The Work of the Holy Spirit*, trans. by Henri de Vries (New York: Funk and Wagnalls, 1900). This work appeared in Dutch in 1888.

6. Charles C. Ryrie, *The Holy Spirit* (Chicago: Moody Press, 1965), p. 119.

Protestant denominations. April 3, 1960, is usually considered the birthday of the Neo-Pentecostal or charismatic movement. On that day in St. Mark's Episcopal Church in Van Nuys, California, the pastor announced he had received the baptism of the Spirit. His speaking in tongues, he believed, proved it. It was not long after this that Neo-Pentecostalism began to appear in all the major Protestant denominations and many Christian organizations.

On April 8, 1967, Neo-Pentecostalism entered and began making significant inroads into the Roman Catholic Church. It began at the now famous Notre Dame prayer meeting. In the same year students, priests, and faculty members, mostly from Notre Dame and Michigan State, met for what was billed as the First Annual National Catholic Pentecostal Conference.

Significant elements in Neo-Pentecostalism in relation to pneumatology have been noted by a historian of the movement:

> With some exceptions most new Pentecostals do not require public speaking in tongues as proof of being baptized in the Holy Spirit. . . . The new Pentecostals follow the established liturgical order when worshiping in their own congregations, rather than the older Pentecostal practice of spontaneous contributions at any given point. The new participants cultivate the "Spirit-led" services at their midweek meetings.[7]

As we will see, evangelicals are rather sharply divided over the gifts of the Spirit. More attention is given today to aspects of the work of the Holy Spirit than in any other period of the church's history.

A Positive Statement of the Doctrine

Orthodox contributions to the doctrine of the Holy Spirit are usually divided between his person and his work, and his personality and deity are usually discussed under "person." The approach taken here will present three major divisions instead of the customary two: the personality, the deity, and the work of God the Holy Spirit.

---

7. Erling Jorstad, ed., *The Holy Spirit in Today's Church: A Handbook of the New Pentecostalism* (Nashville: Abingdon Press, 1973), pp. 22-23.

The Personality of God the Spirit

The importance of the personality of God the Father and God the Son has already been stressed. The personality of God the Spirit is equally as crucial to orthodox doctrine.

Evangelical theology in its doctrine of the Holy Spirit has always attributed to him the essential elements of personality, which are intellect, emotion, and will. These are assigned to him in the Bible. He is seen as the one who knows the things of God (1 Cor. 2:10-11). He is the Spirit of wisdom (Eph. 1:17; cf. Isa. 11:2) and able to teach humans (1 Cor. 2:13). The Holy Spirit is presented as possessing emotions characteristic of personalities. He is grieved or hurt by the believer's sin (Eph. 4:30). The warning is not to act "despite" against him (Heb. 10:29). The Spirit also loves (Rom. 15:30).

The apostle Paul was led or directed in his work by God the Holy Spirit (Acts 16:6-10). He also declared that the same Spirit was the one who gives gifts or abilities for service to the people of God (1 Cor. 12:11).

Too often, sometimes even in evangelical circles, the Holy Spirit is viewed merely as a force or power of God. He is often spoken of as "it." This is dishonoring to him and not in harmony with the biblical teaching. The Holy Spirit does what only persons can do—teach (John 14:26), testify (John 15:26), lead (Rom. 8:14), convict (John 16:7-8), send believers into service (Acts 13:2, 4). These things are not done by an influencing force or energy. Things that humans can do to the Holy Spirit also argue for his personality—lie (Acts 5:3), resist (Acts 7:51), blaspheme (Matt. 12:31).

Throughout Scripture the Holy Spirit is presented in association with the other persons of the Godhead (John 16:14; Matt. 28:19; 2 Cor. 13:14), thereby presenting him as a person as well. The Spirit's intercession for the believer clearly requires his distinction from the Father as another person. Jesus himself said he would send "another comforter" of the same kind as himself—personal and divine. All the arguments for the Spirit's full deity given below also argue for his personality.

The Deity of God the Spirit

Throughout the history of the Christian church the personality and the deity of the Holy Spirit have gone hand in hand. Those who have accepted the one have generally accepted the other, and those who have rejected the one have rejected the other. Both doctrines are vital to the historic Christian faith, and they stand or fall together.

By ascribing deity to the Holy Spirit evangelicals mean he is as fully God as the Father and Son are God. Appeal has usually been made, in defense of this conviction, to the Spirit's characteristics or attributes of deity, his works, and his coidentity with God.

Many of the Father's attributes are also assigned to the Spirit. He is said to possess all knowledge, or omniscience (1 Cor. 2:11-12). The psalmist presented him as omnipresent, present every place at the same time in all his fullness (Ps. 139:7). Through his work in creation the Spirit is seen to be omnipotent, all-powerful (Job 33:4). God the Spirit is the giver of life (Rom. 8:2; cf. 8:11) and possessor of divine wisdom (Isa. 40:13).

Works are assigned to the Spirit which only God can perform, thus arguing for his full deity. The Holy Spirit was involved in the work of creation (Gen. 1:2; Pss. 33:6; 104:30). Both the revelation and inspiration of Scripture were the result of the work of the Spirit (2 Sam. 23:2; Ezek. 2:2; 8:3; 2 Peter 1:21; 2 Tim. 3:16). The Son of God was begotten by the Spirit of God (Luke 1:35). He was sent by the Father and the Son to convict of sin (John 16:8). The Holy Spirit gives life (John 3:6), comforts (John 14:16), intercedes for believers (Rom. 8:26), and sanctifies them (2 Thess. 2:13).

The Spirit of God is identified with the Jehovah-God of the Old Testament. A comparison of New Testament with Old Testament Scripture verifies this (Acts 28:25 with Isa. 6:1-13 and Heb. 10:15-17 with Jer. 31:31-34). Here then is strong support for his deity. Equally strong is the association of the Spirit with God. To blaspheme and lie to the Holy Spirit is to do these things to God (Matt. 12:31-32; Acts 5:3-4). In the Acts passage the Holy Spirit is actually called God. Significantly, the Spirit is associated with God the Father and with God the Son when they are presented together (Matt. 28:19; 2 Cor. 13:14).

Evangelicals do not worship one God who has three names—Father, Son, and Holy Spirit—or three modes of existence. They worship God who is one in three and three in one. The God of the Bible is one, and he exists in three personal distinctions—God the Father, God the Son, and God the Holy Spirit.

The Work of God the Spirit

In both testaments God the Spirit is seen to be very active. Many of the works assigned to the Spirit in the Old Testament are continued by him in the New. From a theological perspective it is significant that some totally new work is performed by God the Spirit in the New Testament, especially after Christ's ascension. Also, some of the Spirit's works begun in the Old Testament continue today, and others do not. Table 3 identifies some of the major works of the Spirit in the different time periods.

TABLE 3 **Works of the Spirit Throughout History**

Selected work of God the Spirit	O.T.	Continued in N.T.	New in N.T.	Continued Today
Creation	X			
Revelation of Scripture	X	X		
Inspiration of Scripture	X	X		
Restraint of sin	X	X		X
Enablement for service	X	X		X
Indwelling	X	X		X
Baptism			X	X
Filling	X	X		X
Sealing			X	X
Anointing			X	X
Regeneration	X	X		X
(Nicodemus was expected to understand this from the Old Testament)				
Sanctification	X	X		X

The Spirit's Work in Relation to Christ[8]

While each of the members of the Godhead partakes of the same essence, each does not occupy the same office. Though different works are carried out by each of the members, there is always complete harmony and cooperation among them. God the Holy Spirit is associated in Scripture with many aspects of God the

8. Two excellent contributions to this doctrine appear in Ryrie, *The Holy Spirit*, pp. 45-51, and Walvoord, *The Holy Spirit*, pp. 81-104.

Son's person and work. This reality serves as an illustration of the unity of purpose in the Trinity. It also is a reminder of the condescension of the Son in becoming man.

The Spirit's Work and the Humanity of Christ. Gabriel's announcement to Mary that she would conceive by the Holy Spirit came as a complete surprise to her (Luke 1:35). Joseph was no less shocked when he heard the news (Matt. 1:20). The human nature of God the Son was the result of Mary's virgin conception. His humanity was therefore sinless because of the direct ministry of the Spirit.

It is important to note that God the Spirit did not work alone in this great miracle. The writer to the Hebrews declared that the Father prepared Christ's body (Heb. 10:5; cf. Ps. 40:6) and that the Son himself embraced humanity (Heb. 2:14).

Walvoord's explanation of the mystery associated with the Son's reception of humanity is to the point:

> The life which was joined to the humanity of Christ was none other than the Second Person, who had existed from eternity. The inscrutable mystery can be stated, then, that Christ was begotten of the Holy Spirit; the life which was joined to humanity was that of the Second Person, and the First Person became the Father of the humanity of Christ. The Scriptures never refer to the Holy Spirit as the Father of Christ.[9]

The Spirit's Work and the Public Ministry of Christ. At several crucial points in Christ's life on earth the Holy Spirit performed important ministries. These include anointing, filling, direction and performance of miracles, and a ministry at the time of Christ's death and resurrection.

In four different passages Christ's anointing is mentioned. The time when this occurred is not specified, but it most likely took place when he was baptized by John in the Jordan, since the baptism introduced him to his public ministry. The divine anointing of the incarnate Son set him apart as the true Messiah through whom the Holy Spirit would manifest himself. God the Father is seen as the one who anointed Christ (Acts 4:27; Heb. 1:9). He was anointed by the Spirit of the Lord to preach the gospel to the poor (Luke 4:18). Again, the Father is said to have anointed Christ with the Holy Spirit (Acts 10:38).

9. Walvoord, *The Holy Spirit,* p. 84.

God the Son was filled with God the Spirit. Before his temptation this was said of him (Luke 4:1). God, presumably the Father, gave the Spirit to him in fullness (John 3:34). It is generally assumed that Christ was filled or controlled by the Spirit from his conception, though Scripture does not tell us this specifically. Support for it is usually drawn from his work described in the New Testament and from Old Testament prophecies concerning him (Isa. 11:2; 42:1; 61:1).

God the Spirit led Christ into the wilderness to be tempted of the devil (Matt. 4:1; Luke 4:1). He also sustained him in that awful hour. Some, perhaps most, of Christ's miracles were performed in the power of the Spirit. Having voluntarily surrendered the independent use of his divine attributes as a part of his condescension, he apparently also chose to do his mighty deeds in the power of the Spirit. There are a few instances, however, where miracles were performed by drawing upon his own divine power (e.g., Mark 5:30; Luke 5:17).

Specific scriptural defense for the Spirit's involvement in the death of Christ is scanty. Hebrews 9:14 is probably the best support to be found: "How much more shall the blood of Christ, who through the eternal Spirit offered himself without spot to God, purge your conscience from dead works to serve the living God!" Even in this passage the problem is that the eternal Spirit could refer to Christ's own eternal spirit and not the Holy Spirit.[10] In favor of identifying the eternal Spirit with the Holy Spirit is the context, which speaks of the Holy Spirit (c. 9:8). Even though there may not be a clear reference to the Holy Spirit's involvement in Christ's death, this may be assumed on theological ground based upon the unity and relationship within the Godhead.

The Holy Spirit's involvement in the resurrection of Christ also lacks definite proof from Scripture. However, as in his relation to Christ's death, it may be assumed. Three passages are generally used to support the Spirit's role in the Savior's resurrection, though each has an element of uncertainty in it: Romans 1:4; Romans 8:11; and 1 Peter 3:18.[11]

Romans 1:4 can be used only if the spirit of holiness means the Holy Spirit. The antecedent of the "he" that is said to have raised

---

10. See Ryrie, *The Holy Spirit*, pp. 48-49, for the arguments on both sides of the issue.
11. See ibid., pp. 49-51, for the arguments on both sides of the matter.

up Christ in Romans 8:11 is God, and may not be God the Spirit but God the Father. The "in the Spirit" of 1 Peter 3:18 must be taken in the instrumental sense, and the quickening must refer in fact to the resurrection and not the death, for this to support the Spirit's part in Christ's resurrection. Both these things are possible, but so are the alternatives; the passage is not determinative.

The Baptism of God the Spirit[12]

Evangelicals are sharply divided over the significance of baptism in, with, or by the Spirit. The different views of the significance of Spirit baptism will be presented, along with documentation to support the various interpretations, in the section on differences. Here it will only be necessary to set forth the basic meaning and scriptural facts regarding the doctrine.

Throughout Scripture, whenever it occurs, baptism has identification as its primary meaning. John's baptism unto repentance showed the identification of repentant Jews with him and his message. The baptism of Christ at the hands of John signified Christ's identification with John, his message, and his people. When a believer is baptized, he is showing his identification with Christ and with all believers. Likewise, the Spirit's work of baptism identifies the believing sinner with Christ (Rom. 6:1-4) and with other members of his body (1 Cor. 12:12-13). The Holy Spirit provides a vital relationship of each believer with Christ and all other believers. This is what is meant by the baptism of God the Spirit.

There is no reference to the baptism of the Holy Spirit in the Old Testament. Acts 1:5 and the several passages in the Gospels are all prophetic, looking forward to the baptism. Relating Acts 2:1-4 to the prophecy in 1:5 and the reference to the prophecy in 11:15-17, it seems clear that the historical fulfillment of the prophecy took place on the day of Pentecost.

Paul's contribution to the baptism of God the Spirit in 1 Corinthians 12:12-13 enlarges a bit on the Acts prophecy and the

---

12. A thorough treatment of this subject may be found in Merrill F. Unger, *The Baptizing Work of the Holy Spirit* (Chicago: Scripture Press, 1953); see also his *The Baptism and Gifts of the Holy Spirit* (Chicago: Moody Press, 1974).

fulfillment. Whereas in the prophecy of the baptism Christ seems to be the one who would baptize with the Spirit, in Paul's summary the Spirit appears to be the agent baptizing believers into the body. Since Christ is the one who sent the Spirit, and by virtue of their relationship in the Trinity, both Christ and the Holy Spirit may be viewed as agents. This peculiarity is discussed further in chapter 8. The realities described here are visualized in figure 1.

FIGURE 1 **The Baptism of the Spirit**

Prophetical	Historical	Doctrinal
Matthew 3:11	*Acts 2:1-4*	*1 Corinthians 12:12-13*
Mark 1:8	*Acts 11:15-17*	*Romans 6:1-4*
Luke 3:16		
John 1:33		
Acts 1:5		

The Indwelling of God the Spirit

The indwelling ministry of the Spirit has to do with his presence in and with the child of God. All who truly belong to the Lord are said to be indwelt by God the Spirit (1 Cor. 3:16; 6:19). It is clear from 1 Corinthians 5-6 that even sinning Christians are indwelt by him. He is God's gift to all in the family of God (John 7:37-39; Acts 11:17; Rom. 5:5; 1 Cor. 2:12; 2 Cor. 5:5). Those who do not have the Spirit do not belong to God (Rom. 8:9b).

In Old Testament times the Spirit's indwelling appears to have been selective and temporary. He is said to have been "in" certain individuals (e.g., Gen. 41:38; Dan. 4:8). The same Spirit came "upon" many (e.g., Judg. 3:10; 1 Sam. 10:9-10). He also "filled" some (e.g., Exod. 31:3; 35:31). Apparently the Spirit could be withdrawn (Judg. 16:20). According to the New Testament, by way of contrast, the Spirit indwells all believers, and he does so permanently (John 14:16-17).[13]

Several scriptural passages introduce problems regarding conditions for indwelling of the Spirit and the time at which the

---

13. Some believe the Spirit's withdrawal from those persons in Old Testament times means that God removed them from the office for which they had been anointed.

Spirit takes up residence in the believer. These have been discussed thoroughly and can be interpreted in harmony with the major teachings of Scripture.[14]

The Sealing of God the Spirit

Without distinguishing which member of the Godhead is in view, God is said to seal the believer and give him the earnest of the Spirit (2 Cor. 1:22; cf. John 6:27).

The Holy Spirit himself is the seal with which the believer is secured (Eph. 1:13; 4:30). To be sealed by or with the Spirit means to be owned by him. Believers are not exhorted to be sealed, just as they are not exhorted to be baptized by the Spirit. Rather, this badge of ownership is a work of the Spirit, true of all believers; it is begun at the time of salvation, just as Spirit baptism is, and continued "until the day of redemption" (Eph. 4:30).

The Spirit's baptizing and sealing work are very closely related, and both occur at the same time though they are not identical. Baptism has to do with providing the vital relationship between the believer and Christ and believers with each other. Sealing signifies ownership and security.

The Filling of God the Spirit

The people of God are not exhorted in Scripture to be baptized, indwelt, or sealed by the Spirit. But they are told to be filled or controlled by the Spirit (Eph. 5:18). The idea of control comes from the analogy of strong drink used in the passage. To be controlled by the Spirit means the individual believer must cooperate with God in order to be under the Spirit's supervision, which is what filling means. In other words, the believer's obedience to God and his Word is essential for the filling of the Spirit.

Since the Holy Spirit is a person of the Godhead, filling does not involve getting more of him. Rather, it allows him to have more of us, to be under his direction and control. It also follows that since this work of the Spirit involves his control—which is dependent, at least in part, upon individual participation—filling is a repeated experience. The present tense and imperative mood used in Ephesians 5:18 further support this fact. There must be a conscious submission and obedience to God's Word, which is what the Spirit uses to produce Christlikeness in us. When we live according to Scripture, we may be sure we are controlled by the Spirit.

14. See Ryrie, *The Holy Spirit*, pp. 70-72, and Walvoord, *The Holy Spirit*, pp. 152-55.

Evidence of being under the Spirit's sovereign control may be found in the fruit he produces in the believer's life (Gal. 5:22-23). Another evidence is an attitude of worship, praise, and submissiveness (Eph. 5:18-20). For some, being under the Spirit's control has a greater impact on the emotions than for others. We need not expect an ecstatic experience to substantiate that we are controlled by the Spirit. The more we know and obey the Word of God, the more control the Spirit will have in our lives.

The Gifts of God the Spirit

All members of the orthodox community believe gifts of the Spirit were operative in the early days of the church. Most believe at least some of those gifts are still operative today.

Gifts of the Spirit are generally understood to be special abilities given by God to serve him and others in turn. They are viewed as distinct from natural abilities but not totally divorced from them. Ephesians 4:12 states the purpose for their existence; gifted individuals are given to the church for the edifying of the whole body. Though Scripture does not state when gifts of the Spirit are given, it seems reasonable and not out of harmony with Scripture to view them as bestowed at the time of salvation. Evangelicals commonly hold that every believer has at least one spiritual gift and that many have more than one. Some evangelicals lay more stress on certain gifts than do others.

Figure 2 lists the gifts named in the New Testament. "T" indicates those gifts usually considered to have been temporary

FIGURE 2 **New Testament Lists of Gifts**

Rom. 12:3-8	1 Cor. 12:8-10, 28-30	Eph. 4:11
Prophecy (T)	*Word of wisdom*	*Apostles (T)*
Ministry	*Word of knowledge*	*Prophets (T)*
Teaching	*Faith*	*Evangelists*
Exhorting	*Healing (T)*	*Pastors*
Giving	*Miracles (T)*	*Teachers*
Ruling	*Prophecy (T)*	
Showing mercy	*Discerning spirits (T)*	
	Tongues (T)	
	Interpretation (T)	
	Apostles (T)	
	Teachers	
	Helps	
	Governments	

and no longer operative by evangelicals who distinguish between the permanent and temporary gifts. Some make no such distinction and believe all the gifts of the Spirit are still operative today. Differences among evangelicals over the number still in existence today will be discussed below.

Major Areas of Difference Among Evangelicals

The Baptizing Work of the Spirit

The difference among evangelicals on the Spirit's baptizing work centers primarily in the meaning of this work, especially as taught in 1 Corinthians 12:12-13. This great work of the Spirit has been identified or equated with a number of other ministries of the Spirit—regeneration, indwelling, sealing, filling. Spirit baptism is also sometimes identified with the second blessing and with water baptism.[15]

One's ecclesiology has a great deal to do with his view of the meaning and significance of Spirit baptism. Many evangelicals, and I number myself among them, see God's program with the church, the body of Christ, as distinct from his program with Israel. Others view them as essentially one and the same. The sections in chapters 8 and 9 discuss dispensational theology and covenant theology as these relate to the matters at hand.

The View of Covenant Theology. Generally those who hold this view see the church not as having begun on the day of Pentecost but as the covenanted community of believers of all ages. They view the baptism of the Spirit referred to in 1 Corinthians 12:13, for example, as the Spirit's means of providing the mystical union of all believers with Christ but not as beginning a new entity.[16]

It is not at all uncommon for those who do not see the church as a totally new thing begun on the day of Pentecost to relate the baptism of the Spirit very closely with believers' baptism. Lenski, representing the evangelical Lutheran family, serves as an example. In reference to 1 Corinthians 12:13 he writes, ''By baptism all of us were made 'one body' and Christ is in all of us.

---

15. These are presented and refuted in Unger, *The Baptizing Work of the Holy Spirit*, pp. 7-23.

16. Louis Berkhof, *Systematic Theology* (Grand Rapids: Eerdmans, 1968), p. 450.

When we see what the Spirit has done with all of us by means of our baptism, namely converted all of us into one spiritual body, we see how Christ can be compared with the human body and its many members. Christ and we are one."[17] Morris, representing a different group of evangelicals, made a similar association. Again, commenting on 1 Corinthians 12:13, he said, "Baptism symbolizes this truth," the truth of "unity in diversity." " Those baptized are brought within the sphere of the Spirit. It is only as there is an activity of the Spirit that baptism has meaning."[18]

Hoekema simply makes Spirit baptism as taught in 1 Corinthians 12:13 synonymous with regeneration: "What Paul says here in the plainest of words is that all Christians have been Spirit-baptized. Spirit baptism is here described as identical with regeneration—with the sovereign act of God whereby we are made one with Christ, incorporated into the body of Christ."[19] By the body of Christ the author does not mean the church distinct from the people of God in the Old Testament, as evidenced by this earlier statement: "Though the Holy Spirit had been present in the church previous to this time, on Pentecost Day he was bestowed on the church in his fulness."[20]

A survey of the writings of those who view the church as the covenanted community of all God's people reveals little stress on and distinction of the baptizing work of the Spirit. The opposite is true of those evangelicals with dispensational sympathies.

The View of Dispensational Theology. Dispensationalists believe the baptism of the Spirit is unique to the present age for two basic reasons. First, Spirit baptism is that which forms the body of Christ (1 Cor. 12:12-13) and the body is the church (Eph. 1:22-23; Col. 1:18). Also, since Christ is the head of the body, it could not have existed before his resurrection and ascension. Second, this work of the Spirit is not once spoken of as being experienced in the Old Testament or in the Gospels. Christ said it was still future and would occur soon (Acts 1:5).

Eleven passages of Scripture are generally viewed by

17. R. C. H. Lenski, *St. Paul's First and Second Epistles to the Corinthians* (Minneapolis: Augsburg, 1963), p. 514.
18. Leon Morris, *The First Epistle of Paul to the Corinthians* (Grand Rapids: Eerdmans, 1970), p. 174.
19. Anthony A. Hoekema, *Holy Spirit Baptism* (Grand Rapids: Eerdmans, 1972), p. 21.
20. Ibid., p. 16.

dispensationalists as teaching Spirit baptism (Matt. 3:11; Mark 1:8; Luke 3:16; John 1:33; Acts 1:5; 11:16; Rom. 6:1-4; 1 Cor. 12:13; Gal. 3:27; Eph. 4:5; Col. 2:12).

All believers since the day of Pentecost are thought to be baptized by the Spirit. Support for this usually comes from the fact that First Corinthians is addressed to all believers (1:2), and this included even the carnal Christians among them. Ephesians 4:5 also seems to include all believers. Finally, no command is ever given to any believers to be baptized by the Spirit. An exhortation would be expected, it would seem, if it were not a universal work among all the regenerated.

There is some division even among dispensationalists as to the agent involved in Spirit baptism. All the references in the Gospels promise that Christ will do the baptizing "in" or "with" the Spirit. This would make the Spirit the sphere into which one is baptized. Only 1 Corinthians 12:13 names the Holy Spirit as the agent taking the *en pneumati* in the instrumental sense—by one Spirit. A great deal of the conflict between these two views—Christ or the Spirit as the agent—is relieved when both are seen to be agents. After all, Christ did send the Spirit, and both members of the Godhead are named.

Dispensationalists see a twofold identification effected by Spirit baptism, which takes place simultaneously with regeneration. According to 1 Corinthians 12:13 the Spirit identifies each believing sinner with all other members of Christ's body. From Romans 6:1-4 it can be seen that each believer is also vitally joined to Christ, the head of the body, by Spirit baptism. Water baptism no doubt is in the background in Romans 6, but that which identifies believers with Christ is not water but Spirit baptism.

The View of Pentecostals. Evangelicals of the Pentecostal persuasion hold a distinct view of Spirit baptism. Some of these could be classified as dispensational in their theology. However, this would not be true of all of them, especially in the neo-Pentecostalism that has entered mainline denominations, some of which are definitely covenant in their approach to Scripture. In any case, Pentecostals do not give high priority to either covenant or dispensational theology.

Jorstad has well summarized the importance of Spirit baptism to Pentecostals: "The doctrine and practice of the baptism in the Holy Spirit give Pentecostalism, in its old and new forms, its unique character within Christianity. Without it, there simply would be no Pentecostalism; with it, the Pentecostalists are convinced they have the miracle-working powers of God through the Holy Spirit as the evidence of their faith."[21]

Pentecostals usually carefully distinguish between water baptism and Spirit baptism. They insist, however, that Spirit baptism is a distinct work of God from salvation and usually identify it with the second blessing or second work of grace, empowering for service. Many of them also identify tongues as the evidence of Spirit baptism.

> According to Scripture, these two baptisms are indicative of two separate, major experiences of the power of God. The first is conversion; the sinner's acceptance of Jesus Christ as Lord and Savior which brings salvation. He [the repentant sinner] gives testimony to his response to the gospel and his acceptance of Christ by receiving baptism in water for the remission of sins. Here we see the new believer as the object of God's redemption. But the Lord is not satisfied with our conversion alone; he has promised us power to be his witnesses. So, a second time we are confronted with the power of God; this time in the baptism in the Holy Spirit through which the Christian is brought into a deeper relationship with Christ and the Holy Spirit for the purpose of making him—not an object, but an instrument of redemption.[22]

Permanent Versus Temporary Gifts of the Spirit

The issue of whether all the New Testament gifts are still present centers in the miraculous sign gifts—miracles, tongues, and healings. There are at least three views taken by evangelicals regarding this question. Some, usually referred to as charismatics, believe the miraculous sign gifts are still present and that these are usually associated with Spirit baptism in some way. Other evangelicals maintain they are not operative in this age, but do not wish to say they have completely ceased and are impossible today. Still others insist that the miraculous sign gifts have ceased completely. I believe this latter view to be biblically defensible.

---

21. Jorstad, ed., *The Holy Spirit in Today's Church*, p. 58.
22. Ibid., p. 60.

Sign Gifts Present Today.[23]All agree that the gift of tongues is to be characterized as a sign gift. It is universally held among Pentecostals that speaking in tongues is a gift operative today. It is often, though not always, associated with baptism in the Spirit. Lists of reasons for believing this vary both in kind and in number. However, a number of the same reasons appear in every list. The following is representative of the kinds of defense usually given for believing the sign gift of tongues is present today.

1 Speaking with tongues as the Holy Spirit gives the utterance is the unique spiritual gift identified with the Church of Jesus Christ. Prior to the day of Pentecost, all other gifts, miracles, and spiritual manifestations had been in evidence during the Old Testament times. On the Day of Pentecost, this new phenomenon came into evidence and became uniquely identified with the Church (Acts 2:4) and 1st Corinthians, chapters 12-14.

2 Speaking with tongues was ordained by God for the Church (1st Cor. 12:28, 14:21).

3 Speaking with tongues is a specific fulfillment of prophecy (Isaiah 28:11; 1st Cor. 14:21; Joel 2:28; Acts 2:16).

4 Speaking with tongues is a sign OF the believer (Jn. 7:38, 39, Mk. 16:17).

5 Speaking with tongues is a sign TO the unbeliever (1st Cor. 14:22).

6 Speaking with tongues is a proof of the resurrection and glorification of Jesus Christ (Jn. 16:7, Acts 2:22, 25, 32, 33).

7 Speaking with tongues is an evidence of the baptism with the Holy Spirit (Jn. 15:26, Acts 2:4, 10:45, 46, 19:6).

8 Speaking with tongues is a means of preaching to men of other languages (Acts 2:6-11).

9 Speaking with tongues is a spiritual gift for self-edification (1st Cor. 14:4).

10 Speaking with tongues is a spiritual gift for spiritual edification for the Church (1st Cor. 14:5).

23. Of the many volumes written in defense of this position the following are exemplary: Lawrence Christenson, *Speaking in Tongues and Its Significance for the Church* (Minneapolis: Bethany Fellowship, 1968); John L. Sherrill, *They Speak with Other Tongues* (New York: McGraw-Hill, 1964); Ernest S. Williams, *Systematic Theology*, 3 vols. (Springfield, Mo.: Gospel Publishing, 1953).

11 Speaking with tongues is a spiritual gift for communication with God in private worship (1st Cor. 14:2).
12 Speaking with tongues is a means by which the Holy Spirit intercedes through us in prayer (Rom. 8:26, 1st Cor. 14:14).
13 Speaking with tongues is a spiritual gift for "singing in the Spirit" (Eph. 5:18-19, 1st Cor. 14:15).
14 The Apostle Paul was thankful to God for the privilege of speaking in tongues (1st Cor. 14:13).
15 The Apostle Paul desired that all would speak with tongues (1st Cor. 14:5).
16 Speaking with tongues is one of the gifts of the Spirit (1st Cor. 12:10).
17 The Apostle Paul ordered that speaking with tongues should not be forbidden (1st Cor. 14:39).
18 Isaiah prophetically refers to speaking with tongues as a "rest" (Isaiah 28:12, 1st Cor. 14:21).
19 Isaiah prophetically refers to speaking with tongues as a "refreshing" (Isaiah 28:12, 1st Cor. 14:21).
20 Speaking with tongues follows as a confirmation of the word of God when it is preached (Mk. 16:17, 20).[24]

Sign Gifts Possible Today. The two defendants of this view cited will illustrate the assertion that some evangelicals who do not agree with the extremes of some charismatics nevertheless believe sign gifts are still possible.

J. Oswald Sanders in his book on the Holy Spirit gives extended discussion to the gifts of the Spirit and makes these observations regarding sign gifts: "There are those who contend that the miraculous gifts completely passed away, but this would be difficult to maintain in the light of church and missionary history."[25] "The position is not taken that there can be no genuine gift of tongues in this day."[26] Further, regarding tongues, he says the excesses and abuses of the gift were "not adequate grounds for denying the possibility of God bestowing the gift in our day."[27]

---

24. Cited by Jorstad, *The Holy Spirit in Today's Church*, pp. 85-86, from Henry Ness, "The Baptism with the Holy Spirit."
25. J. Oswald Sanders, *The Holy Spirit and His Gifts* (Grand Rapids: Zondervan, 1970), p. 111.
26. Ibid., p. 124.
27. Ibid., p. 127.

Concerning the gift of healings Leslie B., Flynn said, "Should the Spirit choose to give the gift of healing to some of his children they should be zealous in exercising their gift. But in the seeming absence of many with such a gift today, the instructions in the classic section should be faithfully followed to benefit from God's method and ministry of healing."[28] Of the gifts of tongues, miracles, and healings, he writes:

> Some evangelicals hold that the gift of tongues (along with miracles and healings) should be considered sign gifts which mainly served to authenticate the early apostolic leaders and then ended once for all. To class all tongues speaking today as spurious is daring, dangerous, and a denial of the right of the sovereign Spirit to endow his servants with whatever gift he pleases.[29]

Flynn then lists limitations of these gifts today.

Sign Gifts Passed Away.[30] In his answer to the question of whether the miraculous sign gifts are still present Anthony A. Hoekema states: "It has been the almost unanimous conviction of the mainline Protestant churches that these miraculous gifts ceased at the close of the Apostolic Age (see, e.g., John Owen, *On the Holy Spirit*, Part II, pp. 474-75; A. A. Hodge, *Popular Lectures on Theological Themes*, p. 111)."[31] He also includes Benjamin B. Warfield's *Counterfeit Miracles* as setting forth defense for the cessation of these gifts. Hoekema then reviews his own reasons why the miraculous charismata are no longer present today. He argues from the testimony of Scripture, history, and the fact that Scripture does not instruct believers to continue to exercise the miraculous gifts of the Spirit.[32]

An excellent study of the sign gift of tongues is Joseph Dillow's *Speaking in Tongues*. He devotes 76 pages to the question, Did the gift of tongues pass from the church? and presents compelling arguments to answer the question in the affirmative.[33]

28. Leslie B. Flynn, *19 Gifts of the Spirit* (Wheaton, Ill.: Victor Books, 1974), p. 177.

29. Ibid., p. 181.

30. In *The Holy Spirit* Walvoord gives separate treatment to what he calls permanent scriptural gifts and temporary spiritual gifts.

31. Hoekema, *Holy Spirit Baptism*, p. 59.

32. Ibid., pp. 60-71.

33. Joseph Dillow, *Speaking in Tongues* (Grand Rapids: Zondervan, 1975), pp. 88-164.

There are a number of facts supporting the view that the sign gift of tongues ceased when the canon of Scripture was closed.[34] First, there is substantial historical evidence that the gift ceased.[35] Second, only two books of the New Testament definitely mention the gift of tongues—Acts and 1 Corinthians. The reference in Mark 16 comes in a section not included in the oldest Greek manuscripts. Of course, a teaching needs only one scriptural statement to be established; however, peculiarities about the tongues references should be noted. In the first place, of the three passages that list the gifts of the Spirit—Romans 12; 1 Corinthians 12; Ephesians 4—only 1 Corinthians includes tongues in the list. This is significant because 1 Corinthians was written before the other two books, which may imply that tongues had ceased before Romans and Ephesians were written. Another peculiarity about the scarcity of scriptural support for tongues is that there is extensive New Testament teaching of the Holy Spirit's person and work without reference to tongues.

Third, since tongues was a sign gift, especially for the nation Israel (Isa. 28:11-12; 1 Cor. 14:20-22), authenticating the apostles and their message, there is the implication that it was limited to the apostolic age. Fourth, it is highly significant that sign gifts were given only through the apostles. Such gifts were always associated with apostolic ministry. It would seem to follow that when the apostolic office ceased, the sign gifts did also. Fifth, we do know that some gifts of the Spirit were temporary. For example, if the gifts of predictive prophecy and apostle have not ceased, the canon of Scripture must be viewed as still open. Sixth, Paul clearly stated that tongues would cease (1 Cor. 13:8). The three gifts of prophecy, knowledge, and tongues are said to be temporary in contrast to love, which is eternal. There are solid exegetical and theological reasons for taking "shall cease" to refer to the closing of the canon of Scripture.[36] However, since there are two different verbs used in 1 Corinthians 13:8, some see tongues

34. Robert R. Lightner, *Speaking in Tongues and Divine Healing* (Schaumburg, Ill.: Regular Baptist Press, 1978), pp. 54-56.
35. See Robert Glenn Gromacki, *The Modern Tongues Movement* (Philadelphia: Presbyterian and Reformed Publishing Company, 1967).
36. These are summarized in Lightner, *Speaking in Tongues and Divine Healing*, p. 33.

ceasing with the early church but not necessarily with the close of the canon.[37]

Finally, it appears that sign gifts were no longer operative among second-generation Christians. The Book of Hebrews was written to such believers about 65-69. The writer strongly implies that when he wrote, signs, wonders, and "divers miracles and gifts of the Holy Spirit" were no longer present.

The Spirit of God and the Child of God

Since the Holy Spirit is a divine person, the believer's response to him is most important. As we have seen, the Spirit of God convicts, baptizes, seals, fills, gives gifts, and indwells the child of God, thus amplifying the need for proper response to him. Likewise it is the Spirit of God whom the child of God is not to resist, grieve, or quench, but to depend upon fully for daily spiritual nourishment.

As the power of evil increases around the world, all evangelicals agree that we need not only Spirit-illumined truth but also Spirit-endued power. Occult movements seek essentially hidden, secret knowledge and ultimately power from Satan. In spiritual warfare they will not be met adequately with truth alone, unattended by the Spirit's work. All evangelicals recognize the need for the Spirit's power in this battle.

Evangelicals are greatly divided, especially over the work of the Holy Spirit with respect to his gifts. This is understandable in view of the sometimes opposing views. The different viewpoints will probably never be reconciled; but we could agree to disagree, and even as we go our separate ways in separate corporate fellowships, we could treat each other as fellow members of the family of God rather than archenemies. Surely the Spirit of God is grieved by the way children of God whom he has joined together in one body often think about and act toward each other.

Evangelicals hold right doctrine about the person of God the Spirit. But is it really consistent with right doctrine to be guilty of wrong deeds? The creed of evangelicals regarding God the Spirit

---

37. See Stanley D. Toussaint, "First Corinthians Thirteen and the Tongues Question," *Bibliotheca Sacra*, Oct.-Dec., 1963, pp. 312-316.

is according to Scripture. But should not the creed or views we embrace make a difference in our conduct seven days a week?

The Spirit of God suffered, has and still does, from both neglect and abuse. Each child of God needs to determine in his own mind that he will not be guilty of either of these sins. The most significant thing we can do to avoid these sins is to hear what Scripture says about the Spirit and then, by his enablement, proceed to live according to Scripture.

The work of God the Spirit in the world and in the believer's life is christocentric. Everything he does and wants to do exalts the Son of God. When we exalt him, we may be sure we are being ministered to by the Spirit of God and being used of him.

Questions for Discussion

1. How would you defend your view of the Holy Spirit's personality and deity to an interested inquirer?
2. Why is the baptism of the Spirit not taught in the Old Testament?
3. What does the work of the Spirit in relation to Christ illustrate about the Trinity?
4. How many relationships can you think of between ecclesiology and pneumatology?
5. Why do you suppose so many people are involved in the charismatic movement?

Suggestions for Further Reading

Kuyper, Abraham. *The Work of the Holy Spirit*. Trans. by Henri de Vries, New York: Funk and Wagnalls, 1900.

Pink, Arthur W. *The Holy Spirit*. Grand Rapids: Baker Book House, 1970.

Unger, Merrill F. *The Baptism and Gifts of the Holy Spirit*. Chicago: Moody Press, 1974.

Walvoord, John F. *The Holy Spirit*. Findlay, Ohio: Dunham Publishing Company, 1958.

5

God's Angels and Satan's Angels

Systems of theology generally include very little about angels, demons, or Satan. Until the mid-twentieth century very few volumes appeared dealing solely with these doctrines. However, with the rise of the occult, demonology and Satanology have become very prominent.

Why these biblical doctrines related to the spirit world would come in so late for discussion is not altogether clear. It is not too difficult to see why doctrines such as trinitariansim, Christology, pneumatology, and bibliology came first. After all, these are cardinal points of the historic orthodox faith. What is not clear is why so many years passed between the development of these doctrines and the current interest in angelology.

Major areas of theology are affected by the biblical teaching on angelic beings. Bibliology is certainly involved, since information to formulate the doctrine of angels must be gathered from the Bible. God's revelation of the law to the children of Israel was through the ministry of angels. Theology proper, or the doctrine of God, is involved because the holy angels are his ministering spirits and the demons and Satan are his adversaries. The Lord Jesus Christ taught much about these spirit beings. He was associated with them in different ways throughout his life on earth and will be also when he comes again. Through his death Christ judged Satan, the prince of this world. Thus Christology is affected. Pneumatology is also touched by one's view of demons and Satan. The Holy Spirit grants power to the believer to war against Satan and all his evil forces.

Holy angels minister to the redeemed, and Satan's angels influence and harass them. Thus the study of angels, demons, and Satan relates to anthropology. God will use holy angels, and the wicked ones as well, as he brings to fulfillment his plan for the world. So eschatology is affected by angelology. Angels—holy and evil—will be employed by God both to minister to the redeemed and to punish the unregenerate.

Angelic beings are referred to often in Scripture, well over a hundred times in each testament. These references are found in thirty-four books of the Bible—seventeen in the Old Testament and seventeen in the New. To the dedicated believer the study of all God's truth is always beneficial. All Scripture is profitable, including that which deals with the spirit world. A better understanding of angels—God's and Satan's—will provide a deeper appreciation of our sovereign God and his ways in the world. Also, his own holiness and grace will be exalted as his ways with angels and demons are discovered. Holy angels are God's ministering spirits, employed to minister to the redeemed. This should give us comfort, challenge, courage, and assurance.

A Historical Perspective

Though the discussion of spirit beings was not given much attention until the modern era, it is nevertheless fascinating to trace these discussions through the centuries.

The Ancient Period

From the very beginning of the Christian era there are indications that Christians did believe in the existence of good and evil angels. It was generally believed that angels were personal beings originally created by God in a state of perfection. Some of them rebelled against God and followed Satan in his rebellion. In the ancient period some held that angels had ethereal bodies—bodies of light. Later it was debated whether they had bodies at all.

The Roman world into which Christianity came was a decaying society. Pagan polytheism and emperor worship were everywhere. These and other influences soon led to the worship of angels among nominal Christians. The Archangel Michael was especially popular.

In this period of the church's history the fathers and apologists were so occupied with the doctrines of God the Father, Christ, the Holy Spirit, man, sin, and salvation that no concentrated effort was given to the study of angels.

The Gnostics of the second century did give some attention to angels, but their view had no scriptural base. The name Gnostic comes from the Greek, *gnosis*, meaning knowledge. The Gnostics held that salvation was received by knowledge. Gnosticism, though held by some Jews, was a Gentile perversion of the gospel. It arose because of the widespread religious unrest and the desire to bring together all religious ideas and harmonize them. It was without doubt a syncretistic movement. Gnostics believed in two original principles, or gods, which were opposed to each other; their dualistic philosophy viewed spirit as good and matter as evil. The good God was spirit, not to be identified with the God of the Bible. Opposing him was the Demiurge, a subordinate god of matter who was identified as the God of the Old Testament. From the supreme good God there emanated a long chain of aeons, angelic beings, which constituted the divine essence and through which the highest God could relate to created beings. Christ was viewed as the first and highest of these aeons.

Important in the discussion of angels in the ancient period is the work of Dionysius the Areopagite, *Celestial Hierarchy*. It is generally believed that Dionysius was an unknown writer who pretended to be the one Paul referred to in Acts 17:34. His work is viewed as perhaps the greatest fraud in church history.[1]

> Dionysius the Areopagite divided the angels into three classes: the first class consisting of Thrones, Cherubim, and Seraphim; the second, of Mights, Dominions, and Powers; and the third, of Principalities, archangels, and angels. The first class is represented as enjoying the closest communion with God; the second, as being enlightened by the first; and the third, as being enlightened by the second.[2]

1. See Karl Barth, *Church Dogmatics* (Edinburgh: T. & T. Clark, 1960) III/3, pp. 385-90, for an extended evaluation.
2. Louis Berkhof, *Systematic Theology* (Grand Rapids: Eerdmans, 1968), p. 141.

Calvin did not think very highly of Dionysius's work:

> If you read that book, you would think a man fallen from heaven
> recounted, not what he had learned, but what he had seen with his
> own eyes. Yet Paul, who had been caught up beyond the third
> heaven (2 Cor. 12:2), not only said nothing about it, but also
> testified that it is unlawful for any man to speak of the secret things
> that he has seen (2 Cor. 12:4).[3]

The Middle Ages

By comparison to the ancient period, there was little sustained
interest in angels on the scholarly level in the Middle Ages.
Berkhof summarized well the prevailing views among the
schoolmen in the period: Angels were believed to have been
created at the same time as the material universe. It was believed
that angels could be in a given place at a point in time. The
schoolmen, or scholastics as they were sometimes called, agreed
that angels possessed limited knowledge. Their knowledge, it was
believed, was an infused knowledge given them at the time of
their creation. Thomas Aquinas said angels could not gain new
knowledge. Duns Scotus insisted to the contrary that they could
acquire such knowledge through their own intellectual activity. In
the Middle Ages the idea of guardian angels was viewed with
favor.[4]

Without doubt the greatest contribution to the study of angels in
the medieval period was made by Thomas Aquinas, who
provided for this period what Dionysius the Areopagite gave to
the ancient period. Neither was very biblical in his approach,
however.

The Reformation

No new development in angelology can be found during the
Reformation period. However, the Reformers did stress the reality
of Satan and the demons of hell. While he was viewed as very
wicked and powerful, it was emphasized that Satan could only do
what God permits him to do.

---

3. Calvin, *Institutes of the Christian Religion*, ed. John T. McNeill (Philadelphia:
Westminster Press, 1967), 1.14, pp. 164-65.
4. Berkhof, *Systematic Theology*, p. 142.

The attention given to holy angels in this period stressed their role in ministering to heirs of salvation. Some believed strongly in guardian angels, and others denied their existence just as strongly. Article XII of the Belgic Confession presents the generally accepted Calvinistic view of the time.

> He also created the angels good, to be his messengers and to serve his elect; some of whom are fallen from that excellency, in which God created them, into everlasting perdition, and the others have, by the grace of God, remained steadfast and continued in their primitive state. The devils and evil spirits are so depraved that they are enemies of God and every good thing to the utmost of their power, as murderers watching to ruin the Church and every member thereof, and by their wicked stratagems to destroy all; and are therefore, by their own wickedness, adjudged to eternal damnation, daily expecting their horrible torments.

The outstanding contribution to angelology in this period came from Calvin. Though not extensive, for the times it was very significant.[5]

The Modern Period

The rationalism of the eighteenth century affected angelology just as it did all the other doctrines of the historic orthodox Christian faith. Along with the rejection of the Bible as the Word of God came the denial of the existence of angels. Liberal theology seeks to retain a semblance of belief in angels while viewing them simply as symbolic representations of God's care and concern.

Not too long ago those who believed in spirit beings were considered hopelessly naive. Not so today, with the rise and invasion of the occult. Astrology, spiritism, witchcraft, and Satan worship are not only common but are growing in popularity all over the world. The book market has been flooded with publications by both occult sympathizers and those opposed to it. Evangelical publishing houses have marketed large numbers of titles that present the biblical doctrine of angels, demons, and Satan. Billy Graham's *Angels: God's Secret Agents* illustrates the interest in the subject. It sold over 750,000 copies quickly and was on the *New York Times* bestseller list for months. On the side of the

5. See Calvin, *Institutes*, 1.14, pp. 3-19.

occult is Jeanne Dixon's _A Gift of Prophecy_, which sold over three million copies. Most daily newspapers in the United States carry astrology columns. Popular magazines continue to carry articles, sometimes cover stories, dealing with Satan worship and demons.

Religion writer Louis Cassels was right when he called the upsurge of public interest in astrology, witchcraft, spiritualism, and other occult arts one of the most curious phenomena of American life. Of course, other parts of the world have experienced occult oppression for centuries. Why this resurgence of interest? Without doubt the basic reason lies in the rejection of a totally inspired and authoritative Bible. When men turned away from God's Word, they turned to themselves for authority. Having experienced humanism's total failure and frustration, man is now turning to the world of evil spirits for answers to his most perplexing problems. Another reason for the contemporary interest in, and sometimes practice of, the occult may be because evangelical theology has said so little about the scriptural doctrines of angels, demons, and Satan. Into the vacuum created by this dearth of information have come subjective and unscriptural teachings.

A Positive Statement of the Doctrine

Those who seek to build their faith on holy Scripture have little difficulty believing in the existence of angels. There are more than enough clear statements in the Bible to establish the reality of both holy and evil angels.

Creation of Holy Angels

It is not difficult to establish from Scripture that all angels were created by God. First, in those broad general statements that speak of God's creative work in general, angels would certainly be included (Gen. 1:1; John 1:3; Heb. 1:2). Second, there is the more specific statement about God the Son's creative role in regard to heavenly thrones, dominions, rulers, and authorities (Col. 1:16; cf. Rom. 8:38 and Eph. 6:12, where similar terminology appears with clear reference to angelic beings). Third, the psalmist's clear statements leave no doubt about God's creation of angels (Ps. 148:2-5; 103:20-21).

Each angel appears to have been a direct creation of God. Angels do not procreate and are not considered a race but an order of creation (Matt. 22:28-30). Precisely when they were created is not clear. Moses stated that the earth was finished along with the heavens and their host (Gen. 2:1), which would seem to include angels. Job tells us that the angels sang with joy at the creation of the earth (Job 38:4-7).

Why did God create angels? Most importantly, it would seem, so that they might bring honor, praise, and glory to him. Paul said they were created "for" God the Son (Col. 1:16). Holy angels worship and serve God now (Heb. 1:6), as they did in John's vision (Rev. 4:6-11).

Existence of Holy Angels. Some Scripture indicates heaven as the abode of those angels that remained holy and did not follow Satan in his rebellion. The seraphim in Isaiah's vision were certainly there (Isa. 6:1-6). Gabriel is said to stand in God's presence (Luke 1:19). Matthew and Mark wrote of angels in heaven, apparently referring to God's presence (Matt. 22:30; Mark 12:25). Paul referred to "an angel from heaven" (Gal. 1:8).

Other Scripture seems to identify the second or stellar heaven as the home of holy angels. There are three heavens, according to Paul's word to the Corinthians (2 Cor. 12:2). The first would be the atmospheric, the second the stellar, and the third the presence of God. While still holy, Satan desired to ascend to the heaven, where God was (Isa. 14:13). Christ is said to have been made for a little while lower than angels when he became incarnate (Heb. 2:9) and to have passed through the heavens to return to God's presence after his work of redemption was finished (Heb. 4:14). He is now above all principalities and powers (Eph. 3:10; cf. 1 Peter 3:22).

It seems best to conclude, based on the above, that holy angels abide in the second heaven but have access to the presence of God in the third heaven. Some holy angels may even abide there with special assignments.

Nature of Holy Angels. Both angels of God and angels of Satan are spirit beings (Eph. 6:12; Heb. 1:14). It is clear from Paul's reference to both celestial and terrestrial bodies that they possess the former kind (1 Cor. 15:39-40). Mortal eyes are not able to behold these, but they are real nonetheless.

Marks of personality also characterize angels. There is more to personhood than intellect, emotion, and will, yet persons do not exist without these. Intelligence may be ascribed to angels since they "desire to look into" our salvation (1 Peter 1:12). They rejoice (Luke 15:10) and worship God (Heb. 1:6), thus possessing emotion and will.

These holy creatures are unmarriageable (Matt. 22:28-30) and therefore do not reproduce after their kind. They are deathless (Luke 20:36), therefore the number of angels has remained, and will remain, the same.

Since God created angels, they are indeed distinct from him, and will remain so forever (Heb. 12:22-23). As they came from the hand of the Creator, each of the angels possessed creature perfection, unconfirmed holiness (Gen. 1:31). These holy creatures were apparently assigned a period of probation during which they were tested as to whether or not they would sin. Adam and Eve experienced a similar probationary period before they fell. The holy angels were in a perfect environment too. Every good and holy influence surrounded them. There was no rebellion and no sin nature. They were not tempted by the world, the flesh, or even the devil until he aspired to be like God. Lucifer, or Satan, did sin, and so did a host of the holy angels. They followed him in his rebellion against God, his prideful self-assertion. For those who sinned there is no compensating grace of God. Those who did not follow Satan remain forever sinless.

Not even the holy angels are omnipotent. Theirs is a derived power, and it is limited. But to say their power is not equal to God's is not to say it is only comparable to man's. They are indeed great in power and might (2 Peter 2:11). During the early days of the church an angel struck Herod for not giving God glory (Acts 12:23). Unusual strength is ascribed to them (Ps. 103:20; Matt. 28:2). In the future certain elements of nature will be under angelic control (Rev. 7:1; 14:18).

Designations and Orders of Holy Angels

The Hebrew word for angel is *malak*, and the Greek is *angelos*. Both are translated "angel" throughout the Bible, with the basic meaning of messenger. Angels are called ministers in Psalm 104:4. Often in the Old Testament the holy angels of God are called hosts (e.g., Gen. 32:1-2; Ps. 103:21). Other general names descriptive of their work are sons of God (Job 1:6; 38:7), watchers (Dan. 4:13,

17), Holy ones (Ps. 89:7), sons of the mighty (Ps. 89:6), and ministering spirits (Heb. 1:14).

Proper names are also assigned to certain angels. Lucifer (Isa. 14:12) led the rebellion against God in heaven. Michael is the chief of the holy angels (Dan. 12:1). Gabriel is the special revealer of God's purposes (Dan. 9:21; Luke 1:26). In connection with the end times certain angels are named because of the specific work assigned to them (e.g., Rev. 9:11; 14:8; 16:5).

Holy angels are described in various ways in the Bible; in 2 Timothy 5:21 they are termed elect. The cherubim among them always seem to be protecting and defending God and holiness (Gen. 3:24; Exod. 25:17-22). Ezekiel saw the four living creatures in a vision during his captivity in Babylon (Ezek. 1:5). John also saw them in his vision on the isle of Patmos (Rev. 4:6-9). These living creatures are probably identical with the cherubim (Ezek. 10:20). The seraphim are closely associated with God's glory and render unceasing worship to him. The name means "burning ones," which may speak of their continuous adoration of God. In Isaiah's vision they were above Jehovah-God and his throne (Isa. 6:2). Principalities and powers are also referred to. The description is used both of good angels (Eph. 3:10) and evil ones (Eph. 6:11-12). Paul also called evil angels "rulers of the darkness of this world" (Eph. 6:12).

Number and Appearances of Holy Angels

Descriptions of the number of God's angels reveal a multitude too large to count. When Christ was born, praise was given to God by a "multitude" of angels (Luke 2:13-15). When the Savior was betrayed, he said he could have called "twelve legions of angels" to come to his defense (Matt. 26:53). At the time a Roman legion was made up of 3,000 to 6,000 men. Angels are called "chariots of God" and said to number "twenty thousand, even thousands of angels" (Ps. 68:17). The heavenly Jerusalem which is to come down from God is partially occupied by "an innumerable company of angels" (Heb. 12:22). In his vision John saw "ten thousand times ten thousand, and thousands of thousands" of angels (Rev. 5:11).

Generally angels are invisible in the Bible. They are spoken of as masculine and appear as men (Luke 24:4; Acts 1:10), with one possible exception (Zech. 5:9). At times holy angels appear with wings (Isa. 6:2; Rev. 14:6) and as youthful (Mark 16:5). On occasion, they have a countenance "like lightning" (Matt. 28:3) and appear in striking ways (Acts 6:15).

The Relationships of Holy Angels

Angels and Humans. Both men and angels are creatures of God, yet each sustains a distinct nature. This is highlighted in Psalm 8:4-6 and in Hebrews 2:5-8, where the psalmist is quoted.

David wrote of man as having been made "a little lower than the angels" (Ps. 8:5). In both Psalm 8 and Hebrews 2 the crucial phrase is "a little lower." The psalmist seems clearly to be relating man to God, angels, and creation. He sees man with dignity and authority as God's vice-regent on earth.

When the writer of Hebrews quoted from Psalm 8, he did so in a context that refers clearly to the world to come (Heb. 2:5) and a future time when all will be put in subjection under Christ's feet (2:8). He also speaks of the humiliation of Christ as being temporary and of the day when he will bring the redeemed to glory (2:9-10). In view of the writer's use of Psalm 8:4-6, some understand the "little while" to mean "a little while lower."

Now the holy angels do occupy a position higher than man's. They are also greater in power and might (2 Peter 2:11). However, in a future time, when the final state is realized, man in his glorified state will judge angels (1 Cor. 6:3). Both men and angels are assigned responsibilities to serve God and are accountable to him (1 Cor. 6:3; Heb. 9:27; Rev. 22:9). Angels are not to be worshiped by man (Col. 2:18; Rev. 22:8-9). God alone is worthy of such honor.

Angels and the God-Man. The Gnostics of the second century viewed Christ as the highest of angelic creatures. He has been degraded ever since by those who do not accept the biblical portrait of him. In chapter 3 of this book the Christ of Scripture was presented. Here it remains to be seen how he as the Son of God is infinitely superior to the holy angels.

Scripture sets forth sharp contrasts between Christ and angels as to both essence or nature and position.[6] Christ is the uncreated,

---

6. A helpful and well-outlined presentation of these appears in C. Fred Dickason, *Angels, Elect and Evil* (Chicago: Moody Press, 1975), pp. 47-53.

eternal One through whom angels were brought into existence (John 1:1-3; Col. 1:16). Angels are referred to as the sons of God (Job 1:6; 2:1), but Christ is God's only begotten Son (John 1:14; 3:16).

The writer of Hebrews made it his point to set forth the superiority of Christ not only to men but also to angels (Heb. 1:5-14). In this passage he draws on the Old Testament at least seven times to illustrate his point (v. 5, Ps. 2:7 and 2 Sam. 7:14; v. 6, Deut. 32:43 and Ps. 97:7; v. 7, Ps. 104:4; vv. 8-9, Ps. 45:6-7; vv. 10-12, Ps. 102:25-27; vv. 13-14, Ps. 110:1).

In the same context in which the relation and contrast between man and angels is set forth, the superiority of Christ over angels is also seen (Heb. 2:9-10). As a vital part of his humiliation Christ became for a little while lower than angels. This he did "for the suffering of death." He died for men, not angels; therefore he passed through the angelic realm and took on himself human flesh that he might "taste death for every man." Because of his completed work, accepted by the Father, at Christ's name all will one day bow, both in heaven and on earth. His being made lower was for the purpose of man's redemption. With that work completed he once again has been exalted far above the highest ranking of the holy angels (Phil. 2:9-11).

The Ministries of Holy Angels

Ministries for God. Worship of and praise to the triune God is a chief concern of those angels who did not sin. The prophet saw them doing this (Isa. 6:3). So did John as he viewed God's throne (Rev. 4:6-11; 5:8-13).

Genuine worship results in service. The psalmist called upon angels to bless the Lord, since they are his ministers (Ps. 103:21). Hebrews 1:7 also calls them God's ministers and "a flame of fire." This indicates they serve him with haste, fervently. The holy angels of God serve him as they oppose Satan and his wicked angels (Dan. 10:13; 12:1). In the future angels will be employed by God in the control of the forces of nature (Rev. 7:1; 16:3, 8-9). In the past the sovereign God similarly used them to bring judgment upon his enemies (Gen. 19:1, 12-13; Ps. 78:43, 49).

When God performed his work of creation, angels were there with joyful praise (Job 38:7). Through the ministry of angels God gave the law to Moses, who in turn gave it to the people (Acts 7:38, 52-53; Gal. 3:19; Heb. 2:2).

Ministries to and for God the Son. Gabriel, sent by God, announced to Mary her privilege of being the mother of the Christ child (Luke 1:26-28). To the shepherds on the Judean hills an angel gave the news of Messiah's birth and was later joined by a multitude of the heavenly host praising God for the miracle (Luke 2:8-15). A holy angel warned Joseph and Mary to flee to Egypt to escape Herod (Matt. 2:13). Later Joseph was told by an angel to return (Matt. 2:19).

During Christ's temptation in the wilderness he was sustained and strengthened by angels (Matt. 4:11). When going through the Gethsemane experience Christ was ministered to by an angel from heaven (Luke 22:43). God the Son had at his command legions of angels he could have called to come to his defense (Matt. 26:53). What was true in connection with his betrayal and death would certainly have been true all through his life on earth.

It was an angel of the Lord who rolled away the stone from Christ's tomb (Matt. 28:2). Two angels appearing as men announced Christ's ascension and predicted his return (Acts 1:10-11). With continued interest God's angels observe and desire to understand the Son's redemptive work (1 Peter 1:12). They share in the joy of God over the salvation of the lost (Luke 15:10).

Continually the angels of God render praise and service to God the Son (Heb. 1:6; Rev. 5:8-13). When the Savior returns for his own, he will do so with the "voice of the archangel" (1 Thess. 4:16). At his second coming holy angels will accompany him (Matt. 25:31).

Ministries to God's People. Holy angels have had a number of special ministries to the people of God in times past. Both the Old and the New Testaments record these. Dickason lists nine of these together with scriptural support.[7] The important question is, How many of these ministries are still operative today? There is little in the New Testament to guide us in answering this question.

Several passages of Scripture do tell us about the general ministries of holy angels to God's people that appear to be operative now. Angels observe carefully and desire to look into the believer's salvation (1 Peter 1:12). Since they have never

---

7. Ibid., pp. 97-100; he lists revealing, guiding, providing, protecting, delivering, strengthening, encouraging, answering prayer, and attending upon the righteous dead.

experienced sin and thus know nothing of the saving grace of God, their interest is understandable. The affairs of the redeemed are observed by God's ministering spirits (1 Cor. 4:9; 11:10; 1 Tim. 5:21). Paul taught the Ephesian Christians that God has ordained to teach angels about his wisdom displayed to them through the church (Eph. 3:9-10). For this to be taught to them they must be made aware of it and observe it.

We do not know all the specific ways God's angels minister to the child of God. However, this should not deter us from believing that they do indeed minister. It is certain they do perform a ministry to the elect of God. They are "ministering spirits, sent forth to minister for them who shall be heirs of salvation" (Heb. 1:14). The only question left unanswered by this promise is, When? Some say from birth to death. Others say from the actual time of salvation to death. Both views can be supported from the passage. Either way, the point remains: holy angels do minister for God on behalf of God's people.

Satan and His Demons

The Existence of Satan. Christians and increasing numbers of non-Christians believe Satan is a reality, but for different reasons. The Bible is the Christian's basis. The occult literature and humanly unexplainable experiences are the bases for the non-Christian.

Seven books of the Old Testament and every writer of the New Testament refer to Satan. Of the twenty-nine specific passages that speak of him in the Gospels, Christ is speaking in twenty-five of them. For the evangelical, then, there can be no debate about the reality of Satan's existence. To reject it is to deny the authority of the written Word and to impugn the person of the Living Word.

Well over a dozen different names are used of Satan in the Bible. Each of these is character revealing, describing some aspect of him and his wicked ways. Satan is his most common name, used fifty-two times. It pictures him as the resister, the adversary. Devil is used thirty-five times and describes him as the slanderer of man to God and God to man.

Satan, though supernaturally powerful, is a creature. He was created by God and was perfect in all his ways until he sinned (Ezek. 28:13,15). There was a time when he was not. He is a spirit being (Eph. 6:11-12), a cherub of the order of cherubim (Ezek. 28:14). Satan is higher than any of the wicked angels he leads (Jude 9; Rev. 12:3-4). Christ described him as a murderer and a liar (John 8:44). He also described him as the ruler of all the fallen angels (Matt. 25:41) and of the world system (John 12:31). Iniquity was first found in him (Ezek. 28:15).

The activity of Satan falls into several categories. In his unfallen state he existed on the holy mount of God (Ezek. 28:14). Since his fall he lurks in the "heavenlies," masterminding his evil works (Eph. 6:11; Job 1). As a result of his defeat at Calvary he will be cast down to the earth during the great tribulation (Rev. 12:7-9). Also, during the personal reign of Christ on earth he will be bound in the abyss (Rev. 20:1-3). At the end of the millennial reign of Christ he will be loosed for a little season (Rev. 20:7), after which he will be cast into the lake of fire, where he will be forever (Rev. 20:10).

The Sin of Satan. Though there is not total agreement, it is generally held among evangelicals that Satan's sin is described in Isaiah 14:12-20.[8] Here reference is made to Lucifer, whereas in the first part of the chapter the king of Babylon is spoken of.

Satan's sin is decribed in the five "I wills" he asserted.[9] The iniquity found in Satan when his heart was lifted up (Ezek. 28:15, 17) was pride, as expressed in the "I wills" of Isaiah 14:13-14. As a result of Satan's terrible defiance of God he was banished from the presence of God (Isa. 14:12). When did Lucifer sin? Scripture is silent, but it must have been before the events of Genesis 3 took place, perhaps even before what took place in Genesis 2.

Man never sins in isolation. Others are always affected by our sin. Satan did not sin in isolation either. He drew with him a large part of the angelic creation (Rev. 12:4) through his "merchandise" in sin (Ezek. 28:6).

The Present Work of Satan. A large number of terms are used in Scripture to describe what Satan is presently doing. However, most of his work can be categorized under either deception or temptation, or both.

---

8. See E. J. Young in *The New International Critical Commentary* (Grand Rapids: Eerdmans, 1965), 1:441, for an opposing view.

9. These are discussed at some length in Lewis Sperry Chafer, *Systematic Theology* (Dallas: Seminary Press, 1964), 2:44-50.

The devil deceives leaders of nations, and in the future he will be chained so he can no longer do so (Rev. 20:3). Before that time of confinement he will somehow gather nations together to the campaign of Armageddon (Rev. 16:14). That process may already have begun.

The unregenerate are deceived by Satan as he blinds their minds so they will not see their need of Christ (2 Cor. 4:4). Could it not be that he uses false teachers as his ministers to do this (2 Cor. 11:13-15)? Paul here described the false apostles and deceitful workers of his day as those who were doing precisely what Satan himself does. The leader of all the demons of hell actively promotes lies now, and will do so in the future (2 Thess. 2:8-11). He will energize the man of sin, who will present himself as God (v. 9).

It is Satan's chief ambition to get the advantage of God's people, to overthrow their testimony for Christ (2 Cor. 2:11). Doubtless, as he tempted Ananias and Sapphira to lie, he continues to do the same to believers today (Acts 5:1-11). The same can be said of many of his temptations to immorality (1 Cor. 7:5). What he did to the Savior without success (Matt. 4:1-11) he all too often does successfully with the people of God today (1 Peter 5:8).

Demons and Their Work

The Existence of Demons. That many holy angels sinned with Satan when he fell is certain. These then became wicked angels, and are identified as Satan's angels (Matt. 25:41). These same evil creatures are called demons (Matt. 12:24). It thus appears that all the wicked angels are demons. Also, both are called spirits (Ps. 104:4; Matt. 8:16), and both engage in similar activities (Matt. 17:14-18; Luke 22:3; Mark 9:17; Rev. 9:13).

Throughout the Gospels especially there are many references to evil spirits and demons. They are seen to possess the same marks of personality as the unfallen angels possess. Though there is only one devil, there are legions of demons. They possess supernatural intelligence and strength.

The Old Testament is replete with demonological phenomena because since the fall of man in the Garden of Eden, God's saints have been the object of satanic attack (cf. Gen. 4:1-6; 6:1-10). Israel was surrounded by pagan nations which manifested the whole gamut of demonological practices and beliefs and clashed with Israel's monotheistic faith. Enlightened Israelites regarded idols as demons worshipped by man (Baruch 4:7; Psalm 95:5; Septuagint, 1 Cor. 10:20) and the *shedhim* (Deut. 32:17; Ps. 106:36,37) and *seirim* (Lev. 17:7; 2 Chron. 11:15; Isa. 13:21; 34:14) were demonic conceptions.[10]

Interestingly, some wicked angels or demons are bound in chains until the day of judgment (2 Peter 2:4; Jude 6). Others are not thus restricted, but are free to roam and afflict the saints on earth (Eph. 6:11-12).

Those demons that indwelt individuals could be rebuked (Matt. 17:18) and cast out (Matt. 8:16). Demons are even said to believe (James 2:19), but not to salvation, of course. Satan's angels embrace deceptive doctrines and somehow promote them among humans (1 Tim. 4:1-4).

The Activity of Demons. Everything demons do is evil and intended to advance Satan's cause. They are not figments of the imagination, but evil supernatural beings who are always at their leader's command. Dickason has well summarized the duties of demons as promoting Satan's program, opposing God and his program, oppressing mankind, and opposing the saints of God.[11]

There is a twofold danger among Christians in their response to demons. On the one hand, we must not regard them as insignificant and live as though they did not exist. They do. And we put ourselves on dangerous ground and place ourselves as pawns before them if we acknowledge their existence academically and theologically but do not take them seriously.

On the other side, the danger is to err by giving undo attention to demons.

More today are oversensitive to demons, seeking a demon under every stone and attributing everything evil that happens directly to demons. They often view themselves as special targets of demonic activity, though in reality they are only flattering themselves into thinking this might be so. Or they sometimes think that they are particularly discerning with respect to possible demon-working in

10. Merrill F. Unger, *Demons in the World Today* (Wheaton, Ill.: Tyndale House, 1971), p. 9.

11. Dickason, *Angels*, pp. 169-78.

the lives of others. Again they flatter themselves into thinking of themselves as special spiritual giants.[12]

Certainly these extremes should be avoided. Demons and demonic activity should not be ignored, but neither should they be given such prominence in our thinking that we find them everywhere and excuse ourselves from responsibility for our own sin. We do indeed face a spiritual and supernatural foe (Eph. 6:12). But as children of God we have been delivered from Satan's kingdom of darkness and have been translated into the kingdom of God's dear Son (Col. 1:13). We must wage battle against evil supernaturalism with the armor of divine supernaturalism.

Demonism has a strong influence in lands where it has not been checked by the gospel of Christ. Testimonies of missionaries confirm this.

> The recovery of important incantation texts and magical papyri from Babylonian, Assyrian, and Egyption antiquity demonstrates the widespread belief in demon inhabitation and use of exorcisms.
>
> The same prevalence of demon inhabitation has been encountered in the worldwide missionary outreach from about 1750 to the present. The penetration of China, India, Japan, Burma, Ceylon, and other countries with the Christian gospel has revealed the hold of demonism on pagan cultures and the varied exorcism of evil spirits. The same phenomena exist among primitive people of South America, Africa, and the islands of the sea.[13]

In God's sovereign wisdom he allows Satan and his evil cohorts to continue their wicked work. The ultimate and eternal destiny of both is everlasting fire (Matt. 25:41; Rev. 20:10). Until that time it behooves the child of God to put on the whole armor of God (Eph. 6:11) so he can do battle in God's power.

Major Areas of Difference Among Evangelicals

Four areas of difference have been selected for presentation here. The sequence in which they are discussed indicates no order of importance. Evangelical scholarship is rather evenly divided over these matters.

12. Charles C. Ryrie, *You Mean the Bible Teaches That* . . . (Chicago: Moody Press, 1974), p. 101.
13. Unger, *Demons in the World Today*, p. 118.

Who Were the "Sons of God" in Genesis 6:2?

Three views of the "sons of God" in Genesis 6:2 prevail among evangelicals. The first sees these beings as the godly line of Seth, the "daughters of men" as the ungodly line of Cain, and their sin as that of mixed marriage, believer to unbeliever.[14] Supporters of this view argue that the context requires the sons of God to be human. Objectors say the text does not so identify either group. The second view sees the sons of God as kings or nobles.[15] This view is an ancient one, and the Bible does call human judges or rulers "gods" (Ps. 82:1). Advocates find additional support in the context and the fact that pagan kings were called sons of God. The third view identifies the sons of God as wicked angels who had rebelled with Satan and who then sinned further by cohabiting with the daughters of men; these diabolical unions resulted in strange progeny called giants and in divine judgment.[16]

Each of the three views must adequately account for the phrase "sons of God," the flood, progeny of the "sons of God" and the "daughters of men," the confining of some demons in Jude 6, and Peter's association of the angels that sinned with the day of Noah in 2 Peter 2:4-5. The third view seems to have the fewest problems.

Who Were the "Spirits in Prison" in 1 Peter 3:19 and Who Preached to Them?[17]

An identification of the spirits makes clear who preached to them. One view has it that "spirits" refers to all the lost; by preaching to them Christ gave them a second chance. Supporters of the view appeal to 1 Peter 4:6, which they see as a parallel passage. Instead, this verse refers to those who heard and

14. Support for this view may be found in C. F. Keil and F. Delitzsch, *Biblical Commentary on the Old Testament* (Grand Rapids: Eerdmans, 1965), 1:127-38.

15. For support see Leroy Birney, "An Exegetical Study of Genesis 6:1-4," *Journal of the Evangelical Theological Society* 13 (1970): 43-52; Manfred E. Kober, *The Sons of God of Genesis 6: Demons, Degenerates or Despots?* (Ankeny, Iowa: Faith Baptist Bible College).

16. For support see Merrill F. Unger, *Biblical Demonology* (Wheaton, Ill.: Scripture Press, 1952), pp. 17-19, 45-52; Gerhard Von Rad, *Genesis* (Philadelphia: Westminster Press, 1961), pp. 109-12.

17. A good discussion of the problem and leading views on the passage appears in Dickason, *Angels*, pp. 225-27.

believed the gospel before they died for their faith. The Bible does not teach a second-chance doctrine.

Some believe the spirits are spirits of men who lived in Noah's day and were preached to by God's spokesman at that time. Advocates of the view appeal for support to Hebrews 1:1-2. The weakness in the view is that Christ himself is said to have done the preaching.

A third view, which seems to have the fewest problems, is that Christ went and announced his own victory at the cross and therefore the future certain judgment upon the wicked angels confined there. It is usually believed by those who hold this view that the demons in the prison are those that sinned by cohabiting with the daughters of men in Genesis 6:6 (cf. 2 Peter 2:4). The prison in which the angels were held because of their terrible sin is thought to be *tartarosas*, translated "hell" in 2 Peter 2:4.

Can Demons Possess or Indwell Believers?

"Demon possession is a condition in which one or more evil spirits or demons inhabit the body of a human being and can take complete control of their victim at will."[18] Evangelicals agree that demons can and do both afflict and possess the unregenerate. But they are not agreed on the question of whether demons can indwell believers.

Those who argue that believers can be indwelt by demons usually appeal to one or more of the following passages of Scripture: 1 Samuel 16:13-14; Luke 13:11-16; Acts 5:3; 1 Cor. 5:5; 2 Cor. 11:4; 12:7. These texts use phrases said to be supportive of the teaching, but it must be admitted that none of these verses say specifically that believers were demon-possessed.

> Surveying the evidence, one is forced to conclude that there is no clear statement of demon possession of a believer after Pentecost. Yet 1 Corinthians 5:5 seems to allow for it, since presumably if Satan can fill a believer's heart (Acts 5:3), he could send a demon to do the same. It is also not without significance that there are no commands in Acts or the epistles to cast out demons from believers.[19]

18. Unger, *Demons in the World Today*, p. 102.
19. Ryrie, *You Mean the Bible Teaches That* . . . , p. 104.

Unger first said Christians could not be indwelt by demons.[20] When his original volume on demons was revised and retitled, he changed his view and said believers could be demon-possessed.[21] Support for this view is usually drawn from testimonies of or about professed believers from whom demons are said to have been cast out and a reexamination of interpretations of passages alleged to deny the possibility.

I and others who believe Christians cannot be possessed do so for two basic reasons: (1) It does not seem likely that the Holy Spirit would share dwelling places with demons. (2) There is no evidence that any persons possessed in New Testament times were believers.

Regardless of whether or not one believes Christians can be possessed or indwelt, there is no doubt that demons do influence and oppress believers.

> In demon influence, evil spirits exert power over a person short of actual possession. Such influence may vary from mild harassment to extreme subjection when body and mind become dominated and held in slavery by spirit agents. Christians, as well as non-Christians, can be so influenced. They may be oppressed, vexed, depressed, hindered, and bound by demons.[22]

What can believers do to avert and counteract Satanic and demonic influence? First, we must accept responsibility for our own sin and not seek to find explanation for it in Satan or demons. Second, it is dangerous to dabble in demonology and it is possible to have an unbalanced approach to what the Bible says about Satan and his emissaries. Concentration should be focused on Christ's victory over Satan and his hosts and on our promised victory in and through him. Third, we must make a special effort not to "give place to the devil" (Eph. 4:27). We give place to him when we do not live according to Scripture, when we sin. Fourth, Scripture exhorts us to appropriate the finished work of Christ and the promised work of the Holy Spirit in our lives.[23]

20. Unger, *Biblical Demonology*, p. 100.
21. Unger, *Demons in the World Today*, pp. 116-17.
22. Ibid., p. 113.
23. For a presentation of the Christian defense against demons see Ryrie, *You Mean the Bible Teaches That* . . . , pp. 101-3.

After the Apostolic Era Can Humans Cast Out Demons?

Those evangelicals who believe demons should be cast out of believers and unbelievers base their view on the fact that the disciples were given this ability by Christ. They feel the ability is a present reality today.

Other evangelicals argue to the contrary for the following reasons: 1) There is no warrant in the New Testament for exorcism in the present age. 2) The ability to cast out demons was a temporary ability since it existed at the same time as the New Testament sign gifts.

Ryrie offers a helpful approach to demonic activity:

Demonic activity should not be treated by exorcism but just like any other sinful opposition. In other words, the believer should treat demon molestation like temptation or the activities of his own sinful nature. Pinpoint the source of attack; examine himself to see if there is any rebellion against the law or will of God; confess any and all known sin; and rely on the power of the indwelling Spirit. Demon activity can be fought successfully by these means and without theatrics, whether the demon operates from within or from without the believer. Even if exorcism seems called for in some unusual instance, the exorcist cannot prevent demons from attacking the same person again, for no human being can guarantee to completely bind demons or send them into the abyss where they would be confined permanently. Paul says we wrestle, or struggle, against the powers of darkness, and that is a lifelong conflict (Eph. 6:12). Therefore, the believer must be alert (1 Pe 5:8); be clothed in the armor of God (Eph. 6:13-18); and maintain vigorous physical, mental, and spiritual health (Ro 12:2; 2 Co 10:5; Phil 4:8).[24]

Those who do not believe the ability to exorcise demons is available today usually agree there is a better approach to help those possessed or harassed by demons. They do not hesitate to pray with and for such oppressed people and implore God to bring deliverance to them on the authority of the finished work of Christ.[25]

---

24. Ibid., p. 105.
25. See Gordon R. Lewis' discussion on discerning the presence of spirits in John W. Montgomery, ed., *Demon Possession* (Minneapolis: Bethany Fellowship, 1976); Mark Bubeck, *The Adversary* (Chicago: Moody Press, 1975).

Angels, Demons, Satan, and the Daily Christian Life

What hope is there for the child of God to be victorious over such formidable foes? In himself there is none. However, God has made provision for his own. Satan and his demons do have limitations; they are creatures. "Greater is he that is in you, than he that is in the world" (1 John 4:4).

The child of God is in conflict with wicked supernaturalism. All the forces of hell are arraigned against him. True, Satan was defeated by the Savior at Calvary. But this does not mean he has no access or power to oppress God's people. God in sovereign wisdom allows him to head an army of demons and carry out a program of wickedness. But the believer has not been left alone to do battle with Satan and demons. Graciously God has provided bountifully in every way for his own. He has given his Word, whereby those who live according to it can live victoriously. Holy angels serve God on behalf of the redeemed. Every child of God is indwelt by the Spirit of God. He carries on ministries of teaching, correction, and guidance for the teachable. The Son of God carries on a constant ministry of intercession for those who are his.

God is real. So is Satan and his army of demons. These enemies of God should not be made the subject of jokes. We need, instead, to do everything we can to deny them an opportunity to gain a foothold in their warfare against us. Constant reminders are needed of Christ's defeat of Satan at the cross and our triumph available in him. The devil does have devices, and we must not be ignorant of them. The daily Christian life demands a total commitment to both the written and Living Word.

Questions for Discussion

1. How can the contemporary interest in spirit beings be explained, since there was so little interest shown in earlier periods?
2. How does one's view of angels, demons, and Satan affect other doctrines of the Christian faith?

3. Do you think the angels of God and the angels of Satan are at war with each other now? Why, or why not?
4. What evidence is there for demon possession today?
5. What methods does Satan use to overthrow God's people?

Suggestions for Further Reading

Alexander, William Menzies. *Demonic Possession in the New Testament*. Edinburgh: T. & T. Clark, 1902.
Dickason, C. Fred. *Angels, Elect and Evil*. Chicago: Moody Press, 1975.
Lewis, C. S. *The Screwtape Letters*. New York: Macmillan, 1961.
Montgomery, John W., ed. *Demon Possession*. Minneapolis: Bethany Fellowship, 1976.
Unger, Merrill F. *Demons in the World Today*. Wheaton, Ill.: Tyndale House, 1971.

6

God's Creation

This chapter is concerned with anthropology and hamartiology, the doctrines of man and sin. How one views man's significance on earth may determine what is done with the nuclear powers that are capable of destroying the human race.

Several major issues concerning man and sin—the origin of man, the essential elements of man, the image of God in man, and the fall of man will be discussed. In contrast to secular humanistic and pantheistic views of man, evangelicals agree that these are basic.

Evangelical theologians differ considerably in certain areas of the doctrines of man and sin. Both sides of crucial issues will be presented, along with recommended readings by proponents of the various views.

It is fitting that we give attention to these two doctrines at this point. The evangelical theology regarding the Bible, God the Father, God the Son, God the Holy Spirit, and angels has already been set forth. Now, before God's salvation for sinners is presented, we need to establish the need for that salvation.

A Historical Perspective

Pre-Christian Thinking

Contrary to popular belief, evolution as an explanation of origins did not originate with Charles Darwin. True, his *On the*

Origin of Species eventually brought widespread exposure and acceptance to the theory. But the idea of evolution was held by both scientists and philosophers long before Darwin.

One form of early Greek philosophy explained the world by a dualistic concept in which spirit was seen as good and matter as evil. Included was belief in the eternity of matter. Another form embraced the process of emanation, making the world the external manifestation of God. Incipient evolution can be found in the writings of early Greek thinkers such as Anaximander (ca. 610-545 B.C.) and Empedocles (ca. 490-430 B.C.). The former believed men had evolved from fish, while the latter held that animals had been derived from plants.

None of the ancient cosmogonies include any concept of a personal God creating out of nothing. To the contrary, they all begin with something on which the gods or forces of nature work to bring the world and its inhabitants to their present status. Opposing such notions is the view of the Christian church based upon the pristine declarations of Scripture.

The Early Church Fathers

The Greek Fathers. Greek writers were far more speculative in their theology than were the Latin fathers. The early Greek dualism manifested itself especially in the doctrine of sin and grace. The opposition of the Greek fathers to Gnosticism had much to do with their views. While Gnostics stressed the physical necessity of evil, the fathers in response emphasized that Adam's being in the image of God did not mean he was ethically perfect before the fall but only morally perfect.

> Adam could and did sin, and thus came under the power of Satan, death, and sinful corruption. This physical corruption was propagated in the human race, but is not itself sin and did not involve mankind in guilt. There is no original sin in the strict sense of the word. They do not deny the solidarity of the human race, but admit its physical connection with Adam. This connection, however, relates only to the corporeal and sensuous nature, which is propagated from father to son, and not to the higher and rational side of human nature, which is in every case a direct creation of God.[1]

1. Louis Berkhof, *The History of Christian Doctrines* (Grand Rapids: Baker, 1959), p. 132.

Origen represents a slight departure from this view. He said every human was tainted with pollution from birth. He explained this, however, by arguing for a pretemporal fall of the soul.

As might be expected, the weak view of sin advocated by the Greek fathers led them to an equally weak view of God's grace. They stressed man's free will as the starting point in making recovery possible rather than the free sovereign grace of God.

The Latin Fathers. At first Greek thought in the East influenced thinkers in the West. Before long, however, it became obvious that the West was tending toward a much more biblically based anthropology than was true of the speculative view in the East.

In the East, Origen advocated what has come to be known as creationism with regard to the transmission of the human soul. His view was that a separate act of creation is performed by God sometime between conception and birth, bringing into existence the soul of the individual. The parents are responsible only for the propagation of the physical, not the spiritual aspect of the new life. Opposing this in the West, Tertullian taught traducianism—the soul as well as the body is miraculously propagated by parents. There is no separate act of creation in connection with each birth. Creationism and traducianism will be discussed further later in this chapter.

> Tertullian represents only the beginning of Latin anthropology, and some of his expressions still remind one of the teachings of the Greek fathers. He speaks of the innocence of infants . . . and does not altogether deny the freedom of the will. . . . He sometimes uses language that savours of the synergistic theory that God and man work together in regeneration.[2]

Later, in the writings of Latin fathers such as Cyprian, Ambrose, and Hilary, the doctrine of original sin became clearer. Though they tended still to adhere to the idea that salvation was the result of a cooperative effort between God and man, they did affirm that the human race sinned in Adam. Their advance toward more biblically based views certainly paved the way for the still stronger view of Augustine.

---

2. Ibid., p. 134.

The Pelagian/Augustinian Controversy

The British monk Pelagius, soon after he arrived in Rome near the end of the fourth century, became involved in controversy with Augustine over man, sin, and grace. Pelagius was a quiet, austere man with high moral standards, and it was his critical response to lax morals among Christians and his own rigorous life style that brought him to his views of human ability, law, and grace. Much of his writing concerned his points of difference with Augustine.

Augustine, after much spiritual struggle and through the help of Ambrose, turned to Christ. Reportedly his conversion took place in a garden at Milan. He was baptized in 387 and became bishop of Hippo in 395. Augustine relates his own conversion to Christianity in his famous *Confessions*. His strong and biblically oriented position on the human condition and its remedy in God's grace alone has had great effect upon orthodox theology.

Pelagian Views. In general, Pelagius' views are best summarized in the list of points condemned at the Council of Carthage (411-412). These were: 1) Adam's sin affected only Adam, not the human race. 2) Everyone is born in the same condition as Adam was before his fall. 3) Law and gospel are both designed for man's acceptance into the kingdom of God. 4) There were men without sin before the coming of Christ.

According to Pelagius, Adam was created in a state of neutrality. He did not possess positive holiness or evil. Adam's sin injured only him. Pelagius did not believe in original sin and rejected any notion that there was a hereditary transmission of a sinful nature. In man's nature there are no evil tendencies or desires leading him to sin.

Without any help from God man can turn from evil to good. God's grace is of some assistance to man but is not demanded. The grace Pelagius spoke of was not a divine inward work of the Spirit of God but rather the external gifts and natural endowments which man possesses.

Augustinian Views. First, on the four points for which Pelagianism was condemned at Carthage, Augustine took the opposing views. It is generally admitted that the celebrated father's early religious experiences, his study of Romans, and his opposition to Pelagian theology greatly influenced his thinking.

Man was created immortal, which does not mean that he was impervious to death, but that he had the capacity of bodily immortality. Had he proved obedient, he would have been confirmed in holiness. From the state of the *posse non peccare et mori* (the ability not to sin and die) he would have passed to the state of *non posse peccari et mori* (the inability to sin and die). But he sinned, and consequently entered the state of the *non posse non peccari et mori* (the inability not to sin and die).[3]

Augustine viewed the race as a unit and conceived of every member as realistically and not just federally in Adam, sinning when he sinned.[4] Because of man's sin in Adam he is incapable of doing anything whereby he can merit favor with God.

Only God's grace can renew the human heart. Augustine spoke of this grace as "irresistible." By this he meant God's grace so works upon man's stubborn will that in response man chooses God's gift of salvation. In other words, God the Spirit makes the sinner willing and able to believe. Augustine's strong emphasis on God's grace in salvation was accompanied by his view of predestination. The elect, he believed, were predestined to salvation. The reprobation of the nonelect, however, was not accompanied by any work of God to secure the intended results as was the predestination of the elect.

The Aftermath. Officially Pelagianism was condemned at the Council of Ephesus in 431. Soon a mediating position arose termed Semi-Pelagianism or Semi-Augustinianism, depending on the proximity of the views to the systems.

Basically the Western branch of the church adopted Augustine's view of man, sin, and grace. Influential leaders were not always as strong as he was in certain areas such as the reprobation of the lost. But all in the West did stress the bondage of the will and the need of God's sovereign grace for salvation.

It may be said that the most important leaders of the Church remained true to the most practical part of Augustinian anthropology for two or three centuries after Augustine. And the Synod of Orange adopted a moderate Augustinianism as the doctrine of the Church. Pelagianism and Semi-Pelagianism were both condemned as contrary to the orthodox faith. The

3. Berkhof, *History of Christian Doctrines*, p. 138.
4. The realistic and federalistic views of the race's relationship to Adam will be discussed later in the chapter.

Augustinian doctrine of salvation by grace only was victorious, but the doctrine of the irresistible grace of predestination was supplanted by that of the sacramental grace of baptism. And the doctrine of a double predestination—predestination also to evil—was abandoned in 529 A.D. Gradually the general decline in the Roman Catholic Church led to a drift in the direction of Semi-Pelagianism, which had long before secured a rather sure footing in the East. In course of time the Latin Church adopted the anthropology of the Greek Church and adhered to it ever since.[5]

The Middle Ages

The views of three important individuals will be summarized here to highlight the doctrines of anthropology and hamartiology in the Middle Ages.

First are those of Gregory the Great, who became pope in 590. Gregory is often considered one of the main interpreters of Augustine in the Middle Ages. Though it is true that he shared views with Augustine on a number of things related to the doctrines under discussion, he unfortunately did not consistently carry them through.

For Gregory, unlike Augustine, sin was a weakness and did not involve guilt. Like Augustine he believed God's grace initiated redemption. Water baptism, he said, works faith in the human heart and cancels the guilt of past sins. Through it man's will is renewed and his heart made to love God. In this way man is put in a position where he deserves something from God. Gregory differed rather dramatically with Augustine on the matter of predestination. Gregory believed God's predestination of the elect to salvation was based strictly on his foreknowledge that they would believe when confronted with the gospel.

Augustine's anthropology was restated and amplified by Anselm of Canterbury. In his famous *Cur Deus Homo* (Why God Became Man) Anselm revealed his views of man, sin, and God's grace. He argued in answer to Boso that "sin was transmitted to all men from Adam and Eve,"[6] and again that "everyone who sins must repay to God the honor that he has taken away, and this is the satisfaction that every sinner ought to make to God."[7]

---

5. Berkhof, *History of Christian Doctrines*, p. 138.

6. Cited from Hugh T. Kerr, ed., *Readings in Christian Thought* (Nashville: Abingdon Press, 1966), p. 91.

7. Ibid., p. 87.

Anselm insisted that Adam's sin was unique because he included within himself the entire human race. His first sin, therefore, was imputed to all of his posterity. Consequently guilt and pollution are transmitted from parent to child, beginning with our first parents and their offspring.

Thomas Aquinas has been called "the most magnificent architect of systematic theology, judged by standards of size, scope, and consistency."[8] His greatest contribution was his *Summa Theologica* (The Sum of Theology).

Aquinas' answers to two questions reveal his basic views. His answer to whether death and other bodily defects are the result of sin is, in part:

> The sin of our first parent is the cause of death and all such like defects in human nature, in so far as by the sin of our first parent original justice was taken away, whereby not only were the lower powers of the soul held together under the control of reason, without any disorder whatever, but also the whole body was held together in subjection to the soul, without any defect. . . . Wherefore, original justice being forfeited through the sin of our first parent, just as human nature was stricken in the soul by the disorder among the powers . . . , so also it became subject to corruption, by reason of disorder in the body.[9]

To the question of whether a movement of man's free will is possible and essential for him to be justified Aquinas answered:

> The justification of the ungodly is brought about by God moving man to justice. For He it is "that justifieth the ungodly," according to Rom. iv. 5. Now God moves everything in its own manner, just as we see that in natural things, what is heavy and what is light are moved differently, on account of their diverse natures. Hence He moves man to justice according to the condition of his human nature. But it is man's proper nature to have free-will. Hence in him who has the use of reason, God's motion to justice does not take place without a movement of the free-will; but He so infuses the gift of justifying grace that at the same time He moves the free-will to accept the gift of grace, in such as are capable of being moved thus.[10]

8. Ibid., p. 102.
9. Ibid., p. 117.
10. Ibid., pp. 118-19.

In the view of the Roman Catholic Church on anthropology and hamartiology during the Middle Ages there was an element of both Semi-Augustinianism and Semi-Pelagianism. The latter soon became the dominant view. Berkhof's summary of Rome's view of original righteousness is well stated:

> The view gradually prevailed that original righteousness was not a natural but a supernatural endowment of man. Man, it was held, naturally consists of flesh and spirit, and from these diverse or contrary propensities there arises a conflict (concupiscence), which often makes right action difficult. To offset the disadvantages of this original languor of nature, God added to man a certain remarkable gift, namely original righteousness, which served as a check to keep the inferior part of man in proper subjection to the superior, and the superior to God. This original righteousness was a supernatural gift, a *donum superadditum*, something added to the nature of man, who was created without positive righteousness, but also without positive unrighteousness.[11]

When man sinned he lost this original righteousness. It follows, therefore, that he lost no natural endowment but simply the gift he had received which, in fact, was not an essential part of his nature. Man returned to a neutral position, being neither sinful nor holy. In Rome's view, then, man did not receive a sin nature and guilt before God because of his sin. Nor did he become the subject of eternal death.

As might be expected, a close relationship exists between the Roman Catholic doctrine of man and sin and the doctrine of salvation, which includes faith plus works.

The Reformation

Luther's Views. Of Martin Luther's many writings, two have been selected to illustrate his views. In his *Preface to the Epistle to the Romans* his comments on the first three chapters of Romans are revealing:

> That is what St. Paul does. He begins in chapter 1 and rebukes the gross sin and unbelief that are plainly evident, as the sins of the heathen, who live without God's grace, were and still are. . . . In

11. Berkhof, *History of Christian Doctrines*, p. 149.

chapter 2, he stretches this rebuke still farther and extends it to those who seem outwardly to be righteous, but commit sin in secret. . . . In chapter 3 he puts them all together in a heap, and says that one is like the other; they are all sinners before God, except that the Jews have had God's Word.[12]

No doubt *The Bondage of the Will* is the greatest piece of theological writing the great Reformer ever penned. In fact, he considered it his greatest. In it he addressed Erasmus, who advocated the freedom of the will. Luther's summary and definitive statements set forth the tone of all the Reformers:

It now then follows, that Free-will is plainly a divine term and can be applicable to none but the divine Majesty only: for He alone "doth, (as the Psalm sings) what He will in Heaven and earth." (Ps. cxxxv. 6) Whereas, if it be ascribed unto men, it is not more properly ascribed, than the divinity of God himself would be ascribed unto them: which would be greatest of all sacrilege. Wherefore, it becomes Theologians to refrain from the use of this term altogether, whenever they wish to speak of human ability, and to leave it to be applied to God only. And moreover, to take this same term out of the mouths and speech of men; and thus to assert, as it were, for their God, that which belongs to His own sacred and holy Name.[13]

Calvin's Views. Contrary to the view of Roman theology, Calvin insisted that original sin was not just a privation. He believed it to be a corruption that came upon human nature, bringing forth God's wrath and condemnation. As a result of Adam's fall he and all his posterity became totally depraved, unable to do anything to merit favor with God.

In his *Institutes of the Christian Religion* Calvin made his view very clear:

But if it cannot be controverted that the righteousness of Christ is ours by communication, and life as its consequence, it is equally evident that both were lost in Adam, in the same manner in which they were recovered in Christ, and that sin and death were introduced by Adam, in the same manner in which they were

12. Cited from Robert L. Ferm, *Readings in the History of Christian Thought* (New York: Holt, Rinehart and Winston, 1964), p. 345.
13. Ibid., p. 356.

abolished by Christ. There is no obscurity in the declaration that
many are made righteous by the obedience of Christ, as they had
been made sinners by the disobedience of Adam. And, therefore,
between these two persons there is this relation, that the one
ruined us by involving us in his destruction, the other by his grace
has restored us to salvation.[14]

Socinianism. Socinianism was an outright rejection of the major
doctrines of the Reformers. It has rightly been referred to as a
revival of the Pelagian error.

Since Adam had no positive righteousness or holiness, he could
not lose it as the result of sin. While he sinned and incurred the
divine displeasure, his moral nature remained intact, and is
transmitted unimpaired to his posterity. Man dies, not because of
the sin of Adam, but because he was created mortal. Men are even
now by nature like Adam in that they have no proneness or
tendency to sin, but are placed in somewhat more unfavorable
circumstances because of the examples of sin which they see and of
which they hear. While this increases their chances of falling into
sin, they can avoid sin altogether, and some of them actually do.
And even if they do fall in sin and are thus guilty of transgression,
they do not therefore incur the divine wrath. God is a kind and
merciful Father, who knows their frailty and is quite ready to
forgive them when they come to him with penitent hearts. They
need no Saviour nor any extraordinary interposition of God to
secure their salvation.[15]

Arminianism. At first a strict Calvinist, Arminius was appointed
in the late sixteenth century to answer the attacks being made
against the Calvinistic position that God in eternity past elected
some to salvation and predestined others to damnation. As a
result of his studies Arminius was convinced of a less severe form
of Calvinism. Immediately he and his view were attacked.

In his *Declaration of Sentiments* Arminius presented his belief in
four decrees of God. Here his views of man and sin are apparent.
In the first decree God appointed his Son to destroy sin by his
death. The second decree had to do with God's decision to receive
those sinners who repent of their sin, believe in Christ, and

14. Ibid., p. 360.
15. Berkof, *History of Christian Doctrines*, pp. 154-55.

persevere to the end. To pass by and damn those who do not obey God's decree to administer the means which were necessary for repentance and faith through his divine wisdom was the third decree. In the fourth God decreed to save and damn on the basis of his foreknowledge.

On man's will, Arminius believed Adam before the fall was so endowed with knowledge, holiness, and power that he was able to do what God wanted him to do, but only through the assistance of God's grace. In man's present sinful state he cannot in and of himself do what God expects of him unless and until the Holy Spirit enables him.

Berkhof, with justification, views contemporary Arminianism as Semi-Pelagian in the doctrines under discussion.

> They maintain that the guilt of Adam's sin is not imputed to his descendants, though its pollution is passed on from father to son. This pollution they do not regard as sin in the proper sense of the word but only as a disease or a weakness. It does not bring man under a sentence of condemnation, but weakens his nature, so that he is incapable of attaining to eternal life, either by reestablishing himself in the favor of God or by discovering for himself a way of salvation. They do not believe in the total depravity of human nature, though they occasionally express themselves as if they do, but leave room for the free will of man in the material sense of the word, that is as a natural power or ability in man to do something that is spiritually good, so that he can also in some measure prepare himself for turning to God and doing his will.[16]

The Modern Period

With the introduction of modern philosophy there also came modification of and departure from the anthropology of the Reformers. Semi-Pelagian and Semi-Augustinian views continued to flourish.

Major developments in the doctrines of man and sin since the Reformation are best seen in liberal theology—both classic and contemporary.

The old liberal theology of pre-World War II days denied the doctrine of original sin as understood by orthodox theology. Man

16. Ibid., pp. 155-56.

was recognized as essentially good, having within him a spark of divinity. To be sure, he is a finite child of nature and thus subject to death, and is less than perfect. He is sick because of the sins of society, but there is nothing radically wrong with human nature. The root of all evil was viewed as ignorance rather than sin. Some even denied the existence of sin altogether.

Contemporary, or postwar, liberals seek to utilize what they consider the gains of their liberal forefathers. Added to these are their reinterpretations and rewordings of the historic Christian understanding of the biblical doctrines of man, sin, and salvation.

> The real reason for the change from the old liberalism to the new is basically because neoorthodoxy removed the fall, recorded in Genesis 3, from an event in time. For neoorthodoxy, Adam was not a real individual but only a representative of man; and the account of Adam's fall is only the account of what takes place with all of us. Thus, neoliberalism is able to believe that not only was Adam created in goodness, but also that all men are born good. It does admit, however, that men may lose this goodness unless they are "redeemed." . . . Neoliberalism is highly influenced by Reinhold Niebuhr, professor at Union Theological Seminary in New York, who represents American neoorthodoxy but whose theology borders on neoliberalism. He takes the fall of man with profound seriousness. He does so, however, by interpreting it as myth rather than as literal fact. By myth, he means that which deals with aspects of reality which are above and beyond science rather than before science. According to Niebuhr, original sin is man's consciousness that he is not what he ought to be. He sees this original sin becoming universal by man's attempt to either rise to God's level or lower himself to the animal level. Neoliberalism follows Niebuhr very closely in speaking with real seriousness of the fall and original sin, while attempting to free the doctrine of all literalistic connotations.[17]

It is true that neoliberals do take man's sinful behavior far more seriously than their liberal forefathers did. Yet they do not believe man is born a sinner. Instead they believe he becomes one as he participates in an evil society. In contemporary liberal theology humans are not born totally depraved and spiritually dead. Often

17. Robert P. Lightner, *Neo-Liberalism* (Nutley, N.J.: The Craig Press, 1972), pp. 63, 65.

biblical language is used to describe sin, but it is invested with new meaning and explained away.

G. Bromley Oxnam, a spokesman for neoliberal theology, revealed his own view of the doctrines under discussion in his review of the church's view of forgiveness:

> There were those who thought in legal terms, and held that penalty must be exacted. Penalty involved punishment. So Christ was offered as a substitute. We hear much of the substitutionary theory of the atonement. This theory is to me immoral. If Jesus paid it all, or if he is the substitute for me, or if he is the sacrifice for all the sin of the world, then why discuss forgiveness? The books are closed. Another has paid the debt, borne the penalty. I owe nothing. I am absolved.[18]

Oxnam's view of man's salvation is not dependent upon the death of Christ but rather upon man's confession, repentance, and commitment.[19]

Roland Frye uses the term *originating sin* in place of original sin. He means by it "the creature's will to exist as his own god." The fall of man, he says, "is the attempt to establish himself as his own god, and to claim for his own private dominion the fruit of the knowledge of good and evil."[20]

W. Norman Pittenger's comment on Frye's statement reveals his own contemporary liberal view:

> Here we have a particularly lucid statement of the point that we ourselves have sought to make clear in earlier chapters: that it is pride, refusal to accept his place in the scheme of things, which is basic to man's problem; and here too we have the recognition that the story in Genesis describing "the fall" is, like the story of man's creation in the same book, a story told about every man—a myth in the proper sense of the word. It is about us in our contemporary state that we are being instructed, not about some remote historical figure.[21]

18. G. Bromley Oxnam, *A Testament of Faith* (Boston: Little, Brown, 1958), p. 144.
19. Ibid., pp. 144-50.
20. Roland Frye, *Perspectives on Man* (Philadelphia: Westminster Press, 1961), pp. 122-23.
21. W. Norman Pittenger, *The Christian Understanding of Human Nature* (Philadelphia: Westminster Press, 1964), p. 96.

L. Harold DeWolf, another spokesman for neoliberal theology, gives considerable attention to the doctrine of sin. He presents the traditional orthodox view and insists no such doctrine is to be found in the Bible. He then seeks to glean some of the "valuable insights" that have been conveyed by the orthodox view.[22]

A Positive Statement of the Doctrine

The Origin of Man

The answer to the question, Where has man come from? must be found either in some form of evolution or in divine creation.

Evolution. Those who deny the existence of God embrace evolution. They rule out God completely in their view of origins. Some theists, however, embrace forms of evolution. These forms are given different labels, but the term *theistic evolution* describes them all. Some of these views among evangelicals will be discussed later, but here we deal only with atheistic evolution and its answer to the question of where man came from.

It is virtually impossible to find a definition of the theory of organic evolution with which all evolutionists agree. Beyond the fact that man was not created by the God of the Bible but has evolved from lower forms of life, there is little agreement. Based upon what atheistic evolutionists have written, and continue to write, their theory of origins may be defined as "the hypothesis that millions of years ago lifeless matter, acted upon by natural forces, gave origin to one or more minute living organisms which have since evolved into all living and extinct plants and animals including man."[23]

Belief in evolution is not always stated in the same way. Some say man is a direct descendant of apes now in existence. Others insist man and higher apes have a common ancestry. Either way, man descended from lower animals in his entirety (material and immaterial parts) by a perfectly natural process.

Evolution as discussed here is not just change but a certain kind of change, from lifeless matter to living organisms. Such a view, of

22. L. Harold DeWolf, *A Theology of the Living Church* (New York: Harper & Row, 1960), pp. 198-200.

23. *Evolution: A Handbook for Students by a Medical Scientist* (Toronto: International Christian Crusade, 1951), p. 7.

course, rules out completely the supernatural. The theory of evolution controls much of modern thought. As Huxley's comment bears out, it is by no means restricted to the fields of biology:

> The concept of evolution was soon extended into other than biological fields. Inorganic subjects such as the life-histories of stars and the formation of the chemical elements on the one hand, and on the other hand subjects like linguistics, social anthropology, and comparative law and religion, began to be studied from an evolutionary angle, until today we are enabled to see evolution as a universal and all-pervading process.[24]

What, then, is the answer of evolution to the question of man's origin? It is that he came into existence through a completely natural process, having his beginning in lifeless matter. The arguments usually advanced in support of evolution are many and varied. Among them are the arguments from comparative anatomy, classifications of living organisms, embryonic recapitulation, mutations, and the fossil record in the geological time column. These, along with all the other arguments defending atheistic evolution, have been addressed by creationists.[25]

Divine Creation. Creationists, as opposed to evolutionists, accept the full authority of the Bible. They readily acknowledge that its primary purpose is to make men saints not scientists. But while the Bible is not a textbook on science, it nevertheless has a good deal to say about origins.[26] Evangelicals insist the Bible is as authoritative when it addresses matters relating to science as when it addresses matters relating to salvation.

Three Hebrew words are used in the Genesis creation account to speak of God's work of creation: *bara* ("to create"), *asah* ("to make"), and *yatsar* ("to form"). These are used interchangeably in the creation narrative (Gen. 1:26-27; 2:7). Though God certainly did create out of nothing (*ex nihilo*), this was not true of all his creative activity.

---

24. Julian Huxley, "Evolution and Genetics," in *What Is Science?* ed. J. R. Newman (New York: Simon and Schuster, 1955), p. 272.

25. The following works are recommended: Arthur C. Custance, *Genesis and Early Man* (Grand Rapids: Zondervan, 1975); Bolton Davidheiser, *Evolution and Christian Faith* (Philadelphia: Presbyterian and Reformed Publishing Company, 1969); Henry M. Morris, *The Twilight of Evolution* (Grand Rapids: Baker Book House, 1963).

26. See Henry M. Morris, "The Bible Is a Textbook of Science," *Bibliotheca Sacra*, Oct., 1964, Jan., 1965.

Contrary to the contemporary liberal and neoorthodox nonhistorical approach to the Genesis account, evangelicals accept it as a record of historical events. Their basis for doing so is the fact that this is the way other biblical accounts view it (e.g., Exod. 20:10-11; 31:17; Matt. 19:4-6; Heb. 4:4; 2 Peter 3:5).

Evangelicals are not all agreed on the time of the creation or the approximate age of the earth and man because of differences regarding Genesis 1:1-2 and the meaning of "days" in the creation account. Some understand the days as regular solar days, while others view them as periods of time undesignated in length. All agree, however, that repeatedly (at least seventeen times in Genesis 1) God is declared to be the Creator. It is also clearly stated how God brought man into existence. Any form of evolution must be read into the passage; it is not there in the account written by Moses.

Several things set off God's creation of man from the rest of what was created. Man's creation came after divine counsel (Gen. 1:26). It was an immediate act of God, in contrast to creation of the earth, which was to put forth vegetation. The creation of man was after the divine type also, "in our image," instead of "after its kind." Both material and immaterial were used—the dust of the ground and the breath of life. After his creation man was given dominion over the earth. The first man and woman became the source for the entire human race.

The Essential Elements of Man

Of what is man made? Evangelicals are divided into two camps in their answers to this question. Trichotomists believe man is made up of body, soul, and spirit. Dichotomists argue for only two parts—body and spirit. Though they differ on the way they view the essential elements of man, evangelicals concur that man consists of material and immaterial.

The Material Part of Man. Several different terms are used to describe man's physical makeup, his body. The term *soma* ("body") is the most common. It is used of both the resurrected and unresurrected body (Matt. 6:22; 1 Cor. 15:44). The Greek *sarx* ("flesh") is sometimes used of the physical body. Paul referred to the "body of sin" as that through which the sin nature expresses itself (Rom. 6:6). He also spoke of the "body of death" (Rom. 7:24) and the "body of our humiliation" (Phil. 3:21).

Many biblical injunctions relate to the physical body. For the believer it is the temple of the Holy Spirit (1 Cor. 6:19). The deeds of the body are to be put to death by the child of God (Rom. 8:13; Col. 3:5). The body is yet unredeemed (Rom. 8:23). The body is not to be ruled by sin (Rom. 6:12). Each believer is exhorted to present his body to the Lord as a sacrifice (Rom. 12:1). Such injunctions make clear that the care of our bodies is very important, since with them and through them we serve God. The Scriptures thereby assume the validity of the physical organism with its many different functions.

The Immaterial Nature of Man. A fact often overlooked is that the immaterial part of man is accounted for only in biblical revelation. Evolutionists have no satisfying explanation for the mind of man, for example.

A number of different terms are used in Scripture to describe the immaterial in man. *Soul* and *spirit* are no doubt the most common. The Old Testament usage of *soul* is rather broad. It is distinguished from the body and sometimes refers to the whole of the inner man (Isa. 10:18). At death it is the soul that departs (Gen. 35:18). The word *soul* is even used to refer to a corpse. Man is said to be a soul (Gen. 2:7). In the New Testament *soul* is sometimes used interchangeably with *spirit* (John 19:30; 10:15); in other instances it is seen to be different.

Spirit is used to stand for a person after death (Heb. 12:23; Matt. 14:26). It is sometimes used interchangeably with *soul* and sometimes synonymously. As we will see later, the debate between dichotomists and trichotomists is to some extent a semantic one and often represents a confusion of substantial and functional categories of thought.

Heart is used to refer to the seat of the emotions and the initial source of actions, especially in the Old Testament. It is sometimes used synonymously with *mind*. According to Jeremiah 17:9 the heart can be defiled and needs cleansing.

Conscience is another term used, especially in the Pauline writings, referring to a function of the immaterial in man. Though affected by the fall, the conscience still functions in the unregenerate (Rom. 2:15). Paul claimed to have lived according to his conscience before his conversion to Christ (Acts 23:1). It is possible to sear, or desensitize, the conscience (1 Tim. 4:2). For the believer the conscience functions in a number of facets of the Christian life (e.g., Rom. 9:1; 13:5; 1 Cor. 8:7, 10, 12; 2 Cor. 1:12; 1 Peter 2:19).

Mind also describes a function of man's immaterial makeup. The unregenerate mind is vain (Eph. 4:17), defiled (Titus 1:15), blinded (2 Cor. 4:4), darkened (Eph. 4:18), and reprobate (Rom. 1:28). The regenerate mind is to be led captive (2 Cor. 10:5); it needs girding (1 Peter 1:13) and renewing (Rom. 12:2).

Image and *likeness* (Gen. 1:26) are both used, sometimes separately and sometimes together, to describe that side of man which is not physical. More attention will be given to these below.

Since there are major differences among evangelicals over both the transmission and the composition of the immaterial in man, both these topics will be discussed in the section on differences.

The Image of God in Man

This doctrine relates to a number of other areas of theology. God and man are the most obvious. Since Christ is the image of the invisible God (Col. 1:15) and believers are to be conformed to his image (Rom. 8:29), there is a definite relationship with aspects of Christology. Certainly the meaning of the image of God in man cannot be fully understood apart from man's fall, since the description is used of him both before (Gen. 1:26) and after the fall (Gen. 5:1; 9:6).

Some of the early church fathers included physical and bodily characteristics in their understanding of what it means to be in the image of God. Others made a somewhat rigid distinction between image and likeness. They identified image with bodily traits and likeness with the spiritual nature of man. Exegetically there does not seem to be any significant difference between these two words. They are sometimes reversed (e.g., Gen. 1:26; cf. 5:1-3). *Likeness* is not repeated in Genesis 1:27 but is coupled with *image* in Genesis 1:26. *Image* is used alone to express the whole idea (Gen. 9:6). In the New Testament *image* and *glory* are used together (1 Cor. 11:7). Image (Col. 3:10) and likeness (James 3:9) are used alone.

The Meaning. Since God does not possess physical parts, the image of God in man cannot refer to physical resemblance; we are not to assume that man has the appearance of God. Also, God made both male and female, and each has unique physical characteristics. Nowhere does Scripture indicate that our physical nature is an aspect of the image of God. It is important, however, to remember that whatever likeness to God man bears must manifest itself through the physical body.

J. Oliver Buswell has devoted much attention to the meaning of the image of God in man.[27] He believes it refers to both man's makeup and function.

The function aspect has to do with man's dominion over the earth and its subjects (Gen. 1:26-28). This responsibility was given before the entrance of sin and repeated after the fall (Gen. 8:15-9:7). Therefore, man is not just a part of nature, as in Hinduism and Buddhism. Man is over nature, but responsible as a steward for ecological resources. Man's right to rule on the earth is thus at least a part of the meaning of being made in God's image. The true destiny of man is stated in Psalm 8:4-9 and Hebrews 2:5-8. When he fell, man lost the right to rule and hold dominion, but he is still considered to be made in God's image. Christ the representative man won back the right for man. The premillennialist insists this right will ultimately be realized in the future millennial kingdom.

Buswell also argues that the image of God in man includes or is related to knowledge, righteousness, and holiness. This is based primarily on Ephesians 4:22-25 and Colossians 3:9-10.[28] Man's intellect, emotion, and will, the essential elements of personality, are certainly a part of the meaning of bearing the image of God. Since God is a person and these elements of personality are found in him, they must relate to his image in man. Finally, it is contended that the image of God in man includes immortality. Only God possesses this as an essential quality. He has it in and of himself (1 Tim. 6:16). Man's immortality is like an endowment but is nevertheless a part of the meaning of the image.

The Significance. Evangelical theology views mankind with deep respect and ascribes genuine dignity to man because it views him in God's image. It is not antihumanistic, though to be sure its view of man clashes with a purely secularistic approach. All mankind is

27. J. Oliver Buswell, *A Systematic Theology of the Christian Religion* (Grand Rapids: Zondervan, 1971), 2:231-54. See also Gerritt Berkouwer, *Man: The Image of God* (Grand Rapids: Eerdmans, 1962).

28. Buswell, *Systematic Theology*, 2:235-36.

important from the biblical perspective, since every member of the human family is in the image and after the likeness of God. All human life is therefore viewed as sacred.

Evangelical Christianity is not against the arts, as it is often accused of being. Instead it has a vibrant interest in what man can and does create as the result of his God-given abilities. A genuinely biblical humanism has great respect for, and promotes, mankind's education and highest achievements. It does not believe man is the measure of all things, as secular humanism does, but it advocates the enrichment of the mind and encourages intellectual pursuits at every level.

The basis for what some have called Christian humanism[29]—to distinguish it from secular humanism[30]—is found in the Bible. The former is supernaturalistic and the latter naturalistic in base and beliefs. "Biblical Humanism is identifiable in Proverbs, Ecclesiastes, and the Song of Songs. Man probes his world, searches his own mind, rationalizes about the meaning of human existence and the absurdity of death. No relationship however obscure, no phenomenon however small and insignificant, is unworthy of examination."[31]

In the New Testament the emphasis on man made in God's image is equally strong. "At the heart [of the Christian faith] stands the confession that God—the originator of everything right and good—himself became man."[32] The fact that man is made in God's image is the basis for all the admonitions of the New Testament epistles. Man is the object of God's grace, and his chief end is indeed to glorify God and enjoy him forever. As man is renewed in Christ, he enjoys the fellowship of the Creator in a way superior even to that which Adam and Eve experienced before the fall.

29. See Norman L. Geisler, *Is Man the Measure?* (Grand Rapids: Baker Book House, 1983), and Robert E. Webber, *Secular Humanism: Threat and Challenge* (Grand Rapids: Zondervan, 1982), for critiques from an evangelical perspective of "Humanist Manifesto I," "Humanist Manifesto II," and the "Secular Humanist Declaration."

30. The following articles, written from the secular humanist perspective, will be helpful in understanding the position: "Toward a New Humanist Manifesto," *The Humanist*, Jan.-Feb., 1973; "Humanist Manifesto II." *The Humanist*, Sept.-Oct., 1973; "The Secular Humanist Declaration Pro and Con," *Free Inquiry*, Spring, 1981.

31. C. Hassell Bullock, *An Introduction to the Poetic Books* (Chicago: Moody Press, 1979), p. 256.

32. Mark Noll, "Christianity and Humanistic Values in Eighteenth-Century America: A Bicentennial Review," *Christian Scholar's Review*, (1976) 6:114-15.

The believer is the representative of God on earth. Therefore, it becomes his duty and solemn responsibility to those who have not been renewed in the image of God through Christ to share the gospel of God's saving grace. Man lost something in the fall, but not the image of God. His personality was marred, but not destroyed. Fallen man in the image of God is so marred and depraved because of sin that only God's grace can restore him.

The Fall of Man

Evangelicals view the Genesis account of Adam, Eve, the garden, the temptation, and sin as a record of historical facts. Unlike liberal and neoorthodox theology, which view it as legend or myth, evangelical theology accepts the account as a record of facts about real individuals who lived in time-space history.

The Temptation. It appears that the sin of Satan and evil angels had already taken place before our first parents were tempted and sinned. Adam and Eve had been given a number of privileges which also involved responsibilities (Gen. 2:15-20). There was, of course, one thing they were not to do—eat of the forbidden fruit. Death would result if they disobeyed. This meant Adam and Eve, though perfect as they came from the hands of the Creator, possessed unconfirmed creature perfection. That is, they were to undergo a period of probation, a time during which their innocence and holiness would be tested.

Satan apparently used the animal to provide the temptation. At least it was the animal God cursed after man fell. Satan did not appear as himself but rather as something with which Eve was familiar. He is called "that old serpent" (Rev. 12:9; cf. Gen. 3:1).

The Fall. Genesis 3 is the account of undoubtedly the most tragic event in the history of the world. Satan's method was first to create doubt in Eve's mind about the goodness of God in placing even one restriction on her (Gen. 3:1-3). He denied that what God had said was true; he called God a liar, in other words. Then he put before Eve the challenge to act independently of God and by so doing become like him. Soon after she ate of the forbidden fruit, Eve gave some to Adam, and he ate as well.

The first human sin was unique. The command our first parents disobeyed was peculiar to that situation. Their transgression can never be repeated. What they did is called the one sin of Romans

5:12, 15-19. Adam and Eve became sinners because they sinned. All since then, except Christ, sin because they are sinners. That first pair got a sin nature because they sinned. All their posterity sin because each one has a sin nature.

The Consequences. Three forms of death resulted from the sin of the first two humans. Adam and Eve experienced spiritual death, separation from God, the moment they sinned. They lost their relationship with God and came under the dominion of Satan. They also began to die physically (Gen. 3:22-24). And they became subject to eternal death; apart from God's gracious provision for them there would be eternal separation from God.

Various specific penalties were assigned by God after man's disobedience. The serpent was cursed (Gen. 3:14). Satan was doomed to be crushed by a fatal head wound (Gen. 3:15). Enmity was placed between Satan and Eve, between satanic hosts and mankind, and between Christ and Satan. Multiplied pain in childbirth, increased sorrow, and increased desire for her husband who was to rule over her were to come to Eve (Gen. 3:16). These effects were also assigned to Eve's posterity. Adam's penalties have also been passed on to his offspring (Gen. 3:17-19). Hard labor on a cursed ground was to be his lot. It was for man's sake the ground was cursed. All of creation was made subject to vanity because of man's sin (Gen. 3:17; 18; 20; Rom. 8:18-20).

Three additional major consequences of the fall will be given separate treatment. The first two—imputed guilt and transmitted depravity—show the relation of mankind to Adam. The third—personal sin—is the natural consequence of the first two.

Imputed Guilt

By imputation is meant the putting over to someone what may or may not be his. It is used in accounting, "to reckon to one's account." Chafer gives this helpful explanation of the theological meaning.

In the matter of man's relation to God, the Bible presents three major imputations: (a) imputation of Adam's sin to the human race, (b) imputation of the sin of man to the Substitute, Christ, and (c) an imputation of the righteousness of God to the believer. Imputation may be either *real* or *judicial*. That which is real is the reckoning to one of that which is antecedently his, while judicial imputation is the reckoning to one of that which is not antecedently his.[33]

Charles Hodge, who differs with Chafer eschatologically, also differs with him on the division of imputation between *real* and *judicial*. Hodge believes all three of the biblical imputations are to be viewed as judicial.[34]

Evangelicals all agree that Romans 5:12-19 is the central passage on the imputation of Adam's sin to the race. They do not agree, however, on the relation of the race to Adam and therefore in what sense the race sinned. This difference will be discussed later in this chapter.

It is also generally agreed among evangelicals that imputed condemnation results primarily in the just penalty of physical death. Distinction is usually made between imputed guilt and the sin nature as well, though the two cannot really be separated. All who are born and inherit a sin nature from their parents are, of course, those who sinned in some sense in Adam and therefore have that sin imputed to them.

Finally, evangelicals concur that the remedy for imputed sin is the imputed righteousness of Christ. That righteousness is the result of his death, though for some it is also to be related to that righteousness he earned in his life of obedience to the law of Moses.[35]

Transmitted Depravity

As a result of the first sin a fallen nature is passed on from parent to child. After Adam and Eve sinned the first time, they were easily inclined to disbelieve and disobey. They passed on to their children a sin nature, and they in turn to theirs, and the process continues. By sin nature is meant not only the capacity to sin but also the desire and tendency to sin. Scripture uses different terms to describe this nature.

Whereas imputed sin relates primarily to physical death, transmitted sin relates to spiritual death. Parents are the mediators

---

33. Lewis Sperry Chafer, *Systematic Theology* (Dallas: Dallas Theological Seminary Press, 1964), 2:296.

34. Charles Hodge, *Systematic Theology* (Grand Rapids: Eerdmans, 1968), 2:194.

35. See the discussion of this in chapter 3.

of this sin nature. Scripture presents every part of man as affected by the sin nature—intellect (Rom. 1:28), sensibility (Rom. 1:26), and will (Rom. 5:6).

Because all have guilt imputed to them, and because all have had a sin nature transmitted to them, all are therefore totally depraved. That is, all have been affected by the fall to such an extent that there is none righteous, not even one (Rom. 3:10). None are able to do anything to merit favor with God. Sin has affected every aspect of man. All are not as wicked as they could be, nor are all guilty of the same kinds of personal sins, but all are totally without merit before God. This is what total depravity means. All are in need of God's saving grace, and without it there is no hope for any.

The penalty for transmitted depravity is spiritual death. It is in this condition that all are born; those who do not become children of God through the finished work of Christ die in the same condition.

Personal Sin

The personal sins referred to here are those committed by the unregenerate. The sins of God's people are discussed in chapter 7 of this book. Question 24 of the Larger Westminster Catechism asks, "What is sin?" The answer given is, "Sin is any want of conformity unto, or transgression of any law of God, given as a rule to the reasonable creature." Chafer felt this definition was too restricted to transgression of the written law of God. God's character, he insisted, would encompass his law but would also include transgression of those areas not included in his law. He defined sin, therefore, as "any want of conformity to the character of God."[36]

In the Bible sin has both a positive and a negative side. It is not only missing the right mark but also hitting the wrong one. To sin is to side against God (James 4:4). Scripture speaks of the state of sin and also acts of sin. Always sin has its effects upon self, others, and God.

Even more difficult than a definition of sin is the answer to the question, Why evil? The Bible presents God as sovereign. This

---

36. Chafer, *Systematic Theology*, 2:267.

means he could have kept sin from entering his world. But he didn't. He could also eliminate all sin and evil now if that were his desire. But he doesn't.

The sovereign God of the Bible is also holy, loving, and just. He is presented in Scripture as the God who hates sin. The fact that he gave his Son as the sacrifice for sin demonstrates his hatred of it and his plan to rescue man from its ruin.

God is not the responsible originator of sin. He did not create it. His sovereign plan, however, did render the entrance of sin as a certainty. The decree of God did not enact sin, but it included the reality of it. Sin was first enacted when Satan and then Adam and Eve sinned, but it was certain in the eternal councils of God. If God the Son was slain before the foundations of the world, it follows that that which made his death necessary was also a part of his eternal plan. Why God permitted the manifestation of sin in concrete acts, and why he continues to permit it, must rest in the ineffably pure character of the God who works all things according to the good pleasure of his will (Eph. 1:5, 11). Philosophers and theologians have found no completely satisfying answer to the question, Why evil?[37]

The divine remedy for man's sin is to be found in the substitutionary death of Christ, who died for our sins (1 Cor. 15:3) and made provision for our sins in his own body on the tree (1 Peter 2:24). When the believing sinner trusts Christ alone as his sin-bearer, he receives forgiveness, remission of sins (Rom. 3:25). At the same time he also is justified, declared righteous (Rom. 3:24).

A summary of what we have been saying is in order. In addition to the penalties God imposed upon the serpent, Satan, Eve, Adam, and the ground, three major consequences of the fall in the garden have been noted. 1) In some sense the race of mankind was involved in Adam's transgression. His sin was imputed to all. 2.) A sin nature is passed from parent to child beginning with Adam and Eve. 3) Because of imputed sin and transmitted sin, personal acts of sin are committed. For these reasons all stand condemned before God and in need of God's gift of salvation.

37. See Norman L. Geisler, *Philosophy of Religion* (Grand Rapids: Zondervan, 1974), pp. 311-403.

Major Areas of Difference Among Evangelicals

There are four major areas of anthropology where evangelicals hold divergent views.

Theistic Evolution or Special Complete Creation

Theistic evolution claims that God used evolution to perform his work.[38] Those who hold this view insist the Bible does not tell us *how* God did his work of creating but rather *that* he did it. Theistic evolutionists usually are far more comfortable with the day-age view of the "days" of Genesis 1 than with viewing those days as solar time periods.

Fiat creation, or special complete creation, refers to God's creating immediately and completely by his word, his command (e.g., Ps. 33:6, 9; Heb. 11:3). God created the worlds not "out of things which do appear" but rather out of nothing, *ex nihilo*. Man was created by God from the "dust of the ground" (Gen. 2:7) after the worlds were framed.

Some have attempted to articulate positions somewhere between those of theistic evolution and fiat creation. Bernard Ramm's progressive creationism represents a variation of creationism that allows for more time. He argues strongly for the sovereign and fiat act of creation as a result of the concept, plan, or purpose which God had in mind before creation. The process, Ramm argues, came after the fiat act of creation. In this process God who had been working outside of nature, turned the task of continuing creation over to the Holy Spirit, who is inside nature.[39]

Edward J. Carnell's threshold evolution is still another variety of creationism. His view is that "there are gaps which exist between the original 'kinds,' while on the 'total' evolution view each 'kind' can be traced back to a more primitive type, and that, to a still more primitive, *ad infinitum*.'"[40] These original kinds "were stock

---

38. See the following for insight into the view: Russell L. Mixter, ed., *Evolution and Christian Thought Today* (Grand Rapids: Eerdmans, 1959); Bernard Ramm, *The Christian View of Science and Scripture* (Grand Rapids: Eerdmans, 1954).

39. Ramm, *The Christian View of Science and Scripture*, p. 116.

40. Edward J. Carnell, *An Introduction to Christian Apologetics* (Grand Rapids: Eerdmans, 1948), p. 239.

out of which, through threshold evolution, all our present types have evolved."[41]

According to Carl F. H. Henry, the problem is not that these views are unorthodox, though they may be questioned.

> The difficulty is that these phrases contribute to a verbal illusion which attracts the interest of the contemporary evolutionist somewhat under false pretenses, and his enthusiasm over their surface impression can only embarrass the evangelical overture. For creation, in its biblical sense, is something quite distinct from what the scientist insists is "progressively" knit into the warp and woof of reality, which "threshold evolution" can hardly be a part purchase of the developmental rationale if it presumes to be biblical. . . . The employment of conventional phrases with a contrary intention therefore runs needless apologetic hazards.[42]

Evangelicals who oppose theistic evolution, as I do, argue that the Bible allows for no type of biological evolution. They view theistic evolution as merely an attempt to bridge the gap between Christianity and science, an attempt that runs the risk of needless concessions. Scripture does say, "God ended his work" (Gen. 2:2) on the seventh day. And in reflection on God's creative activity the psalmist said God "spoke, and it was done; he commanded, and it stood fast" (Ps. 33:9).

Dichotomy or Trichotomy

The question here is, What is the composition of man? Is it twofold or threefold? Again, there are evangelicals on both sides.

The classic dichotomist view is that man in his entirety is composed of two parts—material and immaterial—body and spirit, with no ontological distinction between soul and spirit as to essence and, often, even as to function.[43] Dichotomists defend their view by insisting that there are in fact only two substances in the universe—material and immaterial. Thus the soul and the spirit cannot be two different substances or essences.

41. Ibid., p. 242, n. 24.
42. Carl F. H. Henry, *Contemporary Evangelical Thought* (Great Neck, N.Y.: Channel Press, 1957), pp. 250-52.
43. See Buswell, *A Systematic Theology*, 2:237-51.

They also appeal to Scripture. Man is said to become a living soul (Gen. 2:7). Here the soul is the whole of man, not something man has. Again, the whole immaterial part is called soul (1 Peter 2:11). James presented a twofold composition of man, and he used *spirit* to speak of the whole immaterial part (James 2:26). Again, Paul wrote of only two parts for man, body and spirit (1 Cor. 7:34).

In trichotomy soul and spirit are viewed as separate substantive entities. Therefore, in this view man consists of three realities—body, soul, and spirit. It is often said that body speaks of world-consciousness, soul of self-consciousness, and spirit of God-consciousness.

Arguments supporting trichotomy frequently begin with the three members of the Trinity of which man is said to be a reflection. Appeal is also made to Scripture. Hebrews 4:12 and 1 Thessalonians 5:23 are the major passages used.[44]

To a large extent the debate between dichotomy and trichotomy hinges on whether we are talking about substance or function. If substance is the issue, then it must be admitted there are only two—material and immaterial. On the other hand, if we are talking about function, it is certainly true that the immaterial part of man has many functions.

Creationism or Traducianism

How is the immaterial part of man, whether it is of one part or two, transmitted? In other words, how have humans since Adam and Eve gotten their immaterial natures? Two views are held by evangelicals.

Creationism holds that the immaterial soul of a child is not generated or derived in any way from the parents but is created separately and individually by God.[45] This act of creation is believed to occur sometime between conception and birth. Adherents of the view are not totally agreed on the exact time the creative act takes place.

Defense for the view is usually drawn from Scripture which emphasizes that man's body comes from the earth and his spirit from God (e.g., Num. 16:22; Heb. 12:9). The nature of the soul

---

44. See Emery H. Bancroft, *Christian Theology* (Hayward, Calif.: J. F. May Press, 1949), pp. 140-42.

45. See Hodge, *Systematic Theology*, 2:70-76, for defense of creationism.

and spirit as immaterial is also used to support creationism. The immaterial is indivisible and, therefore, the argument goes, we either have part of Adam's soul or we are a general essence of him. In addition, appeal is made to the person of Christ. If his soul or immaterial part was passed on from Mary, he was sinful, it is contended.

Traducianism holds that children receive from their parents in a miraculous way both the material and nonmaterial parts.[46] It rejects a special act of creation by God for each new birth. I believe this to be the better of the two views.

Traducianists argue that man in his entirety seems to be a unity at birth (Gen. 1:26). The whole man is born the first time by the will of the flesh (John 1:13). God's creative activity was finished on the sixth day (Gen. 2:1-3), which would not be true in the creationist's view. Traducianists frequently appeal also to Hebrews 7:10 to illustrate their view. Here Levi, father of the Aaronic priests, paid tithes to Melchizedek before he was born.

Traducianists ask whether God creates a perfect soul, which later falls, or a corrupt, depraved soul. Either would result in deviation from clear teaching of Scripture that God cannot even tempt to evil. Christ must be viewed as an exception, as he is in so many other areas. Mary did not pass on to the Christ child a sinful soul.

One's view of the transmission of the immaterial in man will have an effect upon his view of abortion. Abortion is much more defensible in creationism than in traducianism, especially if it is held that the soul is not created until late in the pregnancy.

Federal or Seminal View of Adam

One of the most important passages of Scripture in connection with anthropology and hamartiology is Romans 5:12-21. Knowing its cruciality, evangelicals hold tenaciously to either the federal view, sometimes called the representative view, or the seminal view, often referred to as the realistic view. Both seek to explain Paul's emphasis on the "one" and the "many" in the passage.

The federal view, also called the covenant view, accepts the natural headship of Adam, which means all men receive a corrupt

---

46. See W. G. T. Shedd, *Dogmatic Theology* (Grand Rapids: Zondervan [n.d.]), 2:3-94, for a defense of traducianism.

nature and sin is passed on by propagation.[47] But federalists insist Adam was more than the natural head of the race; he was also the divinely appointed federal or representative head. If only the seminal union is involved, federalists argue, why is only the first sin imputed; and why was Adam's sin imputed but not Eve's?

The realistic, or seminal (from seed), view attempts to alleviate the problem of justice a bit.[48] It has the yet unborn race sinning in Adam when he sinned, rather than Adam sinning as their appointed representative. Perhaps its strongest defense comes from the unity of the race and the use of the second aorist in Romans 5:12. Also, it appears to handle two pertinent passages, Hebrews 7:9-10 and Ezekiel 18, better than the federal view does.

The issue dividing the federal view and the seminal view is whether the seminal and natural headship of Adam was actually and literally true or whether it was established by divine decree. The difference is in the kind of natural headship Adam possessed. Was it actual and literal, or did it become actual and real by virtue of God's covenant or decree?[49] Those who argue strongly for the seminal view often do not give sufficient place to the representative emphasis in the Romans 5 passage. By the same token those who stress the federal view sometimes fail to see the seminal sense of Romans 5:12. Both emphases appear to be in the passage. The representative teaching is there, but so is the seminal; neither of these views by itself does full justice to the text.

The Walk of Man Made New

To be in God's image is a blessed privilege and an awesome responsibility. Though every human bears the divine image, yet the child of God, the man made new, is in a special relationship to God through Christ, who is the image of the invisible God and to whose image the new man is to be conformed.

Does it really make any difference how one thinks about man

47. For a defense see John Murray, *Imputation of Adam's Sin* (Grand Rapids: Eerdmans, 1959).

48. For a defense see Shedd, *Dogmatic Theology*, 2:49-94.

49. An excellent contribution to this discussion is S. Lewis Johnson, "Romans 5:12—An Exercise in Exegesis and Theology," in *New Dimensions in New Testament Study*, ed. R. N. Longenecker and M. C. Tenney (Grand Rapids: Zondervan, 1974).

and sin? Indeed it does, and for a number of reasons. The Bible's presentation of man's unacceptable position before God, his guilt and condemnation, exalts the sovereign love and grace of God. It also points to the need for the sinless, substitutionary Savior and the gracious work of the Holy Spirit, drawing, convicting, and enabling the sinner to believe, and bestowing upon him all blessing. When the biblical portrait of man and sin is rejected or even truncated, there is always a corresponding effect upon one's view of God the Father, Son, Spirit, the salvation offered, and other major doctrines of the Christian faith. If any kind of consistency is maintained, it is impossible to err in one such doctrinal area without also erring in others.

Periodically it is good to be reminded of the horrible pit from which we have been rescued by God's marvelous grace. He has lifted us out of the depth of ruin untold. The same grace by which we have been redeemed sustains us day by day. It is terribly easy to forget these things, especially when we are experiencing a measure of success in the Christian life or in life in general.

Man made new still sins. He has been delivered from the otherwise certain results of imputed guilt, transmitted depravity, and his own personal sins by the appropriation of God's salvation in Christ. Nevertheless, as long as he is in the flesh, he will sin. But God's cleansing and forgiveness are his to experience. When they are, the walk of the redeemed goes on, as well as the daily appropriation of the divine provisions.

Questions for Discussion

1. Why do you think theistic evolution is not more acceptable to evolutionists?
2. How important is the human body in serving the Lord?
3. How does the image of God in man relate to the believer's view of a drunkard, murderer, drug addict?
4. What is the relation between imputed and transmitted sin?
5. How does one's view of the transmission of the immaterial part of man relate to his view of abortion?

Suggestions for Further Reading

Berkhof, Louis. *Systematic Theology.* Grand Rapids: Eerdmans, 1968.

Chafer, Lewis Sperry. *Systematic Theology*, 2. Dallas: Dallas Seminary Press, 1950.

Custance, Arthur C. *Genesis and Early Man.* Grand Rapids: Zondervan, 1975.

Davidheiser, Bolton. *Evolution and Christian Faith.* Philadelphia: Presbyterian and Reformed Publishing Company, 1969.

Schaeffer, Francis A. *Genesis in Space and Time.* Downers Grove, Ill.: Inter-Varsity Press, 1972.

_____. *How Should We Then Live?* Old Tappan, N.J.: Fleming H. Revell, 1976.

7

God's Gift of Salvation

Mankind needs God's gift of salvation more than anything else. With God's salvation there is eternal life; without it there is eternal separation from God and all that is holy and good, plus eternal punishment.

Salvation is the most wonderful gift in all the world. To be saved, or born again, is to be translated from the kingdom of darkness into the kingdom of God's dear Son (Col. 1:13). It is to be made acceptable before God. His salvation is complete and without cost to the sinner. The total price has been paid. The work is finished!

The moment the sinner becomes a recipient of God's grace he is delivered from the debt incurred by sin. For him there is no more condemnation (Rom. 8:1). As the believer walks with God and appropriates the finished work of Christ, he is delivered from the binding fetters of sin in his life (Rom. 6:1-13). When we see Christ, we will be delivered from sin completely (1 John 3:1-2). What a wonderful day that will be!

A meaningful discussion of the doctrine of salvation will include a number of other areas of theology. First, there is man's sinfulness which makes the salvation necessary. Man the sinner must be included in a study of soteriology. All three members of the Godhead are vitally involved in the great gift of salvation; each exercises an indispensable role. It is therefore impossible to discuss God's salvation without including aspects of theology proper, the doctrine of God; Christology, the doctrine of Christ; and pneumatology, the doctrine of the Holy Spirit.

Our study will describe the means God has provided whereby sinners can come to salvation. The host of marvelous blessings accompanying salvation will also be reviewed. It is fitting, too, to include the Bible's teaching regarding the walk of the redeemed.

A Historical Perspective

The Ancient Period

The doctrine of salvation did not come in for extensive discussion until the time of Augustine and Pelagius in the fifth century.[1] In the first three hundred years of the church's history attention was on other aspects of theology, such as trinitarianism and Christology. Along with the development of the doctrines of sin and grace came soteriological discussions.

Repentance and faith were stressed by the earliest fathers of the church as necessary for salvation. Their writings reflect this, but without much evidence of what these meant or how they were related to each other. Justification was based on faith, by which was meant confidence in God and commitment to Jesus Christ and his finished work. Faith was set in contrast to the works of the law.

Early in the history of the church there was a drift toward ceremonialism and the belief that water baptism carried with it the forgiveness of sin. Pelagius carried these first beginnings of departure further, stressing the complete freedom of the human will and introducing a clear works salvation. It was his weak view of human depravity and sin which led him to his humanistic view. It is ever the case. A weak view of sin and grace produces a weak view of salvation, and vice versa.

1. See Robert L. Ferm, ed., *Readings in the History of Christian Thought* (New York: Holt, Rinehart and Winston, 1964), pp. 282-99 for writings of Augustine and Pelagius related to soteriology.

Augustine stressed man's total inability to come to God apart from sovereign grace. He insisted that faith marked the beginning of the Christian life and was the basis for good works in the believer. Believing Christ and believing in him were two different things for Augustine. Modifications of the views of Pelagius and Augustine have been labeled Semi-Pelagianism and Semi-Augustinianism.

Berkhof summarizes the influences in the early church that were contrary to the doctrine of grace as the source of all spiritual blessings and of faith as that from which good works proceed: 1) To believe was sometimes confused with merely holding to an orthodox creed. 2) Satisfaction for sins of believers was seen as the result of good works. 3) Many of the fathers distinguished between divine commands and evangelical counsels. 4) Saint worship and increased dependence on the intercession of saints, especially the Virgin Mary, began. 5) Salvation more and more was made to depend on water baptism.[2]

The Middle Ages

The soteriology of the church during the Middle Ages was only mildly Augustinian. The schoolmen, or scholastics, of the period tended toward Semi-Pelagianism. Peter Lombard, Alexander of Hales, Thomas Aquinas, Bonaventura, and others differed on the meaning of grace, faith, justification, and merit. It was this confusion and the development of the doctrine of merit that paved the way for Roman Catholic soteriology and made necessary the Reformation. In the final form of Rome's doctrine of salvation faith did not have a primary place. Instead it was joined with other things such as agreement to what the church taught, understanding of one's sinful condition, determination to obey God's commandments, and a desire for baptism, at which point justification followed.

The Roman Catholic doctrine of penance and all the traffic in indulgences, along with the stress on works for salvation and the elevation of tradition to the level of Scripture, stirred Luther and resulted in the Protestant Reformation.

2. Louis Berkhof, *The History of Christian Doctrines* (Grand Rapids: Baker, 1959), pp. 207-32.

The Reformation

One of the major emphases of the Reformers was salvation by faith alone. This was a call back to the teaching of the Bible. Luther and Calvin did most certainly differ on the *ordo salutis*, the order of salvation, yet they agreed fully on the nature and the importance of justification by faith alone apart from human works. Both believed that only when the righteousness of Christ is accepted by faith is the sinner set free from the law and pardoned by God.

The Arminians developed an order of salvation quite different from both the Lutheran and the Reformed orders. Arminianism holds that God gives to all a universal grace, a sufficient grace, which makes it possible for the sinner to believe. When that preliminary grace is received, more grace is given. If the believer perseveres to the end of his life, he becomes a partaker of eternal life.

Evangelicals ever since the Reformation have been divided over these issues related to soteriology. They have followed either the Lutheran, the Reformed, or the Arminian teaching, or some of each. As with Luther and Calvin, who differed on the order of salvation but agreed on the sinner's helpless state, need of divine grace, and the nature of justification by faith, so it is among evangelicals today.

A Positive Statement of the Doctrine

The Need for Salvation

The Bible is explicit about the condition of all who have not been born again. They are lost (Luke 19:10), condemned (John 3:18), under God's wrath (John 3:36), dead in trespasses and sin (Eph. 2:1), having no hope, and without God in the world (Eph. 2:12), and unrighteous (Rom. 1:19-32).

These passages represent but a sampling of the Bible's teaching regarding God's view of those not in his heavenly family. Man's need of salvation is thus established. It must not be thought that this teaching applies only to pagans and the worst of sinners by human standards. All are under God's wrath and in need of salvation. The religious and the nonreligious, the educated and the uneducated, the rich and the poor—all are in need of God's saving grace and are hopelessly lost without it.

If ever man is to experience salvation, God himself must do the work. True, all are not as wicked as they might be, and not all are altogether wicked, but before God all are in desperate need of his salvation. No one can do anything to merit any favor with God.

Man's need of salvation is occasioned by his sin and God's estimate of him. Since it is God who must be pleased, it does not matter what man thinks of himself or how he proposes to be acceptable to God. What really matters is what God thinks, what he has done to save man, and what he expects, and in fact, demands of man.

As we have seen in chapter 6, all men everywhere stand guilty before God and in need of his gift of salvation for a number of reasons. All sinned in Adam and are therefore participants in the sentence of death pronounced upon him. All have inherited a sin nature, a capacity and propensity to sin, from their parents. Likewise all commit acts of sin both in violating God's laws and in not doing what he has commanded.

Man's sin had a great effect on God. It still does. Surely sin made its mark on Adam and Eve and on the entire human race. Severe penalties were inflicted on our first parents, the serpent, and even the ground because of man's self-centered attitude and action. But what relationship did Adam's sin and our sin in him have to God? This question is seldom given much thought. The answer is not difficult if we remember that all sin is an offense against God. He is the norm, the standard, the criterion of judging right from wrong. Therefore sin is an offense against him, against his holy character.

Simply stated, the question is, How could God remain holy and just and, at the same time, forgive the sinner and allow him into his presence? God's ineffable purity cannot tolerate sin. He is of purer eyes than to behold evil. How then can man ever come before him?

God is the only one who could solve the problem which man's sin presented to him. After man's fall God the Father began in time the plan of salvation which he devised before time began. This divine plan centered in his divine Son: " He gave his only begotten Son " because he "so loved the world" (John 3:16). "Hereby perceive we the love of God, because he laid down his life for us'' (1 John 3:16). ''In this was manifested the love of God toward us, because that God sent his only-begotten Son into the world that we might live through him'' (1 John 4:9).

From the time God clothed Adam and Eve with the skins of the slain animals, the great program of redemption through blood was begun. Genesis 3:15 in particular anticipates the coming of the seed of the woman who was to inflict a fatal wound upon Satan. This seed, or descendant, was none other than Jesus Christ the Messiah. The sacrifices of the Old Testament were types of him who was to come—God clothed in human flesh—to become the substitute for sinners. In the divine solution Christ was the righteous one who alone could satisfy every demand of the offended righteousness of God. In fact, the cross of Christ is presented in Holy Scripture as the declaration of the very righteousness of God (Rom. 3:25).

This is all a part of the divine solution. But there is another factor that to our minds seems hard to reconcile with God's love. The divine plan of salvation formulated in eternity allowed for the entrance and continuance of sin until that day appointed by God when sin and the author of it will be forever banished. We know this because Scripture speaks forthrightly on the matter. In his sermon at Pentecost, Peter, speaking of Christ, said, ''Him, being delivered by the determinate counsel and foreknowledge of God, ye have taken, and by wicked hands have crucified and slain'' (Acts 2:23). Christ was thus delivered to death by the deliberate counsel of God the Father. On another occasion, as Peter and John preached, it was said that those who had gathered to crucify Christ were doing ''whatsoever thy hand and thy counsel determined before to be done'' (Acts 4:28). Peter also said Christ ''verily was foreordained before the foundation of the world'' (1 Peter 1:20).

If the historic death of Christ was a part of the divine solution to the sin question, it follows that the entrance of sin, which made that death necessary, was also known and permitted.

The Salvation Provided by God

Evangelical Christians, in harmony with the historic orthodox Christian faith, worship God who is one in three and three in one, one in essence and three in person. The entire Godhead—Father, Son, and Holy Spirit—is involved in the salvation of the sinner.

The Lord Jesus Christ, the Son of God, died for sinners. He is the Savior! It is customary in evangelical circles to put such emphasis on the second person's part in our salvation that the roles of the Father and the Spirit are often slighted. Our purpose here is to examine the work of each member of the Trinity in man's salvation. Even though it is not always expressed in the same way, evangelicals agree that man's salvation is the product of the Holy Trinity.

The Work of God the Father. Because of his sinful condition man cannot save himself. God the Father made the first move toward man's salvation.[3] Had he not done so, man would be forever lost and without hope.

God the Father's work in salvation centers primarily in what he did before time began. With infinite love and compassion he acted on our behalf even before we were born. Paul told the Ephesian Christians that they had been chosen in Christ by the Father before the foundation of the world (Eph. 1:4). To the Roman Christians the same apostle wrote about the Father's fore-knowledge, predestination, and call of them before time (Rom. 8:29-30). Peter, writing to saints scattered throughout Asia Minor, described them as "elect" of God the Father (1 Peter 1:2). While evangelicals differ on how these and other such passages are to be understood, they all agree that God the Father initiated the plan of salvation in eternity past.

God the Father is sovereign. He must be to be God. Human responsibility is just as biblical as divine sovereignty. Jesus stressed both. Jesus said no one can come to him unless drawn by the Father but he also said none who come to him would be cast out (John 6:37). Truth about God and his sovereign purposes exalts him and produces in the human heart great confidence and assurance. The Father's purposes will be accomplished. Those whom he has called to himself will come to faith in his dear Son. We can count on it: God's purpose will be done on earth as it is in heaven.

God the Father's Plan.[4] The complex miracle of physical birth requires a divine plan and planner. This is even more true of the

---

3. See J. I. Packer, *Evangelism and the Sovereignty of God* (Downers Grove, Ill.: Inter-Varsity Press, 1961).

4. The material in this section has been taken in part from the author's *The God of the Bible* (Grand Rapids: Baker Book House, 1978), pp. 125-34.

miracle of spiritual birth into the family of God. The author of the plan of redemption is none other than the God and Father of our Lord Jesus Christ, the Creator of the universe and of man. He spoke, and by the word of his mouth brought all things into existence and devised a plan of salvation for his disobedient and fallen creatures.

Scripture clearly points to God the Father as the designer of the plan. God declared that those who receive Christ are the recipients of the power of God and, in fact, they are born of God (John 1:12-13). Paul tells us that Christ the Savior is the wisdom of God (1 Cor. 1:30). He also reminds us that it was God the Father who "set forth" Christ to be the satisfaction of our sins. This was the Father's way of remaining just and, at the same time, justifying all who believe in Christ as Savior (Rom. 3:25-26).

We must never view salvation as an afterthought or as the only possible way out of a hopeless dilemma on the part of God. The plan of salvation is as eternal as God is. God was not shocked when Satan and then man fell. He is eternal, and his plan is from eternity past to eternity future. His wisdom is unsearchable and his ways past finding out. The apostle John, under the Spirit's guidance, eliminated every human merit or effort in man's salvation; it was not of blood (human lineage), nor of the will of the flesh, nor of the will or desire of man (John 1:12-13).

The Development of the Plan. The pretemporal plan of redemption which the Father designed in eternity has been realized in time. In his infinite wisdom God solved the problem that man's sin created. Strange as it may seem, the solution in part involved his choice of sinful men on whom he would bestow his grace in salvation. The Father was motivated to redeem man by his own divine love, mercy, and grace. God is gracious. He is the God of all grace. Because he is the God of all grace, and because grace is a part of his essential nature, he is gracious in his dealings with men. We are often led to believe that our salvation began when we made our decision to trust Christ as Savior. The fact is, God was at work on our behalf long before that time. We could not initiate the salvation we enjoy in Christ.

The entire work of salvation is unto "the praise of his glory" (Eph. 1:12, 14). There are questions about many things related to the divine plan of salvation. We do not understand why God has been pleased to do things as he has, and we may never know the answers to many of our queries until we see him face to face. There is one thing we do know, however. We know that God's plan is the best possible plan to bring the most possible glory to his name. His Word tells us he does all things well.

The human mind delights to ponder on the inscrutable mysteries of God. This is not wrong unless such thoughts keep us from carrying out the many responsibilities outlined for us in Scripture. The precious truths of election and salvation, if rightly understood, will not make us proud and unconcerned for the lost. Instead there will be the assurance that God has given us the responsibility to share the good news and that he will honor his Word. Too often God's plan is viewed as a result of arbitrary declaration and decisions. This is not true; God knows the end from the beginning. His plan is the result of his infinite wisdom and love, and is in keeping with his absolute holiness and justice.

The Work of God the Son

Christ and his cross are central to Christianity. Biblical Christianity is based on historic events—the incarnation, life, death, and resurrection of the Lord Jesus Christ. Since aspects of the work of Christ were included in chapter 3, we will discuss here only his work related to redemption.

God the Father's work in salvation is clear from Scripture. The plan of salvation is truly his from start to finish, but this does not mean there was any sort of disagreement between the members of the Godhead. There never has been, is not now, and never will be anything but complete harmony within the Trinity. Each member willingly accepted certain responsibilities, however, in the fulfillment of the divine decree.

"It is finished!" was Christ's cry from the cross. That proclamation from the lips of the dying Savior is fraught with meaning. Surely the Lord was doing more than announcing the termination of his physical life. That fact was self-evident. What was not known by those who were carrying out the brutal business at Calvary was that somehow, in spite of the sin they were committing, God through Christ had completed the final sacrifice for sin. The words "it is finished" would be better translated as "it stands finished." Thus, on the cross the Son was announcing that the eternal plan of God for the salvation of men had been enacted in time.

Four of Christ's major accomplishments in his death are given special consideration here. These reveal the major accomplishments of God the Father through God the Son at Calvary.

Substitution for Sin. The biblical view of the Savior's death is that he died to satisfy the demands of the offended righteousness of God. The Savior died in the sinner's place. This is an essential, indispensable truth in evangelicalism.

It is true that Christ died for the sinner's benefit, but that does not fully describe the nature and purpose of his finished work. He gave his life in the sinner's place. He died as the sinner's substitute. The strongest expression of Christ's substitutionary death is given with the Greek preposition *anti*, translated "for." Christ himself used this word when he said, "even as the Son of man came not to be ministered unto, but to minister, and to give his life a ransom for many" (Matt. 20:28; cf. Matt. 26:28; 1 Tim. 2:6). Christ died in the sinner's place. He died instead of the condemned.

Redemption: The Price Paid.[5] Old and New Testament words for redemption all have essentially the same idea—freedom by the payment of a price.

Three related and progressive ideas are in the New Testament words translated "redeemed," "redemption," "bought." First is the concept of purchase (e.g., 2 Peter 2:1). The purchase price of his blood was paid even for the false prophets and teachers who deny the only possible thing that can save them. The word used here was often used of the purchase of slaves in the slave market.

Second is the idea of security: "Christ hath redeemed us from the curse of the law" (Gal. 3:13). The Greek word translated "redeemed" here is slightly different from the one in 2 Peter 2:1. This word means that what is purchased is removed from the market, never to be on sale again. Paying the price is one thing. Removing the redeemed one from the slave market of sin is another.

Third, freedom is indicated by a word translated "redeemed" (1 Peter 1:18). This Greek word implied that the one purchased in the slave market is ransomed, or released and set free. What a precious truth this is. The believer need no longer be a slave in

---

5. See Leon Morris, *The Apostolic Preaching of the Cross* (Grand Rapids: Eerdmans, 1956), for a full technical treatment of redemption, propitiation, and reconciliation.

bondage to sin and Satan. By accepting the purchased redemption, he is now delivered from sin's fetters and has a new master—Christ.

The means of redemption from sin in Scripture is always through the shed blood of Christ, and is therefore related to his death (Gal. 3:13; Eph. 1:7; Col. 1:14; Heb. 9:12, 15; 1 Peter 1:18-19; Rev. 5:9). His sinless life demonstrated his qualification to be the sin-bearer. One flaw in his character would have disqualified him.

Propitiation: The Father Satisfied. The death of Christ satisfied the righteous demands of God the Father. Because of sin his holiness had been offended, and only a sinless sacrifice could meet his righteous demands. Jesus Christ the Righteous One provided in himself the perfect sacrifice.

Paul set forth Christ as the propitiation for the remission of sins (Rom. 3:25). Because of the blood he shed Christ provided in himself the appointed place where a holy God could meet sinful man. Christ is now our place of meeting—our mercy seat (cf. 1 John 2:2; 4:10).

The need for propitiation stems from the sin of man and the holiness of God. It is man who needs to be reinstated or reconciled with God. God's holiness and righteous demands remain unchanged. Since there must be a basis upon which God may receive sinners, satisfaction must be made for sin: propitiation provided just such a basis through the death of Christ.

Reconciliation—The World Changed. Because of sin in Adam the entire human race is out of balance, at odds with God. Christ reconciled the world to himself, but each individual must appropriate that work before it benefits him (2 Cor. 5:18).

When both the Old and the New Testament words translated "reconcile" or "reconciliation" are taken into account, it is clear that reconciliation is God's work through the death of Christ by which the sinner is brought back to spiritual freedom and harmony with God.

The Old Testament words for reconciliation do not represent a final dealing with sin. Rather, they present sin as being covered temporarily from the sight of God, awaiting final reconciliation through Christ's death. Examples of such usage may be found in: Leviticus 6:30; 8:15; 2 Chronicles 29:24; 1 Samuel 29:4; Ezekiel 45:15.

The New Testament word translated "reconciled" means to change or exchange. Often reconciliation consisted of an arrangement in which both parties contributed to the renewal of relationships (see 1 Cor. 7:11). However, when this doctrine of reconciliation is referred to in connection with salvation, every reference speaks of man as the one reconciled. God is never said to be reconciled in Scripture. His standards and demands of holiness and righteousness remain the same.

Through Christ's work of redemption the price for sin was paid. God the Father accepted this sacrifice. His demands were satisfied. This is propitiation. Therefore, because of redemption and propitiation, the relationship of man to God has been changed. Man has been reconciled. It is now possible for God to bestow salvation upon the believing sinner because of Christ's finished work on the cross. This is what is meant by reconciliation.

There are two principal passages that deal extensively with reconciliation (Rom. 5:6-11; 2 Cor. 5:14-21). A fourfold need of reconciliation may be seen from Romans 5:6-11: 1) man's total inability, "without strength"; 2) man's lack of merit, "ungodly"; 3) man's guilt before God, "sinners"; 4) man at complete enmity toward God and separated from him, "enemies."[6]

In 2 Corinthians 5:14-21 God through Christ has done the reconciling, and it is the world of mankind that is being reconciled. The message of reconciliation is stated clearly in verse 19. The desired result of God's work of reconciliation is that those who accept it serve as ambassadors.

The Work of God the Holy Spirit

Apart from God the Father there would have been no plan of salvation. Without God the Son there would have been no provision for salvation. Apart from the work of God the Spirit there would be no application of this great salvation to man's needs. It is the third member of the Godhead who procures salvation for all who believe. He draws the sinner to himself, enables him to believe, and then applies the finished work of Christ to him. Too often the work of the Holy Spirit is neglected both in beginning the Christian life and in living it.

General Work. Theologians refer to this ministry of the Spirit as the undeserved favor of God which he displays toward all men by

6. John F. Walvoord, *Jesus Christ Our Lord* (Chicago: Moody Press, 1969), p. 183.

his general care for them. They speak of this work as common grace. It does not refer to any abilities or capabilities within man. Neither does it mean that the unsaved man can, because of it, make some contribution to his salvation.

Three things account for the Spirit's work in common grace. First, the fact that God is the supreme ruler and preserver of life would seem to make necessary and, in a measure, explain God the Holy Spirit's work upon all men. From the testimony of Scripture dealing with the Spirit's work in the Old Testament, it would seem that he has had a similar ministry to all men in every age.

Second, the fact that all men are sinners, totally depraved—without any merit before God and without any ability to please God—makes the Spirit's ministry essential. Scripture states clearly that the unsaved man cannot receive the things of the Spirit of God (1 Cor. 2:14). In fact, to the unregenerate the gospel is foolishness (1 Cor. 1:18). No amount of education and training will equip the unsaved to respond to Christ. That is the work of the Holy Spirit alone.

Third, the power of Satan demands that there be a divine restraining force against sin. Otherwise it would be impossible for the child of God to live in this world. It is hard enough as it is, but without the Spirit's work of restraint, holding back the powers of Satan, it would be impossible.

Charles C. Ryrie has well expressed the evangelical view that the general work of the Holy Spirit is displayed in three great works.[7] These three spheres of activity describe the nature of the Holy Spirit's work upon all men. First, providentially, God gives many evidences of his compassion to all men in the natural blessings such as sunshine and rain. Since creation and the fall these blessings have been graciously bestowed upon the saved and the unsaved (e.g., Ps. 145:9; Matt. 5:45; Luke 6:35; Acts 14:17).

Common grace is also displayed in the Spirit's restraint of sin. Again, this work of the Spirit was operative in the Old Testament as well as the New. In Genesis 6:3 "strive" refers to restraint. The Book of Job also illustrates the hand of God in keeping Satan from doing all he would have liked to do to God's servant (see also Isa.

---

7. Charles C. Ryrie, *The Holy Spirit* (Chicago: Moody Press, 1965), pp. 55-60.

63:10-11). The Holy Spirit continues his restraining ministry in the New Testament. Paul's words in 2 Thessalonians 2:6-7 serve as a basic text on the subject. The words *restraineth* and *hindereth* refer to the Spirit's work of keeping sin and Satan from full manifestation. Several interpretations have been given as to that which holds back sin in the passage. It would seem that the issue would have to be resolved by asking, Who is more powerful than Satan and sin? There can be only one answer. The restrainer must be a member of the Godhead. And since the Spirit of God restrained sin in the Old Testament times and since he is in the immediate context, it seems proper to identify him as the restrainer in these verses.

The third sphere of common grace is the Spirit's conviction of sin. According to John 16:7-11 Christ promised that after his departure he would send the Holy Spirit, who would convict the world of sin, of righteousness, and of judgment. This means the Holy Spirit would give demonstrable proof of the truth of the gospel message. The explanation of each of these areas is also given. Men are in a state of sin (note the singular "sin" in John 16:9) because they do not believe in Christ. The Spirit proves that Christ is righteous because he rose from the dead and returned to the Father. Judgment also is involved in the Spirit's work. He proves that judgment is sure to come because it has come in the past through the judgment of Satan at the cross.

In this way the Holy Spirit enlightens the mind of the unsaved, which is blinded by Satan (2 Cor. 4:4). Not all who are thus enlightened respond in faith, however. This work by itself is not sufficient for salvation, but it does provide the sinner with proof of the truthfulness of the gospel message. If and when that message is received, the Spirit's work of giving life becomes operative.

Clearly Scripture teaches that the Word is necessary in reaching the lost (e.g., Rom. 1:16; 10:14). The Holy Spirit of God uses the Word of God, given out by the children of God, to produce other children of God, who in turn are challenged to live for God so the Holy Spirit can continue his work.

Specific Work. The general ministries of the Holy Spirit discussed above fall short of actual salvation. They are not intended to save the unregenerate, but they do leave humanity without excuse before God. The Spirit's work described below involves salvation and the accompanying benefits.

Salvation becomes a reality when at the moment of faith the Holy Spirit imparts life to the believing sinner. When the Holy Spirit moves in this way upon the individual, his ministry is always one hundred percent effective (note in Rom. 8:28-30 that those called are glorified). This work of the Spirit in moving sinners to trust in Christ the sin-bearer has been called irresistible grace, efficacious grace, or effectual grace. All the works of the Holy Spirit described above come before this saving work. They involve a process continuing over a period of time. However, that work of the Spirit which results in the individual's acceptance of Christ as Savior is not a process. Rather, it is an instantaneous act simultaneous with faith. Scriptural support for this effective work of the Spirit is found in those passages which speak of the call that leads to salvation (e.g., Rom. 1:1; 8:28; 1 Tim. 6:12; 2 Peter 1:3, 10).

The work of the Spirit that accomplishes salvation produces regeneration. Though the word regeneration appears only twice in Scripture (Matt. 19:28; Titus 3:5), the concept of being born again occurs often. Regeneration means just that—to be born again. It has to do with the impartation of life from God.

The means by which regeneration is accomplished eliminates all human endeavor. Though personal faith in Christ as Savior is necessary, faith does not produce the new life; it does not regenerate. Only God regenerates. Human faith and divine regeneration occur at the same time, but the one is man's responsibility as he is enabled by the Holy Spirit, and the other is the work of God imparting the divine life.

The work of regeneration is ascribed to each member of the Godhead (e.g., John 5:21; Titus 3:5; James 1:17-18). It is not based on experience, though the life of one who has been regenerated will surely be different. The results of this instantaneous sovereign work of the Spirit include a new nature (2 Cor. 5:17), new righteousness (Rom. 6:18), new life (e.g., 1 John 3:9, 4:7, 5:1), and eternal life (Phil. 1:6).

The Means of Salvation

Proper directions are always of great importance, and this is especially true of the way of salvation. Can you imagine anything worse than to give wrong directions to the driver of the fire engine or ambulance? There is something worse—far worse. That would be to give a sinner wrong directions to heaven. There is no question of greater importance than the one voiced by the Philippian jailer so long ago: "Sirs, what must I do to be saved?" (Acts 16:30).

Our concern here is with the actual fulfillment of God the Father's eternal plan and God the Son's accomplishments in the salvation of the sinner. The great work of God must be appropriated by faith before it benefits the individual. The divine accomplishments are finished. It now remains for the person to respond in faith to the Holy Spirit's work in mind, emotion, and will. Before the full revelation of Scripture was given, faith was placed in the person and promises of God that had been made known to that time (Rom. 4:3). Since God has made known clearly to man the meaning of the death of his Son, faith is now placed in his person and work. Salvation in any age, then, is a work of God on behalf of the believing sinner altogether apart from human works of any kind.

Just what is the gospel, the good news of salvation? What must a man believe to be saved? The Bible knows of only one condition whereby a sinner becomes a saint, and that is through personal faith in Jesus Christ alone as his Savior.[8] There are over one hundred verses in the Bible that make faith in Christ or its equivalent the sole condition of justification. True, man must know he is a sinner and deplore his condition before God (Rom. 3:23). He must know that the wages of sin is death (Rom. 6:23), and that Christ the Savior died for him and for his sins (Rom. 5:8; 1 Cor. 15:3). He must believe these truths, the essentials of the gospel, in order to trust the Christ to whom they refer. But knowing them does not bring salvation. It is personal faith in Christ the sin-bearer and turning from all idols that bring one into the family of God (Acts 16:31; John 1:12).

While repentant faith is necessary for salvation, yet it is not man's faith that justifies him. Faith is not the cause of salvation. It is the channel through which salvation comes to the sinner. Never in Scripture are people said to be saved *on account of* their faith. It is

---

8. See the author's *Heaven for Those Who Can't Believe* (Schaumburg, Ill.: Regular Baptist Press, 1977), for a study of the question: What about those who die before they are able to decide for or against Christ?

always *through* faith that salvation comes. It is not a person's faith that saves; Christ and Christ alone provides the just basis, and the Holy Spirit alone regenerates. The gospel guides sinners away from idols to the Christ who can save.

He who would be faithful to the Word and present the gospel accurately must be extremely careful in this regard. Often the soul-winner presents the gospel as though some special kind or amount of faith is required for salvation. Satan often comes to the newborn child of God and brings doubts as to whether he has had enough faith or has believed in the right way. As far as the Scripture is concerned, God simply requires removal of trust in self and redirection of trust to Christ. It is true that a person must be sincere when trusting Christ, but it must always be remembered that Christ saves, not one's faith. Man's reception of God's great gift of salvation adds nothing to the completed work of Christ. So it is not Christ's substitutionary atonement plus faith in Christ that provides the basis for acceptance with God. Christ's work alone saves; but unless his person and work are received by faith, no benefit comes to the individual sinner.

Man's faith must have a proper object if justification is to result. God did not demand simply belief in the ultimate triumph of good, or faith in the evangelical church, or even faith in his own existence and power. It is always faith in God's Son as the divine substitute for sin's penalty that results in God bringing life to the spiritually dead sinner.

Justice required Christ's death on the cross. According to Scripture there is an offense, a stigma, attached to the cross. The work of Calvary means that God has done everything and man makes no contribution whatsoever to the finished work of Christ or to his own salvation. Paul indicated that the offense of the cross was the absence of human work from God's way of salvation (Gal. 5:11). Man desires to make some contribution, however small, but he cannot; it is finished. Faith in Christ is not a work, and is never considered as such in Scripture.[9] A gift does not cease to be a gift just because the one to whom it is given receives it. Salvation is a gift—God's gift—and it remains a gift even after it is received by faith.

---

9. For further treatment of this point see J. Gresham Machen, *What Is Faith?* (Grand Rapids: Eerdmans, 1925).

The person who is truly born again will want to serve Christ. Life cannot be hidden very long. Life issues in growth, and growth evidences itself in service. Paul's exhortation to Titus is applicable to all believers: Every child of God must be careful to maintain good works (Titus 3:8). This is not so that men might *be* declared righteous, but rather because they *are* justified.

It makes no difference which period of time or what condition one refers to; the salvation of a sinner has always been, and will always be, by God's grace through faith. The basis upon which God forgives sin has always been the substitutionary death of Christ. Men have not always known what we know about the person and work of Christ, simply because all that has been revealed in the New Testament was not made known to the men of God who wrote the Old Testament. Therefore, while God has always required personal faith as the condition of salvation, the content of that faith has not always been explicit.[10] Those who lived before Calvary knew very little of the atoning blood of Christ. Many of the sacrifices and offerings were types of the Savior and the final and complete work he would do, but it is doubtful that the Old Testament Pharisaic types understood all of that. Certainly the believing remnant did not trust in the blood of bulls and goats. Yet God accounted their faith to them for righteousness. He accepted the work of his Son as already finished. The resurrection of Christ is proof of this acceptance.

Blessings Bestowed by Salvation

Many wonderful things take place the moment the sinner trusts Christ alone as Savior. The blessings are bountiful which come to the believer through the new birth. These riches of grace in Christ Jesus are not derived from experience, though they are of course related to and affect one's experience. Nor are the blessings progressive; that is, they do not become more true the longer a person has been saved or the more he matures in Christ.

These blessings are eternal in character. Also, they are unrelated to any human merit whatsoever. They are divine undertakings, and through divine revelation alone we know about them.

10. See Charles C. Ryrie, *Dispensationalism Today* (Chicago: Moody Press, 1965), pp. 110-31.

A few of the major blessings bestowed upon the believing sinner at the time of salvation are described below.[11]

Membership in the Family of God. Several Scripture passages bear on the fatherhood of God. Each contradicts the false idea that God is the Father of all men morally and spiritually and that all men are brothers in the redeemed family of God. Only in the sense of creation is God the Father of all.

Upon receiving Christ as Savior, believing sinners become children of God (2 Cor. 6:18; Gal. 3:26). The only way to become a member of God's family is by being born into it (John 1:12; 3:7; 1 Peter 1:23). Sinners are dead and must be made alive (Eph. 2:1). When they are, they become, by God's grace, "a new creation" (2 Cor. 5:17). This involves the receiving of life, or regeneration (Titus 3:5).

The Bible also speaks of the believer's adoption into the family of God (Rom. 8:15; Gal. 4:5). Adoption in the biblical usage means to be placed as an adult son in God's family, with all the rights, privileges, and responsibilities of sonship. Thus, the believer's citizenship is in heaven (Eph. 2:19; Phil. 3:20). We are fellow citizens with other saints in the house of God (Eph. 3:15).

Justification. To be justified means to be declared righteous. Because of our position in Christ (Eph. 2:13), whereby Christ's righteousness is imputed to us (Rom. 5:17; 2 Cor. 5:21), God declares us righteous because we are clothed with his righteousness (Rom. 5:1). This is of course the work of grace (Rom. 3:24). God's call precedes justification, and man's glorification follows it (Rom. 8:28-30). Justification is more than simply God viewing the sinner as though he had never sinned. Instead, it is God looking upon the sinner to whom the righteousness of Christ earned at the cross has been added.

Forgiveness of Sins. When the sinner trusts the Savior, his sins are forgiven. The penalty incurred by sin is erased, but not because God has become lenient. God's forgiveness is not based on his feeling sorry for the sinner but on the shed blood of Christ. It is because Christ paid the full price that God can forgive us all our trespasses (Eph. 1:7; 4:32; Col. 1:14; 2:13; 3:13). When we trust Christ as Savior, our sins no longer condemn us because Christ

---

11. Lewis Sperry Chafer, *Systematic Theology* (Dallas: Dallas Seminary Press, 1964), 3:234-66, lists 33 riches of grace for those in Christ.

bore the penalty for us. As the believer lives his life and commits sin, additional confession and forgiveness are needed. This, however, relates to his fellowship with God, his walk with God, not to his relationship with the Father as his child (1 John 1:9).

All the sins of the believing sinner—past, present, and future—are covered by the atoning blood of Christ. Never again will they condemn him. This is all a part of God's forgiveness of sins. Justification has to do with being declared righteous. Forgiveness, to the one who comes to Christ for salvation, relates to the erasing of deserved penalty and judgment. It may be said, therefore, that the believer is a sinner minus the condemnation for his sin, plus the righteousness of God in which he is robed.

Partakers of the Holy and Royal Priesthood. Under the law the priesthood was restricted to one tribe and family. The nation of Israel had a priesthood. By contrast each member of the body of Christ is a priest, and together they are called a kingdom of priests (Rev. 1:6). This priesthood is said to be holy and royal (1 Peter 2:5, 9).

The work of a priest involves sacrifice. Since Christ's sacrifice ended the need for all sacrifice for sin, what sacrifice then is the believer priest to bring? According to Scripture the believer's body is to be presented as a living sacrifice (Rom. 12:1). This involves the presentation of self to God. Likewise the praise of our lips and the doing of good works are constituted sacrifices which are well pleasing to God (Heb. 13:15-16). Every believer is a priest unto God with assurance of a future reign with Christ (Rev. 5:10; 2 Tim. 2:12). Therefore, he needs no other mediator. The believer priest can go directly to the throne of grace and the Word of God.

The Walk of the Redeemed

To be sanctified means to be set apart by God. There are three aspects of the believer's sanctification. First, as far as his position before God is concerned, each believer is set apart at the time of salvation (1 Cor. 1:30; 6:11). Second, it is the will of God that each Christian be continuously setting himself apart to holy living (John 17:17; 2 Cor. 7:1). Third, there will be a final and complete setting apart of each child of God when Christ comes again (1 Thess. 3:12-13).

Only the first aspect of positional sanctification takes place at the time of salvation. Sanctification, therefore, becomes one of the great undertakings that accompany salvation. It is not the same as regeneration, though it is a work that occurs simultaneously with it. Sanctification is initial, progressive, and ultimate in the life of the believer. Regeneration, rather, is a single and final work of God the Holy Spirit, whereby he imparts divine life to the believing sinner.

Justification and sanctification are closely related, though not identical. They are, in fact, inseparable. To be justified is to be declared righteous before God, and to be sanctified is to be set apart; the one presupposes the other. Justification has to do with the believer's righteous standing before God. Sanctification has to do primarily with the believer's holiness in life, his walk before men.

The believer, whether he likes it or not, is engaged in a spiritual warfare. The position we have in Christ does not excuse us from fighting the good fight of faith. Our position before God does provide us with equipment with which we can wage the warfare. To be successful each believer must know his real enemy. To be forewarned is to be forearmed. Lack of understanding in this matter leaves the Christian an open target for the enemy. Satan seeks to get the believer's mind off the real enemy and onto secondary issues and would-be enemies.

The source of victory must be known if the believer is to be successful for Christ. It is vitally important that the one who has trusted in Christ for salvation trust him and his provisions for triumphant living as well. Paul has summarized the war that goes on inside the believer in these words: "For that which I do I allow not: for what I would, that do I not; but what I hate, that do I" (Rom. 7:15).

Why does the Christian still experience conflict between good and evil? Why was it that what the great apostle wanted to do he did not do, and what he did not want to do he often did? It is because the one who has trusted Christ as Savior and has passed from death unto life still possesses the same capacity to sin with which he was born. The tendency to sin is still there. This yen to be at odds with God has been called the sin nature.

Before the Christian can attain victory in the Christian life, he must bring himself to acknowledge with Paul: "I know that in me (that is, in my flesh) dwelleth no good thing" (Rom. 7:18). He must also come to grips with the great truth of who he is and what he has in Christ. The saved person is not in the same position of hopeless failure as the unsaved person is. Here is where the riches of grace that accompany salvation come into the picture.

Torn inside with desires to do that which we know is evil and new desires to please God, we experience the rage of the battle. The internal conflict manifests itself in everyday life as the believer is tempted to sin. The source of this conflict is the old sin nature, which is the root cause of the deeds of sin. In the conflict the believer is not passive. He has a vital role in determining to whom he will give allegiance—the old nature or the new nature. From the moment a sinner trusts Christ, there is a conflict in his very being between the powers of darkness and those of light. The one who has just become a member of the family of God now faces conflicts and problems that he did not have before.

The world is the Christian's enemy because it represents an anti-God system, a philosophy that is diametrically opposed to the will and plan of God. It is a system headed by the devil and therefore at odds with God (2 Cor. 4:4). Likewise, the world hates the believer who lives for Christ (John 17:14). The Lord never kept this a secret from his own. He told them often of the coming conflict with the world (e.g., John 15:18-20; 16:1-3, 32-33; cf. 2 Tim. 3:1-12). It is in this wicked world we must rear our families and earn our livelihoods. We are in it, yet are not to be a part of it.

Satan never appears before the Christian as he really is. He is a deceiver appearing as an angel of light. Using clever devices, he tries every possible strategy to trick the child of God. He hinders the work of God (1 Thess. 2:18) and seeks to frustrate the work of God in the believer's life. He is the epitomy of wickedness. His purposes are always malicious. He is a vicious dragon who is diametrically opposed to everything good and righteous. The believer's downfall is his highest concern, and his efforts are always corrupt and evil. Peter, who fell victim to Satan's temptations, said he prowls as a roaring lion, seeking those he may gobble up (1 Peter 5:8). Paul said Satan's wiles could be resisted by the believer as he puts on the whole armor of God (Eph. 6:11). Paul also reminded the Ephesians that their most serious warfare was "against principalities, against powers, against the rulers of the darkness of this world" (Eph. 6:12).

But Satan is defeated. Even before his death Christ spoke with certainty of Satan's overthrow (John 12:31). The sentence of judgment was issued upon him at Calvary. The execution of that sentence will take place when the enemy of our souls is cast into the lake of fire forever. Until then, he and all the demons of hell are arrayed against the people of God.

Through the lust of the flesh Satan seeks to get us to misuse our God-given physical appetites. Depending upon our weakness, he tempts us to impurity of life, overindulgence in food and drink, or improper expenditure of time and money. Living in a land of plenty and in an age given to sin, the believer must constantly guard against sin in these areas.

A multitude of sinful activities, or things that can become sinful, are visible in the world around us. Through the lust of the eyes impure thoughts are entertained (Matt. 5:28). This is true not only of teen-agers; the sex-mad world in which we live makes everyone susceptible to temptation and sin. The lust of the eyes involves more than sex, however. The craving for more and more material things is also common in our affluent society. It is still sin to covet, to place undue emphasis upon things that will pass away. The philosophy of the world—"eat, drink, and be merry, for tomorrow we die"—has become so glamorized that many Christians have unwittingly adopted it.

Perhaps the believer is more susceptible to the "pride of life" than to the other areas of Satan's attacks. Even Christians who are busy serving the Lord often fall prey to this trick of Satan. This is the "I love myself" attitude—thinking more highly of oneself than one should. In short, it is pride, a thing God hates. Often this attitude is concealed under a cloak of hypocrisy. More often it becomes evident to others in words and actions.

Victory over these enemies is made possible through the work of the members of the Godhead within us. By being in love with God the Father, victory can be won over the world (1 John 2:15). Love for the world is evidence of a lack of love for the Father. Living in light of identification with God the Son and all his redemptive work brings victory over the flesh (Rom. 6:1-11; Col. 3:1-3). Finally, victory over the devil and all his evil angels comes through being controlled by, and fighting in the power of, the Holy Spirit (Eph. 5:18).

Major Areas of Difference Among Evangelicals

In the areas discussed above there is general agreement among evangelicals. Shades of difference do exist over points of emphasis, relationships, and in some instances definitions, yet there is a uniformity of belief on the essentials. It is agreed that man is in need of salvation because of his sin and his relation to Adam. God the Father, Son, and Holy Spirit are each involved in man's salvation. Justification is by God's grace through faith in the Lord Jesus Christ. The Savior's substitution for sin and the need of the redeemed to live a holy life find common agreement as well.

Five areas of difference among evangelicals in areas related to soteriology have been selected for discussion here. These are widespread and well-known disagreements, and they cause much division within the evangelical fold.

What About Unconditional Election?

A great division exists in evangelicalism over the doctrine of election. Unconditional election is the belief that God sovereignly, on the basis of his grace, chose before time individuals on whom he would bestow his saving grace. Those who hold this view are Calvinists. Those who reject the teaching are Arminians. There is, of course, a great deal more to Calvinism and Arminianism than belief or disbelief in this doctrine, but it is a hallmark, a watershed.

Unconditional election has had, and continues to have, many able defenders. John Calvin, John Owen, John Murray, Arthur W. Pink, and a long list of Reformed theologians have defended the doctrine. David Steele and Curtis Thomas have presented the view clearly and concisely, marshalling a large number of Scripture passages which they believe support unconditional election.[12] The emphasis in the defense is on the pretemporal, particular, unconditional aspects of election. First, general statements of Scripture are referred to (e.g., Deut. 10:14-15; Ps. 65:4; Matt. 11:27; Rom. 8:28-30; 1 Peter 1:1-2). The authors then move to more specific scriptural teaching regarding the doctrine.

Those who are not happy with either the Calvinist or the Arminian view have presented alternatives. One view has it that election is corporate rather than individual. Only as individuals identify with the elect body do they become elect: ''The certainty of election and perseverance is with respect to the corporate body, the *ekklesia*, rather than with respect to particular men

---

12. David M. Steele and Curtis C. Thomas, *The Five Points of Calvinism* (Philadelphia: Presbyterian and Reformed Publishing Company, 1963), pp. 30-38.

unconditionally. The election is corporate and comprehends individuals only in identification and association with the elect body."[13]

Another variation of the doctrine stresses that God's choice has been particular but not unconditional. Jack W. Cottrell writes that the biblical doctrine of election

> is the idea that God predestines to salvation those individuals who meet the gracious conditions which he has set forth. In other words, election to salvation is conditional and particular. . . . How is it possible that God could determine even before the creation which individuals will be saved, and could even write their names in the book of life? The answer is found in the fact and nature of God's foreknowledge.[14]

For Whom Did Christ Die?

Evangelical theologians and students of Scripture have heatedly debated the question of for whom Christ died. Two basic positions have been taken. Some argue vigorously that Christ died only for the elect, for those who believe and are saved.[15] Others insist, with just as much enthusiasm, that in his death Christ was a substitute for every member of Adam's lost race. I am firmly convinced of this latter position.[16]

Those who hold that the Savior died only for those who believe appeal to certain passages that speak of his death for select groups. For example, the prophet wrote of Christ as the one who was wounded for *our* transgressions and bruised for *our* iniquities (Isa. 53:5). Matthew wrote in a similar way (Matt. 1:21; 20:28; 26:28). John records Jesus' own words: "I lay down my life for the *sheep*" (John 10:15). Paul told the Ephesians Christ died for the *church* (Eph. 5:25). It is true that in such passages Christ's death is said to be for select groups. But it must also be admitted that in

---

13. Robert Shank, *Elect in the Son* (Springfield, Mo.: Westcott Publishing, 1970), p. 54.

14. Jack W. Cottrell, *Grace Unlimited* (Minneapolis: Bethany Fellowship, 1975), pp. 57-58.

15. See, e.g., John Owens, *The Death of Death* (London: The Banner of Truth Trust, 1959); and A. A. Hodge, *The Atonement* (Grand Rapids: Eerdmans, 1953), for defense of a limited atonement.

16. See Norman F. Douty, *The Death of Christ* (Swengel, Pa.: Reiner Publisher, 1972); and Robert P. Lightner, *The Death Christ Died* (Des Plaines, Ill.: Regular Baptist Press, 1967) for defense of an unlimited atonement.

none of these passages—or anywhere else in Scripture, for that matter—is the death of Christ restricted to the elect or to those who believe. In fact there are many passages that speak of Christ's death for the entire world of men.

It is to these passages that appeals are made by those who believe Christ died as a substitute for every member of Adam's lost race. God is said to love the *world* (John 3:16). The Lamb of God is said to have taken away the sin of the *world* (John 1:29). Christ is the Savior of the *world* (John 4:42). In Christ, God the Father was reconciling the *world* to himself (2 Cor. 5:19). It was the *lost* Christ came to seek and save (Luke 19:10). He died for the *ungodly* (Rom. 5:6). He gave himself a ransom for *all* (1 Tim. 2:6). For *every man* Christ tasted death (Heb. 2:9). The Lord bought even those who deny him (2 Peter 2:1). Christ was a propitiation for the sins of the *whole world* (1 John 2:2).

Those who believe Christ died for all do not see the cross as God's only saving instrumentality. Neither do they believe his choice of some on whom to bestow his saving grace and the Holy Spirit's convicting, drawing, and regenerating works are God's only saving instrumentalities. Rather, they see all of these as aspects of God's work of salvation.

Did Christ die for all? Will all be redeemed? Many have already died who never accepted God's gift of salvation, and many more will do the same. Unless the finished work of Christ is appropriated by faith, those for whom it was provided are without God and therefore without hope. It is on the basis of this rejection in addition to their sinful state that the lost stand condemned before God (John 3:18).

Did Christ die to save all? If he did, he is defeated. His finished work of substitution for sin must be appropriated by faith. This faith is the result of the Spirit's work in the human heart. By faith Christ and his gracious provision must be received. When this is done, his work is applied by the Holy Spirit to the individual sinner.

Can Salvation Be Lost?

Ever since the framing of the five points of Calvinism, and even before, evangelicalism has been divided over the question of whether salvation can be lost. Those who hammered out those five points at the Synod of Dort in 1618-19 referred to this doctrine as the perseverance of the saints. There it was affirmed that the elect are those set apart by the Spirit who will persevere to the end. They are the ones who are secure and safe in the Savior.

The doctrine of the security or perseverance of the saints can, I believe, easily be defended on both theological and scriptural ground.[17] The arguments go something like this: 1) There is security because of God's promises (Rom. 8:31-39). 2) God's presence assumes security (John 10:27-30). 3) Because of God's power the believer is kept (1 Peter 1:3-5).

There are a host of Scripture passages that are clearly on the side of security. But there are some difficult and troublesome passages as well, and it is to these that appeal is made in support of the view that one can lose his salvation. The difficult passages become the norm for those who deny the doctrine, and the clear passages are explained so as to harmonize with them. The process is reversed by those who believe in security.[18]

Two prominent spokesmen who reject the doctrine of the security of the believer as represented in Calvinism are Robert Shank and I. Howard Marshall. Shank argues that for the believer to be secure, he must keep on believing; if he does not, his salvation is lost. He bases his argument on the Greek present tense of "believe" in the New Testament.[19] What is not taken into account in this view is the fact that true believers continue to believe because of God's great work in their hearts (see 2 Tim. 1:12; 2:13). Also, at least twice the aorist tense and not the present is used in salvation passages (Acts 16:31; Rom. 4:3).

Marshall contends there is biblical truth in both the Calvinistic and Arminian positions regarding the question. Both positions in their fullness are in error, he insists. The proper balance, he believes, is to be found in his own presentation. He believes in a conditional security. God's power is not the problem in man's security. God will keep the believer provided the believer perseveres in the faith.[20]

---

17. See Lewis Sperry Chafer, *Salvation* (Wheaton, Ill.: Van Kampen Press, 1917), pp. 96-138.

18. See Robert Glenn Gromacki, *Salvation Is Forever* (Chicago: Moody Press, 1973), for an excellent discussion of the whole question of security and an explanation of the difficult passages.

19. Robert Shank, *Life in the Son* (Springfield, Mo.: Westcott Publishers, 1960).

20. I. Howard Marshall, *Kept by the Power of God* (Minneapolis: Bethany Fellowship, 1975).

Must Christ Be Lord to Be Savior?

The difference among evangelicals over the question of Christ's lordship is becoming more and more pronounced. Some respond with an emphatic "yes" to the question, and some answer, just as emphatically, "no."[21] My own position is on the side of those who answer "no." Both parties insist that salvation is by grace alone through faith alone, and yet they insist on different answers to the question, "What must I do to be saved?"

Those who believe that Christ must be received as Savior from sin and Lord of life do so because they believe that without submission to Christ's lordship, faith is incomplete. Those who do not believe that in order to be saved Christ must be accepted as Lord argue that this makes salvation by works.

John R. Stott advocates the view that for salvation Christ must be accepted as both Lord and Savior. He insists, "It is a misunderstanding of the nature of saving faith which lies at the root of this desire to separate Christ as Savior from Christ as Lord."[22] He presents three basic arguments in defense of his position: 1) Saving faith presupposes repentance. 2) Saving faith includes obedience. 3) Saving faith issues in newness of life.

Everett F. Harrison answered "no" to the question whether Jesus must be Lord to be Savior. He presents five reasons for rejecting the idea:

> (1) This position is unsupported by the examples of gospel preaching in the Book of Acts. (2) The view . . . is contrary to the experience of outstanding Christians in the Apostolic Age. (3) The ground of assurance of salvation is endangered if surrender to Christ's Lordship is a part of that ground. (4) The view . . . rules out the necessity for large portions of the practical teaching of the epistles. (5) To adopt this view involves the introduction of a subtle form of legalism.[23]

When proponents of each side state their view clearly, the problem of semantics becomes apparent. If lordship is added to

---

21. See Charles C. Ryrie, *Balancing the Christian Life* (Chicago: Moody Press, 1969), pp. 169-81.

22. John R. Stott, "Must Christ Be Lord to Be Savior? Yes," *Eternity*, Sept., 1959, p. 16.

23. Everett F. Harrison, "Must Christ Be Lord to Be Savior? No," *Eternity*, Sept., 1959, pp. 15-16.

faith as a separate condition of salvation, it must be rejected as foreign to the New Testament. On the other hand, Scripture clearly states that no one can become a child of God unless he fully intends to serve and obey Christ.

What About Sanctification?

The doctrine of sanctification, on which there is essential agreement among evangelicals, has been presented earlier in this chapter. There is division within the ranks, however, as to the relationship between justification and sanctification and between the actual position of sanctification the believer has before God and the practical outworking of that reality in life.[24]

Some Christians believe that this "sanctification debate" is approached from two entirely different viewpoints: the Reformed interpretation and the Keswick interpretation.[25] Certainly both these schools of thought fall within evangelicalism. The debate, it seems to me, centers somewhat in semantics. The Reformed view seems to confuse the positional aspect of sanctification with the practical, and the Keswick view does not place enough emphasis on the relationship between justification and sanctification.

John Murray summarized the Reformed view when he said, "Justification and sanctification are inseparable and a faith divorced from good works is not the faith that justifies."[26] This view has it that every truly born again person is in fact experiencing progressive sanctification, at least to some extent. The believer's works and growth in grace are a necessary affirmation and assurance that he is a child of God.[27]

The Keswick view gets its name from the annual Bible convention in Keswick, England, where a significant evangelical conference was held in 1875 following the Moody-Sankey revival. In this approach, the relationship between justification and sanctification is not stressed. The former does not guarantee the

24. See Charles C. Ryrie's full discussion of the sanctification debate in Donald K. Campbell (ed), *Walvoord: A Tribute* (Chicago: Moody Press, 1982), pp. 189-201.

25. John L. Benson, "The Sanctification Debate," in *Pastor's Manual* (Denver: Baptist Publications, Fall, 1980).

26. John Murray, "Sanctification," *Christianity Today*, May 11, 1962, p. 30.

27. See Zane C. Hodges, *The Gospel Under Siege* (Dallas: Redencion Viva, 1981), for an opposing viewpoint.

practical outworking of the latter. In this view stress is placed on
the positional aspect of sanctification enjoyed by all believers.
Only a relative few ever really appropriate their position of union
with Christ and therefore experience practical sanctification.

There does seem to be a view that encompasses both the
positional and the progressive sides of the believer's sanctification.[28] The Bible does not divorce these, nor does it stress the one
to the neglect of the other. Neither should we.

Saved to Serve

One of the major purposes of our salvation is so that we might
love and serve God. Indeed, the saved one is God's
"workmanship, created in Christ Jesus unto good works, which
God hath before ordained that we should walk in them" (Eph.
2:10). Jesus said, "By their fruits ye shall know them" (Matt.
7:20).

Whether we believe in so-called lordship salvation or not, as
evangelicals we must all agree that the child of God is to serve
God in the power and strength of the Holy Spirit. The idea that
salvation is simply a free ticket to heaven and the assurance of
missing hell is foreign to the Bible.

Good works in the life of the believer are terribly important, not
to be saved or to stay saved, but as a natural expression of
gratitude to God for his great salvation.

Questions for Discussion

1. What does the fact that the Father, Son, and Holy Spirit each
   has a part in man's salvation say about the Trinity?
2. How would you respond to the unsaved person who brings
   up election and predestination when you try to present the
   gospel to him or her?

28. See Ryrie, *Balancing the Christian Life,* pp. 61-74.

3. As you think through the material in this chapter, what other doctrines are crucial to an understanding of soteriology?
4. Since infants and mentally incompetent people cannot respond in faith to Christ, what do you think about their eternal destiny? Why?
5. Do you think people are really saved who say they trust Christ but show no evidence of it?

Suggestions for Further Reading

Boice, James M. *God the Redeemer*, Foundations of the Christian Faith, Vol. 2. Downers Grove, Ill.: Inter-Varsity Press, 1978.

Gromacki, Robert Glenn. *Salvation Is Forever*. Chicago: Moody Press, 1973.

Horne, Charles M. *Salvation*. Chicago: Moody Press, 1971.

Kantzer, Kenneth S., and Gundry, Stanley N., eds. *Perspectives on Evangelical Theology*. Grand Rapids: Baker Book House, 1979, pp. 81-116.

Murray, John. *Redemption: Accomplished and Applied*. Grand Rapids: Eerdmans, 1955.

8

God's Church

Ecclesiology is primarily a New Testament doctrine. The reference is both to the church and to the churches. The word *church* does appear in the Old Testament, but it has the meaning simply of an assembly of people called together for a specific purpose. Only in the New Testament is the church identified as the body of Christ, a peculiar people especially gifted, with a distinct program. Likewise only in the New Testament are there references to local assemblies called churches. It must be admitted by all evangelicals that something new and unique began on the day of Pentecost.

The church as the body of Christ is predicted by him in the Gospel of Matthew (16:18). The apostle Paul described the church as Christ's body on two different occasions (Eph. 1:22-23; Col. 1:18).

The Savior also gave instruction concerning discipline and forgiveness of members of a local church (Matt. 18:15-17). A number of the New Testament epistles were addressed to local assemblies of believers (e.g., Phil. 1:1; 1 Thess. 1:1; 2 Thess. 1:1). Seven local churches are addressed by John in Revelation 2-3. The local church is called "the house of God, . . . the church of the living God, the pillar and ground of the truth" (1 Tim. 3:15).

A Historical Perspective

In the history of doctrinal development the doctrine of the church came in for discussion rather late. This does not mean the early Christians were uninterested in the church. To the contrary, they were very interested and involved on the personal level.

Doctrinal formulations concerning a given truth grew out of controversy. Only when the scriptural teachings were challenged did the ancients bring forth definitive statements concerning the truth in question. The rise of heresies forced the early Christians to set forth precisely what they did believe in contrast to the opposing views. This is certainly true of the doctrine of the church.

The Ancient Period

Up until around A.D. 600, the centers of doctrinal controversy were the Trinity, Christ, the Holy Spirit, man, and sin. The fathers of the church gave their first attention to these issues because the earliest heresies arose over these doctrines. Two rather obvious emphases related to the church ran through the period. There was the stress on external unity on the one hand and internal purity on the other. The latter was clearly a reaction to the former. Both these emphases have to a certain extent continued to the present time.

It must be kept in mind that the ancient writers wrote primarily devotional literature for the laity and not theological treatises.

Yet the emphasis on the external unity of the church is discernible in the writings of such men as Clement of Rome, Ignatius, and Polycarp. There is evidence in their writings that they believed in both a universal church and local churches. Frequently the burden for the unity of all the local churches can be seen, and the concern was not at all unnatural. After all, Christianity did need to stand united in the face of the increasing number of religious views that were arising. With the attempts to unite Christians there also came the necessity of some sort of centralization of authority and power.

The early development of ecclesiasticism can be traced through three stages: "First was the appearance of the monarchial bishop to whom fellow elders were obedient. . . . Secondly, there was the development of the ecumenical domination. . . . The final step, then, was the development of Roman supremacy. The concept of the universal church, which began to find expression in Ignatius and was definitely advocated by Irenaeus, demanded a centralizing of authority and control."[1]

Three individuals in the ancient period deserve special attention because of their profound impact upon the doctrine of the church, especially as it relates to external unity.

Irenaeus, in *Against Heresies*, reveals a definite shift of emphasis. Instead of the stress being on Christ's relation to the local church, there is emphasis on the need for the organic unity of the visible universal church. Irenaeus also advocated the perpetual succession of bishops from Christ. He said, "We are in a position to reckon up those who were by the Apostles instituted bishops in the churches, and (to demonstrate) the succession of these men to our own times."[2] Seed was sown by Irenaeus for the establishment of a system that would recognize one head over the entire church.

Cyprian wrote a famous work on the doctrine of the church entitled *On the Unity of the Church*, which developed the doctrine of the episcopal church. Cyprian believed in the unity of the catholic, or universal, church and in the full authority of the bishop. He taught the priesthood of the clergy based on their sacrificial work. Rebellion against any bishop was viewed as rebellion against God. For Cyprian the bishops made up an organization that represented the entire church. Outside the church there was no salvation. He wrote, "If you abandon the church and join yourself to an adulteress, you are cut off from the promises of the church. If you then leave the church of Christ, you will not come to Christ's rewards, you will be an alien, an outcast, an enemy. You cannot have God as your Father unless you have the church for your mother."[3]

Augustine, in his *City of God*, gave added impetus to the stress on the unity of the visible church, enlarging on Cyprian's concept. The result was a confusion of the scriptural teaching on the church and the churches. As we will see later, this same confusion characterizes the modern ecumenical movement.

1. Earl D. Radmacher, *What the Church Is All About* (Chicago: Moody Press, 1978), p. 50. This work is extremely helpful in its development of the history of the doctrine of the church.
2. Irenaeus, *Against Heresies* 3.3.1-2.
3. Cyprian, *On the Unity of the Church* 6.

The ancient period saw, in addition to the stress on external unity, an accompanying stress on internal purity. In fact, the latter was a direct result of the former. As a result of the emphasis on external unity, there developed a gradual secularization and lessening of spiritual emphasis in the churches. This created the need for a renewal of internal purity.

Emphasis on internal purity was advocated most strongly by those not identified with the orthodox church. These individuals set forth their opposition to the prevailing view that there was no salvation outside the church. They also disagreed sharply with the notion that the true church was the visible Catholic Church, which was composed of both good and evil. Instead, they stressed that the true church was composed only of the redeemed.

Three individuals were of special importance in this regard—Marcion, Montanus, and Donatus. Though the adherents of Marcionism, Montanism, and Donatism held differing points of view, they all agreed that the church needed reform, and all attempted to accomplish that reform.

The Middle Ages

There was little doctrinal development during the Middle Ages, and the doctrine of the church fared no better than other doctrines. The theologians of the time, called schoolmen or scholastics, accepted the doctrine of the church as developed by such men as Irenaeus, Cyprian, and Augustine.

Students of the medieval period are in general agreement that there was virtually no development in ecclesiology. They also agree that in spite of this fact there developed an almost absolute hierarchy within the church. This, of course, made the Reformation necessary.

The Reformation

The Lutheran Contribution. Martin Luther spoke out against the Roman Catholic concept of the church. Contrary to Rome, he believed the church consisted of all true believers in Christ everywhere. He wrote, "This community or assembly consists of all those who live in true faith, hope, and love; so that the essence, life and nature of the church is not a bodily assembly, but an assembly of hearts in one faith.'"[4] It is clear also from the scriptural proof Luther used to support his view (e.g., Luke 17:20-21; John 18:36) that he, like Augustine before him, equated the church and the kingdom.

According to Luther, the term *church* was not to be used to describe the external organization, though he did believe in the local assembly. That there were two churches Luther never questioned, but he chose to call the universal church "a spiritual inner Christendom." The local church he called "a bodily external Christendom.'"[5]

The relation between these two Luther did not develop; whatever may be said of his contribution, two things stand out clearly: 1) he did little to advance the New Testament teaching of the local church; 2) the state did gain control of the church under his tutelage.

The Calvinistic Contribution. John Calvin was much more specific and definite in his views on the church than was Luther. He viewed the church in a threefold sense. First, he saw the invisible church as including all the elect. Second, Calvin said *church* referred to all who profess to know Christ: "Often, however, the name 'church' designates the whole multitude of men spread over the earth who profess to worship one God in Christ. . . . In this church are mingled many hypocrites who have nothing of Christ but the name and outward appearance.'"[6] Third, Calvin did advance the close church-state relationship held by the church he left.

Cyprian's concept of the church is everywhere evident in Calvin's teaching. He simply restated and developed Cyprian's view, even to the point that he did not believe one could have God as his Father who did not have the church as his mother. This great Reformer did not believe the universal church existed beyond the sum total of all the local churches.

The clarion calls of the Reformation were *sola scriptura* and *sola fide*. Everything else was secondary to the Reformers—even the doctrine of the church.

4. Martin Luther, "The Papacy at Rome," *Works of Martin Luther* (Philadelphia: A. J. Holman, 1932), 1:349.

5. Ibid., p. 355.

6. Calvin, *Institutes of the Christian Religion* 4.1.7.

The Anglican Contribution. The Anglican Reformation in England did not have one outstanding leader as the Lutheran and Calvinistic movements did. Through the Act of Supremacy in 1534 the church in England separated from the Roman papacy. It separated organizationally at this time, but not theologically.

The Thirty-nine Articles of Faith became the official creed of the Anglican Church; they remain so today, with little change from the original statements. No specific reference is made to the invisible or universal church in the Articles. Reference is made to "the visible church of Christ," and here is where the emphasis rests. When Anglicans say "invisible church," they refer to those members of the local church who have gone to be with the Lord.

There were both Lutheran and Calvinistic strands in the Anglican Church. There were also persons who felt too many Roman Catholic trappings remained in the church. Those who wanted to purify the church were called Puritans. At first the Puritan movement was not Presbyterian or Congregational in polity. But it was not long until both these forms became apparent and developed into two parties within Puritanism. Both remained within the Anglican Church while stating their strong differences with it.

At the same time there were those who advocated complete separation from the state church. These were known as Separatists, and two doctrines set them apart. In their churches only those who could demonstrate they were born again could be members. Also, each local church was completely independent from any other ecclesiastical control.

The Anabaptist Contribution. Technically the Anabaptist Free Church movement was not really part of the Protestant Reformation. Unlike the Reformers, the leaders of the so-called sects were never a part of the Roman Catholic Church. Their protestations were from without, not from within. Also, unlike the Reformers the Anabaptists were not interested in reforming the existing ecclesiastical system. Rather, they wanted to reconstruct the church according to the New Testament teaching as they understood it.

Reformers such as Luther, Calvin, and Zwingli had great respect for the church which mothered them. It was not their intent at the beginning to leave Rome and thus unchurch themselves. As far as they were concerned, the existing church was indeed the true church. It had fallen upon evil days, to be sure, but it was still the true church.

> The Anabaptists however, set out to discard the territorial church pattern and replace it with the pattern they saw in the New Testament. Their objective was not to introduce something new, but to restore something old. "Restitution" was their slogan—a restitution of the early church. From the Anabaptist point of view, the difference between the Reformers and themselves was the difference between reform and restitution.[7]

A cursory reading of the Reformation literature might give the impression that the difference between the Reformers and the Anabaptists was over water baptism, but this was not the case. Totally divergent views of the church constituted the real difference. The issue of water baptism only served to bring the real difference out into the open.

The term *Anabaptist* was assigned to these people in a derogatory way by the Reformers themselves. The word means "rebaptize." But the ones to whom the name was given rejected it. They insisted that since infant baptism was not true baptism, they were not rebaptizing.

The Anabaptists stressed believer's baptism. They also repudiated the union of the church and state, a view that went hand in hand with infant baptism. For them the church had fallen when Constantine made Christianity the state religion.

The Modern Period

That there is a determined effort on the part of many to build a world church is no secret. The modern ecumenical movement is a reality. W. A. Visser't Hooft, the first general secretary of the World Council of Churches, surveyed the developments in the organization's history:

> The first had been the period of the pioneers. . . . The second period was that of the architects who sought to give a more clearly defined shape to the ecumenical movement. . . . The task was now to insure that the ecumenical movement should really become

7. Radmacher, *What the Church Is All About*, p. 69.

ecumenical, that it should become the ecumenical movement of the churches, and that it should develop adequate structures. . . . The story of the years since 1948 is essentially the story of the process through which the ecumenical movement became universalized. It is a story of ecumenical mobilization of practically all Christian churches.[8]

According to Visser't Hooft, the word *ecumenical* refers to "that quality or attitude which expresses the consciousness of and desire for Christian unity." Early in its usage the word meant "pertaining to the whole earth." Later it came to mean "pertaining to the whole church." Today the term is used to describe the desire for the union of all Christian groups into one conglomerate called the church.

The drive for church union is without much regard for doctrinal agreement and did not begin in the church pew (no major heresy, in fact, ever began there). Instead, it began in academic centers, then found its way to the pulpit, and finally to the pew and then out into the world.

Church unionism has made its mark in every major denomination. Great strides have already been made toward bringing together under one ecclesiastical umbrella all denominations without significant regard for doctrinal beliefs.

The Theological Background. The modern ecumenical movement can be traced to the rise of theological liberalism. This liberalism grew out of the man-centered philosophies of the Renaissance and the period that followed.

A profound interest in the world, along with faith in reason and man's own capabilities, characterized the Renaissance period. Widespread skepticism regarding the Bible and biblical Christianity prevailed. The attacks on Christianity became stronger and more direct as time passed. The philosophies of the period had a direct influence on the theologians of the day, many of whom in turn became the fathers of theological liberalism.

The liberal establishment which spearheads the mad drive for a monstrous world church is no more orthodox now than it has ever been. Through a deceitful game of semantic delusions, it is seeking

---

8. W. A. Visser't Hooft, *The Ecumenical Advance: A History of the Ecumenical Movement 1948-1968*, Vol. 2, ed. Harold E. Fey, pp.3-4.

to sell the public a thoroughly heterodox bill of goods, and what is sadly true is that multitudes of laymen are being persuaded to buy the product. Most of them are not aware of the fact that their purchase will ultimately involve the surrender of whatever remains of their church's liberties and will align them whether they like it or not with those men and movements which are diametrically opposed to the faith once delivered unto the saints—the faith of our fathers.

The basic problem of the rejection of the inspiration and authority of the Bible which plagued the founders of liberal theology and was embraced by the attempt of church union from the very beginning still characterizes the present ecumenical leadership. The doctrine that the Bible is the inspired and inerrant Word of God is rejected by them.[9]

The Historical Context. Without doubt the rise and spread of theological liberalism paved the way for the church union movement. From the very beginning the enthusiasts for church union rejected the cardinal doctrines of the Christian faith. Among these are the total inspiration of the Scriptures and the full deity of Christ the Savior.

Those who pioneered the church union movement did so through various organizations, which are described below. Except for the first, these were all started and promoted by theological liberals.

1 The World Evangelical Alliance. This organization was founded by evangelicals in 1845. From the very beginning the WEA placed great stress on the Bible as the Word of God and Christ as the Son of God. Some of the members of the WEA were influenced by the higher critical view of the Scriptures. These were in the minority, however, and they withdrew in 1894 after they saw they could not win the movement to their liberal persuasions.

2 The Federal Council of Churches of Christ in America. Those who withdrew from the WEA organized the Open Church League, which later became the National Federation of Churches and Christian Workers. In 1905 this organization

9. Robert P. Lightner, *Church Union* (Des Plaines, Ill.: Regular Baptist Press, 1971), pp. 26-27.

became the Federal Council of Churches of Christ in America. The FCC had a very minimal doctrinal basis. The preamble stated it recognized Jesus Christ as "divine Lord and Savior." This brief statement was open to varied interpretations by the constituent bodies.

3 The World Council of Churches. The WCC had its beginning in several earlier organizations—the Conference on Faith and Order, the Conference on Life and Work, and the International Missionary Council. Theological liberals staffed each of these. Attempts were made in 1938 to form the WCC, but the outbreak of World War II made it necessary to delay the plans. The WCC was formed in 1948 in Amsterdam, Holland. From the start theological liberals have occupied key places of leadership in the WCC. The basis for membership is concurrence with a very brief statement: "The World Council of Churches is a fellowship of churches which accept our Lord Jesus Christ as God and Savior according to the Scriptures and therefore seek to fulfill together their common calling to the glory of the one God, Father, Son, and Holy Spirit."[10] While this statement sounds good as far as it goes, there is no attempt made to determine how the members interpret it. This is apparent in view of the admission of groups like the Hicksite Quakers, who deny the deity of Christ.

4 The National Council of Churches of Christ in the U.S.A. In 1950 the old Federal Council of Churches became the National Council of Churches. Over thirty denominations are members. Its brief doctrinal statement, "Jesus Christ as divine Lord and Savior," is also open to varied interpretations, as is evidenced by the membership. From the very beginning to the present, avowed and well-known deniers of the historic Christian faith have wielded tremendous influence in the NCC. The same efforts carried on by the WCC on a world level are performed by the NCC on a national level.

---

10. See ibid., pp. 34-39, for further documentation.

5 The Consultation on Church Union.[11] On December 4, 1960, Eugene Carson Blake, then the stated clerk of the United Presbyterian Church in the U.S.A., preached in the Grace (Episcopal) Cathedral of San Francisco, and proposed what became the Consultation on Church Union. COCU represents the largest single attempt toward a superchurch. A perusal of the views of the leaders of this gigantic effort reveal quickly that they are not in harmony with the historic Christian faith. The initial proposals of COCU were not well received by the memberships of the consulting bodies. In response the leaders have retreated a bit and are making less bold attempts to accomplish the same goal—a superchurch without regard for the faith once delivered to the saints.

What of the future? What the future holds with respect to the present church union efforts is difficult to predict. It could be that COCU will replace the NCC as the major arm of the ecumenical movement in the United States. One thing is certain: God will one day judge any false world church that might be brought into existence. The liberal church union effort will collapse. Not only that, it will experience the judgment of God (Rev. 17:1-2).

That false teachers would arise who would trouble the church is clearly taught in the New Testament (e.g., Acts 20:28-32; Gal. 1:6; 2 Peter 2:1). Equally clear is the scriptural teaching that the believer is to separate from false teachers and teachings (e.g., 2 Chron. 19:2; Amos 3:3; Eph. 5:11; Gal. 1:8-9; 2 Cor. 6:14-16; 1 Tim. 6:5; 2 Tim. 2:19; 3:5; 2 John 9-10; 2 Thess. 3:6).

A Positive Statement of the Doctrine

The Universal Church

The Meaning of Ekklesia. The word *ekklesia,* translated "church" throughout the New Testament, comes from two Greek words: *ek,* "out," and *kaleo,* "to call." The two words together mean "to call

---

11. As of this writing the participating denominations of COCU are: United Methodist, Episcopal, African Methodist Episcopal Zion, Christian Methodist Episcopal, African Methodist Episcopal, Presbyterian Church (U.S.A.), Christian Church (Disciples of Christ), United Church of Christ, and National Council of Community Churches.

out." It follows therefore that *ekklesia* refers to a called-out assembly or a gathering of people. In the New Testament there are several usages of *ekklesia*.[12]

(1) An assembly of people. Israel in the wilderness was called "the church in the wilderness" (Acts 7:38). Even the heathen mob assembled at Ephesus was called a church (Acts 19:39). Likewise, *ekklesia* was used for a group of people assembled for a religious purpose (Heb. 2:12; cf. Ps. 22:22).

(2) An assembly of Christians in a local church. Frequently the New Testament speaks of the church which was in some particular place: "the church which was at Jerusalem" (Acts 8:1); "the church that was at Antioch" (Acts 13:1); "the church which is at Cenchrea" (Rom. 16:1); "the church of God which is at Corinth" (1 Cor. 1:2). *Ekklesia* is also used in the plural for a group of local churchs (1 Cor. 16:19; Gal. 1:2).

(3) All professing Christians. In this sense *ekklesia* takes on a meaning almost synonymous with Christendom. Paul said to the Romans, "The churches of Christ salute you" (Rom. 16:16). To the Galatians he wrote that he had "persecuted the church of God" (Gal. 1:13). In such instances no particular church is in view, but rather all Christians being persecuted everywhere.

(4) The body of Christ. Paul identified the church as Christ's body when writing to both the Ephesians (1:22-23) and the Colossians (1:18). All members of the church are vitally united with each other and with Christ, the head of the body and the Lord of the church. This union was consummated by the baptism of the Spirit.

The Reality of the Universal Church. There are a number of usages of *ekklesia* that do not seem to refer to a local assembly of believers. Instead, they speak of that company of believers formed on the day of Pentecost into the body of Christ, which has been growing ever since as sinners trust Christ alone as Savior and are added to it. This company of the redeemed is called the church without consideration of whether or not those who are a part of it are members of local churches. However, there are some evangelicals who do not believe there is any so-called universal church that exists outside the local assembly. This difference of opinion will be addressed later.

12. See Radmacher, *What the Church Is All About*, pp. 115-31, for an excellent summary of the usage of *ekklesia* in classical Greek and the Septuagint.

The Means of Entrance. By the baptizing ministry of the Holy Spirit the universal church was formed. At the time of salvation each believing sinner is made a member of the body of Christ (1 Cor. 12:12-13). The Holy Spirit of God is the primary agent who identifies the believer with other believers. Each one is a member of the body, and each member is united with the other members and with Christ (Rom. 6:1-4).

In the Gospels, where the promise of Spirit baptism is first given, Christ is said to be the one who would baptize in the Spirit (Matt. 3:11; Mark 1:8; Luke 3:16). The same is true in the prophecy recorded in Acts 1:5. But in 1 Corinthians 12:12-13 Christ is not named as the one baptizing but the Spirit is. The believer is to be identified with the "body." This body is defined as the church in Ephesians 1:22-23 and Colossians 1:18. On the basis of this, we conclude that both the Holy Spirit and Christ are agents in the work of forming the body of Christ. The Spirit may be viewed as the primary agent and Christ the secondary agent in that he sent the Holy Spirit to begin his new work after his ascension.

Foundation. Four passages of Scripture are of special significance to the teaching of Christ as the foundation of the church.

1. Matthew 16:18-20. In the history of the church several views have been advanced as to the meaning of Christ's words "upon this rock I will build my church."

The view of the Roman Catholic Church is that Peter is the foundation of the church. The view is based on the Aramaic forms of the two English words *Peter* and *rock* in Matthew 16:18. However, there is no trace of Matthew's Gospel in Aramaic. In the Greek New Testament the words are different and have different meanings. It is not too much to say that Rome's interpretation of Matthew 16:18 is indispensible to the whole theological superstructure of the Roman Catholic Church.

Peter's confession of faith is viewed by some as the foundation of the church. This view is closely related to the prominent evangelical belief that Christ is the foundation of the church. Though the views are not identical, they can hardly be separated from each other; together they constitute an evangelical consensus.

Peter in Greek is *Petros*. The word is masculine in gender and means rock. In Christ's statement that he would build his church upon the rock, he used *Petra,* a different word, which is used sixteen times in the New Testament. Eleven of those times it is used of a big boulder-type rock. Five times it is used metaphorically of Christ. *Petros* and *petra* always seem to be used in a different sense, and that certainly appears to be the case in this passage. Very likely as Christ spoke, he pointed first to Peter when he said, "Thou art Peter." Then he pointed to himself as he said, "And upon this rock I will build my church."

Several other considerations regarding Peter's subsequent behavior substantiate this interpretation.[13] Peter never claimed any authority over the other apostles; instead he denied it (see 1 Peter 1:1; 5:1-3; Acts 10:25-26). His actions, especially in relation to Christ, did not conform to his being the one on whom the church was to be built. Just after Christ's promise to build the church, Peter denied that Christ should even die (Matt. 16:22). Furthermore, Peter slept in the garden while Christ prayed, and later denied him openly. If Peter was the foundation of the church, why was he not more active in the choice to replace Judas among the apostles (see Acts 1:15-26)? Why was James the leader of the great Jerusalem council and not Peter (Acts 15)? Finally, in addition to the teaching in Matthew 16:18 that Christ is the foundation of the church, there is supportive teaching in other passages (1 Cor. 3:11; Eph. 2:19-22; 1 Peter 2:4-8).

A word about the keys and the binding and loosing of Matthew 16:19 is in order. To Peter, Jesus said, "And I will give unto thee the keys of the kingdom of heaven, and whatsoever thou shalt bind on earth shall be bound in heaven; and whatsoever thou shalt loose on earth shall be loosed in heaven." To begin, it should be noted that Jesus gave the same word to the other apostles (cf. Matt. 18:18). This was not therefore the exclusive right of Peter. However, he was used in a special way to open the door of opportunity to the Gentiles (Acts 2, 8, 10). The figure of the keys in our Lord's words to Peter had to do with locking or unlocking, opening or closing the gospel to the Gentiles. It was a declarative power given to Peter here, not a saving power. Peter himself made it abundantly clear that he had no saving power (see Acts 2:21; 10:43).

---

13. See Loraine Boettner, *Roman Catholicism* (Philadelphia: Presbyterian and Reformed Publishing Company, 1962), pp. 104-24.

The binding and loosing in Christ's word to Peter relate to delivering the message of the gospel. When he gave the message, the people were able to be released from their sins. If he withheld the message, they would remain bound in their sin.

2. 1 Corinthians 3:11. Here Paul used the metaphor of a building as he wrote of the church. The local church at Corinth was primarily in view, and Paul's early work in starting it. And yet, as he labored among the people, he built upon Christ by proclaiming him and his finished work. It was not his own message he proclaimed, but that which he received from Christ. The foundation Paul laid as a wise master builder (Eph. 2:10) was that of Christ himself and his teaching.

3. Ephesians 2:19-22. In this passage the building metaphor is used differently from the way it is used in 1 Corinthians 3:11. There the emphasis was on the truth of Christ, upon which the church was built. Here the emphasis is on those individuals, Christ himself and the apostles and prophets, who constitute the foundation of the church. Here Jesus Christ himself is said to be "the chief cornerstone." The building referred to is the universal church, which is viewed as a "habitation of God through the Spirit." The fact that there is only one definite article with two nouns points to apostles and prophets constituting one class in their relation to the church. The apostles being placed before the prophets also supports this view.

4. 1 Peter 2:4-8. It is highly significant that Peter considered himself not as the foundation of the church, but as having a role no different from the other apostles in the construction of the church. He made it clear by his quotation from Isaiah 28:16 that Christ alone is the "head of the corner." The specific meaning of the cornerstone is open to some question. However, one thing is very clear from the figure: Christ occupied an absolutely essential place in the church structure.

We may conclude from Christ's own words (Matt. 16:18) that he is the foundation of the church; in complete harmony with this are the other three passages discussed above.

The Local Church

Those who endeavor to base their views on the Scripture turn to the practices and precepts of the local church in the New

Testament. By practice is meant the inspired record of what the church in the New Testament actually did. By precepts is meant the equally inspired record of the specific instruction declaring how the local church is to exist and function. In formulating doctrine precepts take the priority. When there are none, the practices are generally viewed as normative.

There is more in the New Testament about the practices of the early church, and practice must not be set aside as unimportant. Many biblical truths we hold precious are not specific commands as to what we should believe or do, but are simply what in fact New Testament Christians believed. We often believe and behave, in other words, because we are told what was believed by New Testament Christians and how they behaved as the people of God.

Reality and Identity. The most common usage of *ekklesia* is in reference to an organized assembly of believers in a particular locality. At least ninety times the word is used with this meaning.

The *ekklesia* of the New Testament had stated a time of meeting (Acts 20:7). Leaders were chosen (Acts 20:17). Corporate discipline was practiced (1 Cor. 5). In these assemblies believers were united in raising money for the work of the gospel (2 Cor. 8-9). In the total teaching of the New Testament certain things were true of the local church. Each assembly was made up of those who were regenerate and had banded together to observe the ordinances and engage in worship, Christian fellowship, and the spread of the gospel. They were organized and had chosen leaders to assist them in doing the will of God.

The local church is, in a real sense, a miniature of the universal church: To be a member of the universal church one must be divinely related to Christ. The most basic requirement of membership in the local church, if it is true to the New Testament pattern, is the same as the universal church—union with Christ. Christ is the living exalted head of the church, which is his body. He desires to be the head of each local church as well. By means of Spirit baptism, believing sinners are identified with Christ and with other believers. Believer's baptism in water is an ordinance of the local church and is the means by which one's union with Christ in his death, burial, and resurrection is made public.

Membership. That the local church of the New Testament had an accountable "membership" seems certain. The number of converts was known (Acts 2:41; 4:4). We know that there were special requirements for widows (1 Tim. 5:9), and this would imply other requirements as well. The very fact that official leaders such as elders and deacons were chosen assumes responsibility and accountability on the part of the church (Acts 6:2-5; 20:7). The teaching of church discipline also assumes such responsibility and accountability (1 Cor. 5:13). How could an individual be disciplined unless he was a member of the assembly with certain privileges and responsibilities? Further, the office of elder or bishop seems to require membership. The one holding this office was to rule (Heb. 13:7). Evangelicals are in general agreement on these requirements, though there are differences over how they are to be implemented.

Organization and Ordinances. The same arguments cited in support of membership requirements also argue for a measure of organization and structure in the church. The early church was marked by a very simple kind of structure, which arose to take the place of direct apostolic authority (Acts 4:35; 5:1-11; 6:2). The organization grew in response to the needs and problems that developed (e.g., Acts 6; 15:6, 22). Certainly the organization of the New Testament church was definite in principle, yet it was not detailed or specific in all areas. There was room for expansion and development as the churches grew.

Elder, bishop, and pastor refer to different ministries of the same person. Paul used the terms *elder* and *bishop* when writing about the same person (Acts 20:17, 28; Titus 1:5-7). The terms were used interchangeably. Further, as he described the work of the pastor, he related it to shepherding (Eph. 4:11-12). From the references to elder and bishop we learn that theirs is the same kind of work. Pastor refers to a gift given by the Spirit of God. Elder and bishop refer more to the office than to the function of the office.

The qualifications for those who would be elder or bishop were carefully delineated by Paul (1 Tim. 3:1-7; Titus 1:6-9). These are high indeed. Unfortunately they are not always taken into account today when the office is filled. Duties of the elder, bishop, or pastor are also quite specific (Acts 20:28; 2 Tim. 4:2; Titus 1:13; 2:15; 1 Peter 5:2). The local church itself has responsibilities toward the elder. These are described in Scripture (1 Tim. 5:1, 17-19; 1 Thess. 5:13). A "crown of glory" (1 Peter 5:4) and "crown of righteousness'' (2 Tim. 4:7-8) await the faithful leaders of God's people.

Deacons were also officers in the New Testament church. It is generally believed their origin is to be found in the experience recorded in Acts 6. The word translated "deacon" means servant. It is used in an unofficial sense (e.g., Rom. 12:6-7) and in an official sense (e.g., 1 Tim. 3:8-13) with respect to special church officers. In the early church the deacons assisted the apostles in caring for the needy in the assembly. The qualifications of these specially designated servants of God are essentially the same as those of elders. Very high standards of conduct are also given for deacons (1 Tim. 3:8-13).

The terms *ordinance* and *sacrament* are both used among evangelicals. Ordinance seems more acceptable, since sacrament is generally understood to convey the idea of saving merit or grace.

An ordinance refers to an outward rite appointed by Christ to be ministered by the church as a visible sign of the saving truth of the gospel. Most evangelicals observe two ordinances in their local churches. While footwashing is also observed as an ordinance by some,[14] water baptism and Communion, or the Lord's Table, are the two ordinances most practiced among evangelicals.

Believer's baptism is a public testimony of one's union with Christ. The act symbolizes a believer's identification with Christ in his death, burial, and resurrection. The act is a solemn reminder to the individual and to all who observe that there is no turning back.

The Lord's Table, or Communion as it is commonly called, is generally observed more regularly and given more prominence than believer's baptism by many evangelicals. The number of times the ordinance is observed each year varies. Also, there are differences as to the kind of elements to be used. The greatest difference among evangelicals over this ordinance concerns its meaning and significance.

Mission in the World. The universal church, the body of Christ, is manifested in the world through local churches; the invisible church is seen through the visible local assembly. In the New Testament the local church is of divine appointment and charged with responsibilities under God. Paul made this clear when he

14. See Herman A. Hoyt, *This Do in Remembrance of Me* (Winona Lake, Ind.) for arguments supporting footwashing as an ordinance of the church.

told Timothy that the local church was the "pillar and ground of the truth" (1 Tim. 3:15).

It seems obvious that the mission of the church is vitally important. What is God's intended purpose for this divine institution? Surely he has a purpose for the church's existence, but what is that purpose? Why did Christ build the church anyway? While the church has many responsibilities in the world, its primary mission centers in three duties: the exaltation of the Savior and the Scriptures, the edification of the people of God, and the evangelization of the lost. Evangelicals are in general agreement that the church's mission is threefold, but divergence of practice prevails in attempting to accomplish this mission.

1. The exaltation of the Savior and the Scriptures. When Christ, the incarnate Word, and the Bible, the written Word, are honored, exalted, and obeyed, God is worshiped. To glorify God is truly the highest privilege and responsibility ever afforded man. Paul's repeated exhortations to Timothy and Titus demonstrate the importance of these two Words of God (1 Tim. 4:13-16; 2 Tim. 3:14-17; 4:2; Titus 1:9). When the written Word is studied and obeyed, the Living Word is exalted. To love and obey the one is to love and obey the other. The apostle, who was such a student of Scripture and was used of God to bring it to us, preached Christ in all his fullness (1 Cor. 1:23; 2 Cor. 4:5).

First and foremost, the local church in all its activities has the responsibility of equipping the saints with the Word of God. All that it does must be anchored in the Word of God and performed for the glory of God.

2. The edification of the people of God. In broad outline Christ's great commission sets forth the answer to the question, Why does the church exist? The evangelization of the lost is a major responsibility of the church (Matt. 28:19). "Go ye therefore and teach all nations" is better translated, "Go ye therefore and make disciples of all nations." This is the evangelization command of the commission. The edification command is in the baptizing and teaching which follow. The church exists in the world to evangelize it. The church exists as a gathered community of believers to edify or build up those who are a part of it.[15] The

15. Gene A. Getz, *Sharpening the Focus of the Church* (Chicago: Moody Press, 1974), pp. 21-28.

emphasis throughout the New Testament is evenly distributed between these two responsibilities.

The Lord Jesus forcefully stated the responsibility to feed his lambs and sheep (John 21:15-17). Much of Paul's missionary travel was for the purpose of edifying or building up the saints (e.g., Acts 14:23; 15:41; 16:4-5). He exhorted the Ephesian elders to "feed the church of God" (Acts 20:28). There is no lack of biblical support for this charge.

Unfortunately it is often thought that only the pastor or church leaders are to edify the saints. To be sure, this is a major responsibility of the undershepherds of God's flock. But Scripture abounds in admonitions to individual believers to edify each other through prayer, exhortation, bearing of burdens, and sharing with those in need.

3. The evangelization of the lost. This is indeed a primary responsibility of the church (see Matt. 28:19-20; Luke 24:47, 49; Acts 1:8, 13:2-3, 38-39; Rom. 10:12-15). The church's mission is to make Christ known to the whole world. Evangelism of the lost is basic to the very nature of Christianity. To be true to the New Testament each local church must be responsible for those in its immediate vicinity. The early Christians were to take the message first to Jerusalem and then beyond their borders (Acts 1:8).

As members of local churches we must not wait for the unregenerate to come to our assemblies. Each believer is to be a light for Christ in his world, pointing men and women, boys and girls to him. This is not to say people can't or shouldn't trust Christ as personal Savior in the church. But it is to say that evangelization is to be done by individual believers in the workaday world outside the church as well.

In summary, then, the threefold mission of the church is to exalt the Savior and the Scriptures, to edify the people of God, and to evangelize the lost. This means the primary function of the church is not to Christianize society. Local churches in the New Testament were not given a so-called cultural mandate. They were never told to exert their influence in the world in such a way and to such an extent that all the social evils of the day would be corrected. As the pillar and ground of the truth the church has as its primary task the solemn responsibility to declare the whole counsel of God to a lost and dying world.

Major Areas of Difference Among Evangelicals

Denial of the Universal Church

By the universal church is meant the *ekklesia*, identified as the body of Christ (Col. 1:18). The term *universal* is preferred to *invisible*, the latter term is especially open to misunderstanding because to some it implies unreality.

The truth is that a significant number of Christians do not believe in the existence of a universal church as distinct from local churches.[16] Rarely is the term *universal church* used by these people. Occasionally the body of Christ may be referred to, but it is used to describe the sum total of all the New Testament local churches. In this view when one becomes a Christian, he becomes a member of the family of God, the spiritual kingdom of God, but not the universal invisible church. In other words, no one is a member of the body of Christ who is not a member of a local church. To them the local church is the body of Christ, and vice versa.

If the above view is correct, the following Scripture passages are difficult to interpret.

Matthew 16:18. Here Christ promised that he would build the church in the future. This meant it was not in existence at the time he spoke. No particular local church was in view here, because he used the singular and because he promised perpetuity for the church that he promised to build. No local church is eternal, but the body of Christ is.

1 Corinthians 12:12-13. Here Paul identifies the church with Christ, the name of the one whose body it is. In view of this the question is, To how many local churches could that name apply

16. This denial characterizes several independent fundamental Baptist groups such as Old Landmarkism, Bible Baptists, Missionary Baptists, and the North American Baptist Association. These organizations do not include statements on the universal church in their doctrinal statements. Some works which promote the denial of the universal church are S. W. Anderson, *Real Churches or a Fog* (Texarkana, Texas: Boggard Press, 1975); B. H. Carroll, *Ekklesia—The Church* (Louisville: Baptist Book Concern); Richard V. Clearwaters, *The Local Church of the New Testament* (Conservative Baptist Association of America); Chester E. Tulga, *New Testament Baptists in the Nature of the Church* (Chicago: Conservative Baptist Association of America).

The view of the above is not too dissimilar from Roman Catholicism, which also denies the universal church. It teaches that no one can be a part of Christ's mystical body who is not a member of the visible Roman Catholic Church.

without blasphemy? In this passage all who believe are described as parts or members of the body of Christ, whether they are members of the local church or not. There can be no mistaking it; all believers are baptized by the Spirit and are therefore members of the body of Christ (see Rom. 6:1-4).

Ephesians 1:22-23. The church is here identified as the body (cf. Col. 1:18). Furthermore, it is said to be "the fulness of him that filleth all in all," which would seem to describe the universal church rather than a local assembly, or even a group of them.

Ephesians 2:11-17. The "one body" referred to here is made up of Jews and Gentiles, who are constituted "one new man" in Christ. If the body is interpreted to mean the local church, it would follow that each local church must have in it both Jews and Gentiles.

Ephesians 3. In this chapter the "one new man" and the "one body" of 2:15-16 are described further. The union of Jews and Gentiles in one body, so that Gentiles are "fellow heirs and of the same body" with the Jews, is called the mystery — that is, something not revealed before. The truth had been "hid in God." The reference to the church in verses 10 and 21 must be understood in view of this. It is through the church that "principalities and powers in heavenly places might be known," the very "wisdom of God." Also, through this church glory comes to Christ "throughout all ages." That all these references to the church refer to the local assembly seems highly unlikely.

Ephesians 4:4-16. Once again the emphasis is on "one body," the "body of Christ," and "the whole body." The divinely given abilities for service are also described in this chapter. These gifts of the Spirit are given as means for the "perfecting of the saints for the work of the ministry." The "body" referred to in this chapter must be seen as the "new man" referred to earlier (2:15) and cannot be the local church.

Ephesians 5:23-27. Several references to the church appear in these verses. Christ is said to be the church's head and also "the saviour of the body." He loved the church, and proved it by his death. It is Christ's purpose to provide for himself a spotless and holy church. How could these statements possibly refer to the local church? If they do, the question is, To which one do they refer?

Hebrews 12:22-23. "The church of the firstborn" is included here among the occupants of the heavenly Jerusalem. The church spoken of here could not in any sense be earthly.

Views of the Beginning of the Church

Roman Catholicism. The Roman Catholic Church regards itself as the continuation of Israel. Rome claims spiritual power is higher and more important than political power, and therefore the church claims authority over the state.

Roman Catholicism emphasizes the visible and external nature of the church but does not deny the mystical or invisible church. However, this church is defined as the fellowship of believers who are part of the visible church, that is, the Roman Church. Roman theology insists there is no church invisible or universal that is not a part of the visible or local church. In 1950 Pope Pius XII denounced all who denied that the mystical body of Christ and the Roman Catholic Church are the same.

The Reformers. The Reformers had little quarrel with Rome's doctrine of the church. They were far more concerned to defend the doctrine of salvation by faith alone and the authority of the Bible alone. And yet the Reformers did recognize the true body of believers, even though they placed great stress on the visible organization. For them the church had its roots in Judaism and included all the saints of all ages. The church was the inheritor of Israel's promises.

Luther believed the church was "the assembly of all the believers in Christ upon earth."[17] Calvin said, "The church includes not only the saints presently living on earth, but all the elect from the beginning of the world."[18] Thus, it could be said that the Reformers, as represented by these two, believed the church began with Adam.

Covenant Theology.[19] This system generally sees the church beginning with God's covenant with Abraham and his seed.

17. Luther, "The Papacy at Rome," p. 349.
18. Calvin, *Institutes* 4.1.7
19. Covenant theology may be defined as that system of theology which is based on the theological covenants of works and grace, with a minimizing of the biblical covenants, and has as the primary purpose of God the redemption of mankind.

Therefore, covenant theologians do not distinguish between God's program with Israel and his program with the church. They also see the church as the inheritor of Israel's promises. Although the church did not come to maturity until the Spirit's ministry on the day of Pentecost, covenant theology sees the church in the Old Testament and the church in the New Testament as essentially the same. "The church under the new dispensation is identical with that of the old. It is not a new church, but one and the same. It is the same olive tree (Rom. 11:17, 24). It is found in the same covenant, the covenant made with Abraham."[20]

Some Independent Baptist Views. Certain Baptist groups, especially in the south, insist the church began with Christ. Clearwaters is a spokesman for this viewpoint: "The church, therefore, was established in the days of Jesus'sojourn in the flesh. The work of its construction was begun with material prepared by John the Baptist, later the twelve apostles of our Lord."[21]

Dispensational Thought. Certain forms of dispensational theology,[22] commonly regarded as ultra or hyper by other dispensationalists,[23] see two churches. They believe there was first the Jewish (Acts 2) and later the Gentile church. A sharp distinction is made between the church begun on the day of Pentecost and the one in the epistles of Paul. There is no agreement among these dispensationalists as to precisely when the church did begin. Some say it started in Acts 9, others in Acts 13, and still others after Acts 28.

The New Testament Concept. Since Christ promised to build the church (Matt. 16:18), it seems clear that it did not exist when he spoke. He provided teaching for the church when it would exist (John 13-17). Christ gave himself for the church (Eph. 5:25). He purchased it with his own blood (Acts 20:28) and is the resurrected head of the church (Col. 3:1-3). Therefore, the church depended not only on his death but also on his resurrection for its existence.

---

20. Charles Hodge, *Systematic Theology* (Grand Rapids: Eerdmans, 1960), 3:549.

21. Clearwaters, *The Local Church of the New Testament*, p. 26.

22. Dispensational theology may be defined as that system of theology which sees the Bible as the unfolding of the distinguishable economies in the outworking of God's purpose and which sees the ultimate purpose of God to bring glory to himself in all his relations with all his creatures.

23. See Charles C. Ryrie, *Dispensationalism Today* (Chicago: Moody Press, 1965), pp. 192-205, for an excellent summary and critique.

If the Holy Spirit formed the church by his baptizing work (1 Cor. 12:12-13), it could not have begun until that work was operative. There is no evidence of the baptism of the Spirit until Acts 2.

The bringing together of Jews and Gentiles in one body is called a mystery (Eph. 3:1-6), which means it was not revealed before. A biblical mystery is defined in Romans 16:25. Paul says the mystery was not made known in other ages ''as it is now revealed unto his holy apostles and prophets'' (Eph. 3:5). The *as* clause may be taken either in a restrictive sense, meaning the truth was partially revealed before, or it may be taken in a descriptive sense, indicating it was totally unrevealed before. Since the same truth was declared by the same writer on another occasion (Col. 1:25-26) without the *as* clause, it seems best to understand it in the descriptive sense in Ephesians 3:5. Though this does not tell us precisely when the church did begin, it does mean it did not exist in the Old Testament.

The beginning of the church is definitely related to the day of Pentecost (Acts 2). First, the Spirit's baptism is future from the ascension of Christ (Acts 1:5). Second, the day of Pentecost is the time when the promise in Acts 1:5 was fulfilled. Third, we know this because of Peter's reference to prophecy and his discussion of what happened in the house of Cornelius (Acts 11:15-16). Fourth, Paul declared that as a result of the baptism of the Spirit the body was formed (1 Cor. 12:12-13). Fifth, we are told that the body formed by the Spirit's baptism is the church (Eph. 1:22-23; Col. 1:18).

The Plurality of Elders

Must there always be a plurality of elders, bishops, or pastors—whatever they are called—in every local church if it is to be true to the New Testament pattern? I do not believe so. Though the term *elder* does appear consistently in the plural, there are strong reasons why plurality is not always demanded,[24] even though many evangelicals insist this is the case.

First, there were house churches rather than large public meeting places in New Testament times. Therefore the use of the

24. See Manfred E. Kober, *The Case for the Singularity of Elders* (Ankey, Iowa: Faith Baptist Bible College).

plural need not mean that each and every church had a plurality of elders. It may be understood to refer to one elder for each of the house churches in the city. Second, there is an interesting switch from the singular bishop to the plural deacons (1 Tim. 3:1-2, 8). This change lends some support to the validity of having only one elder or bishop in some instances. Third, the "angel," or messenger, in Revelation 2-3 most likely referred to the single elder of each of those churches. It would seem strange to give divine messages regarding human conduct to angelic beings. There are other instances where the same word obviously refers to humans (e.g., Mark 1:2; Luke 7:24; 9:52; James 2:25).

Deaconesses

Some believe the New Testament supports the office of deaconess.[25] There is not much specific support for this, however. Only two references speak of women as deacons, and in each case the word may refer to an unofficial servant and need not be taken in an official sense (Rom. 16:1-2; 1 Tim. 3:11).

The Mode of Believer's Baptism

Water baptism is a public testimony of one's union with Christ. The act symbolizes the believer's identification with Christ in his death, burial, and resurrection. Two basic modes of baptism are practiced by evangelicals today—sprinkling and immersion.

Those who sprinkle believe their view is the correct one for the following reasons: 1) Sprinkling is a better practice than immersion to picture what the Holy Spirit does when he comes upon a believer. 2) The meaning of *baptizo* is to bring under the influence of, not simply to immerse. 3) Immersion seems impossible in a number of cases (e.g., Acts 2:41; 8:38; 9:18; 2:41; 16:33). 4) The water rituals related to baptism in the Old Testament included not only immersion but also sprinkling and pouring.

Arguments supporting immersion are as follows: 1) The primary meaning of *baptizo* is to immerse; the secondary meaning is to bring under the influence of. 2) Every instance of believer's

25. See Homer A. Kent, *The Pastoral Epistles* (Chicago: Moody Press, 1982), pp. 135-40 for arguments for deaconesses.

baptism in the New Testament allows for immersion. 3) Immersion results from the natural meaning of the prepositions *ek*, "out," *en*, "in," and *eis*, "into." 4) The Greek language has a word for sprinkle, *rontizo*, which is never used of believer's baptism. 5) The early church practiced immersion until the third century, when pouring was permitted in the case of illness. 6) Immersion best pictures a believer's total identification with Christ in his death, burial, and resurrection.

The Lord's Table

The Lord's Table is also understood differently among evangelicals. Protestant evangelicals have held three principal views of the relation of the elements to Christ. All three of these views differ drastically from the Roman Catholic view, transubstantiation, which means the bread and the wine actually are changed to the body and blood of Christ as the priest prays.

The Lutheran view is called consubstantiation. In this view the elements do not change, but there is a spiritual participation, a real presence of Christ, in the elements. The Reformed position holds that the elements do constitute a means of grace through partaking of them. There is a spiritual presence of Christ in the bread and the cup, but there is no real presence of Christ in them. Zwingli argued that there was no change in the elements, no participation of Christ in them, and not even a spiritual presence. They were simply memorials, not means of grace. This is probably the most popular view among evangelical Christians today and finds the greatest support in the Scriptures.

The Government of the Church

Evangelicals all agree the local church needs to be governed. All who name the name of Christ give assent to Christ as the head of the local church, just as he is the head of the universal church. But he is not here in the body, giving instructions to each local assembly. Human leaders must determine his will for the church from the pages of Scripture. But these Christians do not agree on how the local church should be run.

There are basically five types of local church government: 1) The papal form is practiced by the Roman Catholic Church. In this approach authority rests ultimately in the pope. 2) The episcopal form places authority in the bishops. 3) Presbyterianism practices the representative form, with final authority resting in the sessions and the synods. 4) The congregational form of church government places final authority with the congregation. 5) A number of modifications and combinations of these four types have developed through the years, especially among independent church groups. The elder-rule approach, where the elders are self-appointed, often for life, and rule without allowing for much congregational involvement is a relatively recent example of this.

The congregational form of government does not mean the congregation decides on every single matter. There is no such thing as a pure congregationalism, any more than there is a pure democracy. The New Testament church appointed leaders who had specific responsibilities. They were responsible ultimately to the congregation, however, and of course the congregation was responsible to Christ.

Organization stopped at the local level in the New Testament church; there was no authority outside the local assemblies. Each one was autonomous and self-supporting, carrying on its own affairs without direction from a larger group.

That the congregation of believers in a local church has the responsibility of governing the church through chosen leaders seems certain from the following: Instruction for dealing with an erring brother was to take the matter to the church (Matt. 18:16-17). Before elders or deacons were chosen, the emphasis was on group action (Acts 2:41-47). The whole church was involved in electing leaders (Acts 6; 15; Titus 1:5). Barnabas was sent to Antioch by the church (Acts 11:21-23). Likewise, Barnabas and Paul were also sent by the church (Acts 13:1-3). The church "ordained" men (Acts 14:23). In resolving the conflict in the Jerusalem council, the emphasis is clearly on the church, the "multitude," the "brethren" (Acts 15). It is highly significant that throughout the epistles the churches are addressed. Corporate discipline was enjoined upon the church (1 Cor. 5:4-5, 7, 11). In the same vein, the church was to restore the erring brother. The church is warned about accepting false teachers (e.g., 2 Cor. 11:4). This seems strange if in fact the church had nothing to do with their selection. Epaphroditus was sent by the church of Philippi as its messenger (Phil. 2:25). The church at Colossae was warned about false teaching (Col. 2:8, 18). Finally, the complaints were against the churches in Asia Minor (Rev. 2-3).

The Church and the Church Member

What can we learn from the development of the doctrine of the church in history, and what difference does that history make for us now? The need to distinguish between the church and the churches seems urgent. A proper biblical balance between the two is very important. We also need to keep in proper perspective the stress on external unity and internal purity.

We should ask ourselves, What can I do as a member of my local church to make it a truer representation of the universal church? How can I use my abilities to greater advantage in my church? How can I receive a broader vision of the church beyond my own local assembly? Is the Bible really opposed to the building of a superchurch without regard to crucial doctrinal beliefs? Am I in any way contributing toward such a goal? These are some of the questions which should be answered.

Every member of the body of Christ is needed, even those with whom we disagree. Each has a part to play in the body of Christ; each member of the local church is needed to accomplish the task God has for it. The church is not the building, but the individuals who meet there for worship and service.

Questions for Discussion

1. What characterized each of the periods of church history with regard to the doctrine of the church?
2. How would you define the universal church and the local church?
3. Can you defend your view of when the church began?
4. What approach would you use to defend the existence of the universal church as distinct from local churches?
5. How would you evaluate the modern ecumenical movement?

Suggestions for Further Reading

Jackson, Paul R. *The Doctrine and Administration of the Church.* Des Plaines, Ill.: Regular Baptist Press, 1968.

Radmacher, Earl D. *What the Church Is All About.* Chicago: Moody Press, 1978.

Saucy, Robert L. *The Church in God's Program.* Chicago: Moody Press, 1972.

Shelley, Bruce. *The Church: God's People.* Wheaton, Ill.: Victor Books, 1973.

9

God's Plan for the Future

Jesus taught his disciples that he would die, be raised from the dead, return to the Father, and come again for his people. A study of the New Testament reveals that the earliest Christians expected Christ to return at any moment in their lifetime. They lived in light of his imminent appearance.

No attempt was made to determine an order of events associated with the Savior's return until late in the history of Christian doctrine. The person and work of Christ and other great biblical themes occupied the minds of post-New Testament Christians long before eschatology was discussed. For hundreds of years students of Scripture were content simply to affirm their belief in the certainties of future resurrection and judgment, the return of Christ, and the eternal bliss of the righteous along with the eternal damnation of the wicked.

Evangelicals are probably more divided over the doctrine of eschatology than any other doctrine. Why this is so has not been fully determined. However, this conflict should not deter us from a serious study of what in fact the Bible does teach about future things. The many portions of Scripture dealing with what lies ahead for mankind are as important as the other parts of the Word of God.

Eschatology has suffered from both neglect and abuse. Some are afraid to study the subject or to commit themselves to any particular point of view. Others seem to thrive on the study and try to come up with the identification of some current happening or person with the teaching of Scripture. As in all other areas of biblical doctrine balance is needed in the study of eschatology.

A Historical Perspective

Among evangelicals today there are three basic views regarding the future: premillennialism, amillennialism, and postmillennialism. Adherents of each of these viewpoints claim their system has roots in the ancient past. Each of these systems is defined fully and diagrammed in charts below. Here only brief descriptions need be given.

Premillennialists believe there will be a literal millennium, a thousand-year reign of peace on the earth; Christ will return with his saints and establish this kingdom, which was promised in the Old Testament. Amillennialists do not believe in a future earthly kingdom; eternity begins at Christ's second coming, according to their view. Postmillennialists also reject a future thousand-year reign of peace on the earth in fulfillment of Old Testament prophecies; their belief is that before Christ returns, the church will succeed in Christianizing society. When Christ returns, Christian influence will prevail and his coming will usher in eternity.

A highly respected work names fifteen church fathers of the first century who were premillennial.[1] Barnabas is claimed to be the single exponent of amillennialism, but even that claim is sometimes disputed.

According to premillennialists there is no trace of amillennialism in the second century until its very close. Gaius and Clement of Alexandria, writing at the end of the second century and the beginning of the third, along with their students Origen and Dionysius, are the first bona fide amillennialists. The rise and spread of Platonic philosophy and a less-than-literal interpretation of Scripture lie at the heart of the shift from premillennialism to amillennialism and the decline of the former. Actually, there are no undisputed exponents of amillennialism before Augustine.

The leaders of the Protestant Reformation were far too concerned about the doctrines of Scripture and salvation to give any attention to eschatology. They followed the Roman Church,

1. George N. H. Peters, *The Theocratic Kingdom* (Grand Rapids: Kregel Publications, 1952), 1:494-95.

which had followed in large part Augustine, who held that the present age is the millennium. He believed Revelation 20 pictured a recapitulation of the present age, which he felt was described in the earlier chapters of the book. The present age, in Augustine's view, is a progressive triumph that is to conclude with the second coming of Christ and the final judgment (see figure 5).

In the mid-nineteenth century a new type of amillennialism arose, which was a reversal of Augustine's understanding of Revelation 20. The millennium in this view is distinct from the present church age but does come before the second coming of Christ. Benjamin B. Warfield, an exponent of this approach, saw the millennium as a state of blessedness of the redeemed in heaven and not a time period on earth (see figure 6).

It is generally agreed that Joachim of Floris, a Roman Catholic writer of the twelfth century, was the first postmillennialist theologian. Daniel Whitby was largely responsible for the spread of the teaching. Cocceius and Witsius are also important names in postmillennialism.

Until this generation postmillennialism prevailed as the most popular and influential millennial theory, but world wars and other difficulties brought about its near demise. There are strong indications of a revival of the system in some quarters of evangelicalism today. Contemporary postmillennialism and theonomy (from the Greek for *God* and *law*) usually go together.[2] Postmillennial theonomy advocates argue that the church, like Israel of old, has the solemn responsibility to pressure civil governments to confirm God's laws, including those given through Moses—the precepts and the penalties.[3] In this way the secular state will be brought to submission to God and his laws. When this has been realized, God's kingdom on earth will have arrived. After God's kingdom has come, his Son will come again and usher in the eternal state.[4]

There is, of course, more to eschatology than the return of Christ and the millennium, which are matters of general eschatology. There is also individual eschatology, which includes such things

2. See by way of contrast Norman L. Geisler, "A Premillennial View of Law and Government," *Bibliotheca Sacra* (Dallas: Dallas Theological Seminary) July-Sept, 1985, pp. 250-66.
3. See my three-part series, "Theological Perspectives on Theonomy," *Bibliotheca Sacra* (Dallas: Dallas Theological Seminary), Jan-Mar. 1986, Apr.-June 1986, July-Sept. 1986.
4. See Greg L. Bahnsen, *Theonomy in Christian Ethics* (Phillipsburg, N.J.: Presbyterian and Reformed Publishing Company, 1984); David Chilton, *Paradise Restored* (Tyler, Tex.: Reconstruction Press, 1985).

as physical death, the immortality of the soul, the intermediate state, resurrection, judgment, and the eternal state. The major concern of individual eschatology relates to how those who have died will participate in the final events of the future. From the beginning of the Christian era belief was expressed in all these elements of individual eschatology, but there was no attempt at first to relate these to each other. They were seen as separate parts rather than parts of the whole. It was not until some time after the Reformation that the elements of individual eschatology were woven into the doctrine of eschatology.

A Positive Statement of the Doctrine

There are several future realities on which evangelicals are in hearty agreement. Differences do exist over specifics, mostly related to time factors, yet there is a united voice in several crucial areas.[5]

The Immortality of the Soul

Contrary to nonevangelicals, evangelicals have always believed that there is a definite relation between sin and death. Different views have been held as to the exact way in which mankind was associated with Adam and his sin, as we saw in chapter 7. But that there is a relation between the two has always been affirmed by evangelicals, whether that be viewed seminally or federally.

The historic orthodox Christian faith has from the earliest days included in its doctrine the immortality of the soul. Basing their beliefs on both the Old and New Testaments, evangelicals agree in maintaining a continued existence after death for both the righteous and the wicked. In the most absolute sense, of course, God alone is immortal (1 Tim. 6:15-16). Made in God's image, man was endowed with immortality as he came from God's hand (Gen. 1:26-27). In this state of immortality there was still the possibility of becoming subject to sin and death, and our first parents experienced both.

5. Portions of this section have been taken from the author's *Prophecy in the Ring* (Denver, Colo.: Accent Books, 1976).

But there is a higher sense in which the redeemed are immortal. Immortality in the highest sense designates "that state of man in which he is impervious to death and cannot possibly become its prey. . . . This immortality would have resulted if Adam had complied with the condition of the covenant of works, but can now only result from the work of redemption as it is completed in the consummation."[6]

The Intermediate State

The intermediate state describes the condition between death and the resurrection of both the saved and the lost. There has been general agreement among evangelicals regarding this doctrine. The subject is concerned with the relation of those who have died with the eschatological events still in the future. The intermediate state is classified as a matter of individual rather than general eschatology.

In the Old Testament, Sheol was the place of existence for life after death.

> This was a shadowy, limited existence compared to this life, but it was a very real existence. Belief in Sheol was a doctrine of immortality, not of annihilation. Furthermore, side by side with this common conception of the life after death, passages exist here and there that reveal glimpses of a more wonderful life after death for the believer and a few which hint at a more terrible life after death for the unbeliever.[7]

Sheol is translated "hell" in the Authorized Version but does not refer to the place of eternal punishment. Instead, it means the gloomy place where both the good and the evil exist after death. Job has both of these existing together (Job 3:17-19), but Isaiah describes different levels of existence there (Isa. 14:15-20). The Old Testament presents Sheol as a place of darkness (Job 10:21-22), of silence (Ps. 94:17), of forgetfulness (Ps. 88:12), of separation from God (Ps. 6:5), and a place without awareness of what takes place on earth (Eccles. 9:5-6, 10).[8]

---

6. Louis Berkhof, *Systematic Theology* (Grand Rapids: Eerdmans, 1968), p. 673.
7. Harry Buis, *The Doctrine of Eternal Punishment* (Philadephia: Presbyterian and Reformed Publishing Company, 1957), p. 2.
8. Ibid., pp. 2-3.

Alongside the Old Testament descriptions of the shadowy and gloomy side of Sheol there are passages that reveal a bright and joyful life after death for the people of God. Most of these are found in the poetic literature (e.g., Gen. 15:15; 25:8; Job 19:25-27; Pss. 16:9-11; 17:15; 49:12-15).

> In summary: the Old Testament clearly teaches a life after death, commonly in the form of an existence in Sheol, where good and evil alike share a similar dreary fate. However, there are also passages of inspired hope in a better life beyond death for the believer, a life of glorious fellowship with his God. Although there is in these passages no direct teaching with regard to the eternal punishment of the unbeliever, there is the beginning of a differentiation between the lot of the unbeliever and that of the believer. While the believer is rescued from Sheol, no such hope is expressed for the unbeliever.[9]

The New Testament Greek Hades corresponds to the Hebrew Sheol. It is used to indicate the abode of the unbeliever between death and the judgment at the great white throne. The lost in Hades are conscious and in torment (Luke 16:23-24). In the future, at the time of the final judgment, Hades will be cast into the lake of fire (Rev. 20:13-15).

The rich man in Hades, who was an unbeliever, was able to see both Abraham and Lazarus, even though a great gulf separated them from him (Luke 16:23-26). On the basis of Ephesians 4:8-10 some hold that at the time of Christ's resurrection the believers were removed from Hades and taken to the presence of the Lord. Since the Savior's resurrection, to be absent from the body is to be present with the Lord (2 Cor. 5:8). Paul said that to depart from this life is to be present with the Lord (Phil. 1:23). And Jesus told the repentant thief on the cross he would be with him in paradise that very day (Luke 23:43). Paradise is described as a place of great joy and bliss (2 Cor. 12:1-4).

The Future Return of Christ

All who take the Bible seriously believe the Lord Jesus Christ will come again, just as surely and as literally as he came the first time.

The Old Testament prophets did not distinguish between

9. Ibid., p. 12.

Messiah's coming as a babe in the manger in Bethlehem and his coming the second time as King of kings and Lord of lords in power and great glory (Isa. 7:14; 9:6-7; Zech. 14:4). It was Christ himself who first announced his future return after he told his own of his certain death. Those who witnessed Jesus' ascension heard the angelic messengers say, "Ye men of Galilee, why stand ye gazing up into heaven? This same Jesus, which is taken up from you into heaven, shall so come in like manner as ye have seen him go into heaven" (Acts 1:11).

Before he returned to the Father, Jesus taught his own that he would come again. On one occasion as he sat on the Mount of Olives, he told his disciples about the future. They were warned of difficult times ahead and were assured of their Lord's return (Matt. 24:21-27). In his upper room discourse he brought comfort to his disciples by announcing that he would come again for them. They did not, however, want to think about his death. "I will come again, and receive you unto myself," Jesus assured them (John 14:3). The very last book in the Bible holds out the promise of Christ's second coming. John, in vision, saw Christ, "the Word of God," coming from heaven along with the armies of heaven (Rev. 19:11-16).

Evangelicals do not fight over these prophecies. They all agree they have not yet been fulfilled. Will Christ come first in the air for all his children (1 Thess. 4:13-18)? Is this coming to be distinguished from his coming to the earth (Rev. 19:11-16)? Evangelicals have different answers to such questions, but they all concur that Christ is literally coming to the earth again just as surely as he came the first time.

The Resurrection of the Dead

When Jesus was on earth, some believed in the resurrection of the dead and others did not. The Pharisees accepted the doctrine, but the Sadducees rejected it (Matt. 22:23; Acts 23:8). Their differences did not, of course, keep them from joining together in their opposition to the Savior. They were perfectly willing to overlook their differences so they could form a united front against Christ.

Evangelicals base their view of future resurrection on the clear teaching of Scripture. They see implicit and direct teaching of the doctrine in the Old Testament (Job 19:25-27; Pss. 49:15; 73:24-25;

Prov. 23:14; Isa. 26:19; Dan. 12:2). Berkhof summarizes the evangelical view:

> It is true that we find no clear statements respecting the resurrection of the dead before the time of the prophets, though Jesus found that it was already implied in Ex. 3:6; cf. Matt. 22:29-32, and the writer of Hebrews intimates that even the patriarchs looked forward to the resurrection of the dead, Heb. 11:10, 13-16, 19. Certainly evidences are not wanting that there was a belief in the resurrection long before the exile. It is implied in the passages that speak of a deliverance from *sheol,* Ps. 49:15; 73:24-25; Prov. 23:14. It finds expression in the famous statement of Job 19:25-27. Moreover, it is very clearly taught in Isa. 26:19 (a late passage, according to the critics), and in Dan. 12:2, and is probably implied also in Ezek. 37:1-14.[10]

The New Testament contains even more teaching about the resurrection of the dead. Jesus himself argued for the resurrection in opposition to the Sadducees (Matt. 22:23-33). As he did so he cited Genesis 17:7; 26:24; 28:21; and Exodus 3:6, appealing to these texts in defense of his teaching.

On another occasion in reply to his critics Jesus set forth the doctrine of resurrection: "The hour is coming, in the which all that are in the grave shall hear his voice, and shall come forth: they that have done good, unto the resurrection of life; and they that have done evil, unto the resurrection of damnation" (John 5:28-29).

Repeatedly Jesus promised to raise up at the last day those who belong to him (John 6:39-40, 44, 54). He claimed to be the resurrection and the life (John 11:24-25). On the basis of these and other clear passages of Scripture there is common agreement among evangelicals that all the dead will be raised at God's appointed time in the future. Regardless of other differences all who name the name of Christ can join in repeating the Apostles' Creed: "I believe in . . . the resurrection of the body."

The Judgment to Come

That all men, as well as Satan and all the wicked angels, will one day stand before God in judgment is universally accepted by those

10. Berkhof, *Systematic Theology,* p. 721.

who embrace the Bible as God's Word. The question among evangelicals is not whether God will bring all to judgment. They agree he will. Will all be judged at the same time; that is, will the unsaved, the saved, Satan, and all his angels appear before God together at the same time? On that question there is a great deal of difference.

Differences over the order of events does not mar evangelicals' agreement on the certainty of future divine judgment. Their high view of God and his Word leads them to the conclusion that divine judgment is ahead. True, God does judge sin in the present. He does indeed visit evil with punishment and good with reward and blessing. Yet Scripture makes clear that the judgments of God experienced in the here and now are not final.

From the beginning of the Christian era belief in future divine judgment was associated with belief in the certainty of the resurrection of all men. The dead are to be raised so that they might be judged. The Apostles' Creed, earliest apostolic testimony about Christ, puts it succinctly when it states that Christ "shall come to judge the quick and the dead."

That all the unregenerate will one day appear before God in judgment is clear from John's record of his revelation. He saw the dead, small and great, standing before God and judged by God; if their names were not found in the book of life, they were cast into the lake of fire (Rev. 20:11-15).

Scripture is equally clear in its prophecy of the certainty of believers standing personally before God to give an account to him. The apostle Paul reminded the Christians in Corinth and Rome of this. He told the Corinthians that all believers must one day appear before "the judgment seat of Christ" (2 Cor. 5:10; cf. 1 Cor. 3:13-15). The Roman Christians were given the same teaching (Rom. 14:10-12).

Final judgment also awaits the devil and his demons. The everlasting fire of hell was prepared for the devil and his angels (Matt. 25:41). In his vision John was given to see "the devil that deceived them . . . cast into the lake of fire and brimstone where the beast and the false prophet are" (Rev. 20:10). There they are to be tormented day and night forever and ever. Peter and Jude were both directed by the Holy Spirit to tell us of wicked angels being reserved in chains until the day of their final judgment (2 Peter 2:4; Jude 6).

The Bible teaches us to look forward to a final judgment as the decisive answer of God to all such questions [questions like, Why does sin often seem to go unpunished? and, Where is the God of judgment?], as the solution of all such problems, and as the removal of all the apparent discrepancies of the present, Matt. 25:31-46; John 5:27-29; Acts 25:26; Rom. 2:5-11; Heb. 9:27; 10:27; 2 Pet. 3:7; Rev. 20:11-15. These passages do not refer to a process, but to a very definite event at the end of time. It is represented as accompanied by other historical events, such as the coming of Jesus Christ, the resurrection of the dead, and the renewal of heaven and earth.[11]

All evangelicals believe in a future divine judgment. They take the words of the psalmist seriously and as yet unfulfilled when he said the Lord "cometh to judge the earth; he shall judge the world with righteousness, and the people with his truth" (Ps. 96:13).

The Eternal State

Among evangelicals there is no doubt or debate that time will not go on forever. Eternity is as much a future certainty as time is a present reality.

When will time end and eternity begin? How will eternity be ushered in? These questions are answered differently by evangelicals, but that there is a real future world out there is not disputed by God's people. No believing student of the Bible accepts the notion that death ends it all. Evangelicals believe in an eternal existence for man, either in heaven or hell. They also agree that one day there will be a new heaven and a new earth. And they believe these things because the Bible teaches them.

Concerning heaven Jesus said to his own, "I go to prepare a place for you" (John 14:2). Where he would be, he wanted them also. The historic Christian faith has always held that heaven is a place, not a subjective condition that may be enjoyed now and projected into the future at death. Those rightly related to God through his Son are said to be with him and within, in contrast to those outside (Matt. 22:12-13; 25:10-12). Eternal life is the reward of the righteous (John 3:16; Rom. 2:7), which all the redeemed share alike, but there will be rewards given commensurate with service rendered on earth by the believer (1 Cor. 3:11-17).

11. Ibid., p. 729.

Hell, Jesus taught, is also a place and not simply a condition. He presented it as a place of eternal torment for the devil, his angels, and the sons and daughters of Adam who rejected him and his sacrifice for their sins. It is a place of damnation where the fire is not quenched (Matt. 23:33; Mark 9:48). Those who have not received God's forgiveness in Christ will spend eternity in the place called "the lake of fire." Berkhof summarizes the Bible's teaching on hell in these words:

> Positively, it may be said to consist in (a) a total absence of the favor of God; (b) an endless disturbance of life as a result of the complete domination of sin; (c) positive pains and sufferings in body and soul; and (d) such subjective punishments as pangs of conscience, anguish, despair, weeping, and gnashing of teeth, Matt. 8:12; 13:50; Mark 9:43, 44, 47, 48; Lk. 16:23, 26; Rev. 14:10; 21:8. Evidently, there will be degrees in the punishment of the wicked. This follows from such passages as Matt. 11:22, 24; Luke 12:47, 48; 20:17. Their punishment will be commensurate with their sinning against the light which they had received.[12]

Evangelicals agree that there will be a new heaven and a new earth in the future. The prophet Isaiah recorded Jehovah's answer to the prayer of the believing remnant: "Behold, I create new heavens, and a new earth; and the former shall not be remembered, nor come into mind" (Isa. 65:17). "For as the new heavens, and the new earth, which I will make, shall remain before me, saith the Lord, so shall your seed and your name remain" (Isa. 66:22).

In New Testament times Peter was still predicting judgment upon the "heavens and the earth which are now . . . . The heavens shall pass away with a great noise, and the elements shall melt with fervent heat; the earth also and the works that are therein shall be burnt up" (2 Peter 3:7, 10). But he prophesied further: "We . . . look for new heavens and a new earth, wherein dwelleth righteousness" (3:13). John in his apocalyptic vision saw Christ on a throne, and from his face "the earth and the heaven fled away" (Rev. 20:11).

The present heavens and earth have not yet been destroyed. The prophecy that they will be awaits future fulfillment, and so does the prophecy of the creation of a new heaven and earth.

12 Ibid., p. 736.

Evangelicals do not differ on these things. They agree that the eternal state has not yet begun.

Major Areas of Difference Among Evangelicals[13]

Evangelicals have much in common in the area of eschatology. They agree on the basic essentials of God's plan for the future. And yet the people of God do differ on many of the specifics related to unfulfilled prophecy.

The battle over the future did not just begin; it has been waged for a long, long time. If anything, the conflict seems to be getting worse rather than better, both from the standpoint of its intensity and the kinds of weapons being used in the battle. Sides are often taken without a thorough understanding of the position or its subsequent effect on other doctrinal beliefs.

We need to be doubly sure our motives and attitudes are pure in approaching this subject. If ever there was a time when we needed to manifest the fruit of the Spirit and every Christian grace, it is in the study of future things. Always we must remember that we are dealing with other members of the body of Christ, fellow members of the household of faith, fellow citizens of the kingdom of God's dear Son.

As a committed premillennialist who also embraces the pretribulational dispensational viewpoint I will make every effort to heed the above in the discussion that follows.

The Biblical Covenants

God made some staggering promises to his people through chosen representatives. These promises are presented to us in Scripture in the form of covenants. Evangelical Christians all agree with this. What they do not all agree on is the nature and meaning of these covenants. To whom, specifically, were they given? Are they conditional, depending on man's obedience for their fulfillment, or are they unconditional, depending solely on the ''I will'' of God for their fulfillment?

There are four basic covenants in the Old Testament that relate especially to things to come. It is not too much to say that one's

13. Portions of this section have been taken from the author's *Prophecy in the Ring*.

view of these covenants determines his view of things to come. In each, God promised specific things to his people.

Figure 3 shows the importance of the Abrahamic covenant and the relation of the other three to it. The major features of the Abrahamic covenant—land, seed, blessing—are developed further in the later covenants.

FIGURE 3 **Four Biblical Covenants**

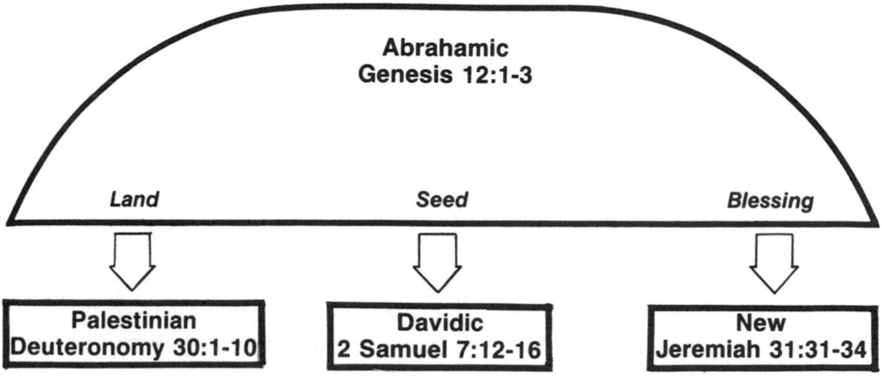

The word *covenant* appears frequently in the Bible. Relationships and agreements between God and man, between men, and between nations are called covenants. A covenant is a compact, an agreement, a contract. Some of the covenants in the Scripture—for example, the Mosaic—are obviously conditional; stated conditions must be met. Other biblical covenants do not stress conditions and seem to be unconditional with respect to their inauguration and eventual fulfillment.

The Abrahamic Covenant (Gen. 12:1-3). Confirmation and enlargement of this great covenant is recorded in several other places (e.g., Gen. 12:6-7; 13:14-17; 15; 17:1-14; 22:15-18; Ps. 69).

God promised to bless Abraham and give him a great name, make him a channel of blessing to others, deal with others as they dealt with him and his seed, and to give him an heir by Sarah. These promises all concerned Abraham as an individual.

A great nation was to be born from Abraham's seed (Gen. 12:2; 17:6). This nation was promised the land of Canaan as an everlasting inheritance (Gen. 17:8). Also, God promised that the covenant would be established with Abraham's seed and would be everlasting (Gen. 17:7). God promised Abraham that ''in thee shall all families of the earth be blessed." "All families of the earth" reached beyond Abraham and even beyond his physical seed. This aspect of the covenant is generally referred to as universal.

The burning questions are, Have any of these promises to Abraham, the father of the Jewish race, been fulfilled? Has the fulfillment of all of them occurred? If any of them have been fulfilled, which ones? How were they fulfilled? What about the remaining promises? Does the nation of Israel really have a future in God's program? The answers to these and similar questions have great bearing upon one's view of things to come and result in differences among evangelicals.

The Palestinian Covenant (Deut. 30:1-10). This covenant is called Palestinian because it concerns the land of Palestine. At the close of Moses' leadership, when Joshua was about to begin his work, the people of Israel were still not in possession of the land God had promised them. They were at the entrance of it, but not in it. In fact, there were enemies in the land. Was the land of Palestine really going to be theirs? Was God going to fulfill his promises in spite of their own unbelief and in spite of their enemies' opposition? God's answer to these questions came in the form of a covenant.

Several tremendous promises are enumerated in this covenant. Because of unfaithfulness the nation would be taken from the land (Deut. 30:1-3). Israel's Messiah would return (vv. 3-6); Israel would be restored to the land (v. 5); as a nation Israel would be judged (v. 7); full blessing would come to the nation Israel in God's time (v. 9).

At a later time in Israel's history God confirmed this covenant (Ezek. 16:1-7). Apparently Ezekiel viewed it as yet unfulfilled. Has the covenant ever been fulfilled completely? Has the nation Israel ever possessed all the land promised by God in this covenant? One reason evangelicals differ in their answers to such pertinent questions is because they understand the biblical covenants differently.

The Davidic Covenant (2 Sam. 7:12-16). Concerning Solomon, God said to David, "He shall build an house for my name, and I will stablish the throne of his kingdom for ever" (2 Sam. 7:13-16). These words came after David had expressed his desire to build a temple for the Lord. He wanted to replace the temporary portable tabernacle with a beautiful and permanent temple for the worship of God. His intentions were certainly commendable, though God did not permit him to fulfill them. The covenant was confirmed by God in Psalm 89, indicating it had evidently not yet been fulfilled by that time.

Three specific promises of God to David stand out in this covenant: He would have a son, a posterity, called in the covenant his "seed." The "throne" of David was to be established forever. Finally the "kingdom" of David was also to be established forever. Three things were promised to Solomon, David's son, in the covenant: He would be the one to build the temple which David had aspired to build. Solomon's throne would also be established forever. The chastening hand of God would come because of disobedience, yet the covenant would be fulfilled.

Again the questions must be asked: Has this covenant ever been fulfilled? If it has, how and in what sense has it been realized? If it has not, will it ever be fulfilled, and how? Evangelicals are divided over their answers to these probing questions.

The New Covenant (Jer. 31:31-34). All who believe the Bible to be God's Word agree that God promised his people a new covenant through his "weeping prophet." Most important of all, the new covenant assures those to whom it was given of a new heart. God's law will be written in the hearts of the people. Their iniquity will be removed, and their sin will be remembered no more. The Holy Spirit of God will teach the people and will find their hearts obedient and responsive. Great material blessing will accompany Israel when it is brought into the land (Jer. 32:41; cf. Hos. 2:19-20).

Several pressing questions confront the student of Scripture as he seeks to understand this covenant. To whom was it given? Was it conditional or unconditional? Has it ever been fulfilled? Does it await fulfillment in the future? How are we to understand the references to the new covenant in the New Testament?

Two Views of the Covenants

Two differing views of the biblical covenants exist. Premillennialists generally hold to the one, and amillennialists and postmillennialists to the other. These viewpoints will be explained more fully later in this chapter. Here we simply want to show how they see the covenants.

Premillennialists argue strongly that each of these four biblical covenants is unconditional; that is, they believe the fulfillment of the covenants does not depend on man's response, but solely on God. This does not mean, of course, that man's behavior in response to God is not important. It does mean that while man's obedience or disobedience affects his relation to the blessings of the covenants, his disobedience does not nullify God's eternal covenants; God will do precisely what he has promised.

Staunch defenders of the premillennial system are united in their belief in the unconditional nature of these covenants. John F. Walvoord, for example, argues that all of Israel's covenants were unconditional except one—the Mosaic.

> The Abrahamic covenant is expressly declared to be eternal and therefore unconditional in numerous passages (Genesis 17:7, 13, 19; 1 Chronicles 16:17; Psalm 105:10). The Palestinian covenant is likewise declared to be everlasting (Ezekiel 16:60). The Davidic covenant is described in the same terms (2 Samuel 7:13, 16, 19; 1 Chronicles 17:12; 22:10; Isaiah 55:3; Exekiel 37:25). The new covenant with Israel is also eternal (Isaiah 61:8; Jeremiah 32:40; 50:5; Hebrews 13:20).[14]

Altogether Walvoord presents ten reasons for believing in the unconditional nature of the Abrahamic covenant.[15] Charles Ryrie, another who champions the premillennial cause, also argues that all four of the biblical covenants are unconditional.[16]

In addition to the belief that these covenants are unconditional, it is generally agreed among premillennialists that they were originally given to the people of Israel and not to the church. Further, most insist that the national promises embodied in these covenants will be realized by the nation to whom they were given. The promises to the Jewish nation have not been, nor will they ever be, transferred to the church. "Israel means Israel and her promises have not been fullfilled by the church. Since they have not they must be fulfilled in the millennium if God's Word is not to be broken."[17]

14. John F. Walvoord, *The Millennial Kingdom* (Findley, Ohio: Dunham Publishing Company, 1959), p. 150.
15. Ibid., pp. 150-52.
16. Charles C. Ryrie, *The Basis of the Premillennial Faith* (New York: Loizeaux Brothers, 1953), p. 112.
17. Ibid., p. 125.

Classic and contemporary amillennial understanding of the covenants sees them as either conditional in nature, and thus abrogated because of Israel's disobedience, or as transferred to "spiritual Israel," the church. Oswald T. Allis, a leading exponent of amillennialism, cites six reasons for believing the Abrahamic covenant was conditional.[18]

A convert from premillennialism to amillennial thinking said this about the Abrahamic covenant: "Since the covenant was conditional the contract is broken and God is not bound to *Israel as a nation.* His covenant now is with the faithful remnant and with the Gentile believers. These two groups constitute the Christian church, which today is the Israel of God (Gal. 6:16)."[19] Of the new covenant the same writer said, "Although the covenant was made with Judah and Israel of the Old Testament, it was fulfilled in the spiritual Israel of the New Testament, that is the church. Even this however, was prophesied in Scripture (e.g., Zech. 2:11; cf. also Rom. 15:8-12)."[20]

The postmillennial interpreters present a somewhat different view of the biblical covenants from that expressed in the amillennial system, though they by no means agree with the premillennial school.

For example, Loraine Boettner, a champion of the postmillennial faith, made this observation in his explanation of Scripture setting forth the new covenant:

These are very precious promises and certainly they point forward to conditions that have not yet been enjoyed on this earth. They are in fact so far reaching and expansive that they stagger the imagination. Some amillennialists, finding no place in their system for these conditions, attempt to carry them over into the eternal state. But references to the "nations" (Isa. 2:2, 4) judging the people with righteousness (Isa. 65:20); etc., point unmistakeably to this world.[21]

18. Oswald T. Allis, *Prophecy and the Church* (Philadelphia: Presbyterian and Reformed Publishing Company, 1945), pp. 32-36.
19. William Cox, *Biblical Studies in Final Things* (Philadelphia: Presbyterian and Reformed Publishing Company, 1967), p. 7.
20. Ibid., p. 8.
21. Loraine Boettner, *The Millennium* (Philadelphia: Presbyterian and Reformed Publishing Company, 1964), p. 123.

While expressing his dissatisfaction with the amillennial interpretation of the new covenant, Boettner also revealed dissatisfaction with the premillennial views.

> The promise given to Abraham that his seed would be very numerous and that through his seed all the nations of the earth should be blessed, finds primary fulfillment not in the totality of his physical descendents, as at first sight would have seemed to be indicated, nor even in the descendents through Jacob who stood in a special relationship to God, but in those who are his spiritual descendents (Gal. 3:27-29); and the seed through which all the nations of the earth were to be blessed were not his descendents in general but one individual which is Christ.[22]

A postmillennial interpretation of the thousand years in Revelation 20 and the possibility of Christ's literal reign as the son of David reveals how the biblical covenants are viewed: "The term *thousand years* in Revelation 20 is a figurative expression used to describe the period of the Messianic kingdom upon earth. It is that period from the first advent of Christ until the second coming. It is the total or complete period of Christ's kingdom upon earth."[23]

Charles Hodge, a postmillennial theologian of years gone by, expressed a similar view of the biblical covenant—a view not at all in harmony with premillennialism. In his presentation of arguments against the restoration of the Jews in the Holy Land he said: "The idea that the Jews are to be restored to their own land and there constitute a distinct nation in the Christian sense is inconsistent, not only with the distinct assertions of the Scripture, but also with its plainest and most important doctrines.[24]

Without doubt, a basic disagreement among evangelicals is over how to understand the four biblical covenants. Differences which divide evangelicals over God's plan for the future come to a climax in Revelation 20. They begin with how the biblical covenants are understood.

The Millennium

Among those who accept the divine authority of the Bible there are three major views about God's future program for mankind

22. Ibid., pp. 102-3.
23. J. Marcellus Kik, *Revelation 20—An Exposition* (Philadelphia: Presbyterian and Reformed Publishing Company, 1955), p. 29.
24. Charles Hodge, *Systematic Theology* (Grand Rapids: Eerdmans, 1968), 3:810.

and the world. The distinctions between these systems are by no means unimportant. To the contrary, there are far-reaching consequences associated with each of the views.

Dedicated men and women who love the Lord and his Word hold to these views, and their honesty and sincerity must never be questioned. One thing is sure, however; all three systems with their proposed order of events cannot be right. They are very different, and in some places they contradict each other.

Each position has a different view of end times just before Christ returns. There is no agreement over when he will come with respect to the future kingdom or even if there will be a future kingdom on earth. There is division as to the nature of his coming. Will he first come in the air for the redeemed, and then later to establish his kingdom on earth? Or will these comings be so closely related in time that they will be essentially one? Answers to these kinds of questions reveal real differences between members of the family of God.

These three different viewpoints actually constitute systems of theology. The least popular view at the present time will be presented first.

Postmillennialism.[25] According to this system as held by evangelicals, Christ will return after society has been Christianized by the church. In this view the church is not the kingdom, but it will, through the spread of the gospel, build a kingdom. Postmillennial means Christ will come after the kingdom has been established. The "thousand years" in Revelation 20 is not taken literally.

The Baptist theologian A. H. Strong, who subscribed to postmillennialism, described the view this way: "Scripture foretells a period called in the language of prophecy 'a thousand years,' when Satan shall be restrained and the saints shall reign with Christ on the earth. Comparison of the passages bearing on this subject lead us to the conclusion that this millennial blessedness and dominion is prior to the second advent."[26] Boettner defines the system in these words:

25. Postmillennialism among some evangelicals is becoming more popular. Two rather recent contributions are a chapter in *The Meaning of the Millennium,* ed. Robert G. Clouse and Rousas John Rushdoony, *God's Plan for Victory* (Downers Grove, Ill.: Inter-Varsity Press. 1977).

26. A. H. Strong, *Systematic Theology* (Philadelphia: American Baptist Publication Society, 1907), 3:1010-11.

Postmillennialism is that view of the last things which holds that the kingdom of God is now being extended in the world through the preaching of the Gospel and the saving work of the Holy Spirit, that the world eventually will be Christianized, and that the return of Christ will occur at the close of a long period of righteousness and peace commonly called the *millennium*. . . . It should be added that on postmillennial principles, the Second Coming of Christ will be followed immediately by the general resurrection, the general judgment, and the introduction of heaven and hell in their fulness.[27]

Until rather recently postmillennialism was a most important and influential millennial view. It arose in the mid-seventeenth century as a result of and a reaction against humanism and liberal theology. The near demise of postmillennialism came with the collapse of utopian dreams in the world wars. Today it is a minority view among evangelicals, though there has been a revival of interest in it.

The evangelical postmillennial viewpoint is visualized in figure 4.

There are slightly different variations within the postmillennial position, depending on how literally the millennial prophecies are taken. Those who take some of them literally have the millennial state realized in the rather remote future established by the Christianizing influence of the church on the world. Others who see less literalism in the prophecies view the entire time between the advents of Christ as the fulfillment of the millennial prophecies.

As the diagram shows, the postmillennial view does not anticipate a future seven-year period of tribulation or an earthly kingdom with Christ on the throne in Jerusalem. There will be but one future coming of Christ. At that time, or closely associated with it, there will be a general resurrection when both the righteous and the unrighteous will be raised. Also there will be, at the same time, a general judgment that will include both the righteous and the unrighteous. Eternity then begins after the creation of a new heaven and a new earth.

Amillennialism. The prefix *a* means "no." Amillennialism is the view that denies a future literal reign of Christ on the earth in fulfillment of the Old Testament promises of God. One of its

27. Boettner, *The Millennium*, p. 4, 14.

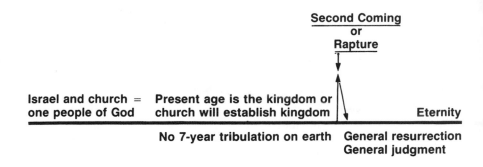

FIGURE 4 **Evangelical Postmillennial View**

advocates, J. G. Vos, has defined it thus:

> Amillennialism is that view of the last things which holds the Bible does not predict a "millennium" or a period of worldwide peace and righteousness on this earth before the end of the world. Amillennialism teaches that there will be a parallel and contemporaneous development of good and evil—God's kingdom and satan's kingdom—in this world, which will continue until the Second Coming of Christ. At the Second Coming of Christ, the resurrection and judgment will take place, followed by the eternal order of things—the absolute, perfect kingdom of God, in which there will be no sin, suffering or death.[28]

Jay Adams, who embraces the amillennial interpretation, calls the term *amillennialism* an unhappy one. He does not believe it describes the position accurately.

> *Amillennialism* is not only a misnomer because it is negative, but the distinction which it makes is a false one. No amillennialist denies that the Bible teaches a millennium, but the word amillennialism means no millennium. The issue is not whether Revelation 20 teaches a millennium, amillennialists believe it does. . . . The true difference between amillennialism and the other system involves two things. One, the nature of the millennium. Two, the chronological position of the millennium in the economy of God. The word amillennialism fails to draw either of these distinctions.

28. J. G. Vos, "Blue Banner of Faith and Life" (Jan.-March, 1951), cited in Boettner, *The Millennium*, p. 109.

Instead it expresses a belief which no conservative holds—that there is no millennium. The term cannot be defended and certainly should be abandoned. Amillennialists simply are not amillennialists.[29]

Adams suggests a new term to refer to the position which has been known as amillennialism.

Accurately speaking the biblical system may be distinguished from the two other systems as *realized millennialism.* Whereas both pre- and postmillennialists look forward to a future unrealized millennium, realized millennialists contend that the millennium is a present reality. This chronological difference necessarily involves the *nature* of the period. If the millennium is a present reality, it is most certainly of a non-Utopian type. Both of the other systems maintain that the millennium is future exactly *because* they cannot conceive of its nature as identical with the present church age. Both will look for an earthly Utopia apart from that fiery purging which alone will bring what the Bible calls "the new earth." They anticipate a golden age prior to the judgment of all men. Adherents to *realized* millennialism on the other hand maintain that such a belief confounds the millennium with the eternal state described in the last two chapters of Revelation, 2 Peter 3:12-14, Isaiah 65:17, and other prophecies. While realized millennialists believe there is a future golden age, they teach that it follows the millennial period. It will not come until the old earth has "fled away" (Rev. 20:11).[30]

Perhaps the term *realized millennialism* is a better description of the position traditionally known as amillennialism. But the fact remains, regardless of what the view is called, that this interpretation does not allow for a future earthly kingdom. To that extent it is distinct from premillennialism and postmillennialism.

Anthony A. Hoekema is a contemporary spokesman for amillennialism.[31] He supports his amillennial view with a unique interpretation of the Book of Revelation, which he sees as depicting the struggle between Christ and the church on the one hand and the enemies of Christ and the church on the other. He believes chapters 1-11 describe the struggle on earth and chapters 12-22 present the deeper spiritual background of the struggle. In

29. Jay Adams, *The Time Is at Hand* (Nutley, N.J.: Presbyterian and Reformed Publishing Company, 1970), p. 8.

30. Ibid., p. 9.

31. See Anthony A. Hoekema's chapter in *The Meaning of the Millennium,* ed. Clouse, pp. 155-87.

his view the Book of Revelation consists of seven sections that run parallel to each other and depict the church and the world from the time of Christ's first coming to the time of his second coming. The seven sections are chapters 1-3, 4-7, 8-11, 12-14, 15-16, 17-19, 20-22. Hoekema is to be credited for his attempt to state positively what amillennialists believe rather than simply refuting premillennialism. His view of Revelation is most helpful. Viewing the book as he does frees him from the literal stance in the premillennial approach.

All amillennialists reject dispensationalism.[32] Ryrie defines a dispensation as "a distinguishable economy of the outworking of God's purpose." Going on to describe the dispensational system of biblical interpretation he says:

> Dispensationalism views the world as a household run by God. In this household world God is dispensing or administering its affairs according to his own will and in various stages of revelation in the process of time. These various stages mark off the distinguishably different economies in the outworking of his total purpose and these economies are the dispensations. The understanding of God's differing economies is essential to the proper interpretation of his revelation within those various economies.[33]

Amillennialists believe dispensationalism is a recent human invention foisted upon the Scriptures. Instead of a dispensational theology amillennialists, and postmillennialists too for that matter, hold to what is known as covenant theology,[34] which represents the entire Bible as covered by two covenants: the covenant of works and the covenant of grace.

The covenant of works was an agreement between God and Adam. God promised him life for obedience and death for disobedience. Adam, and mankind in him, failed. To save man from his disobedience a covenant of grace became operative. This is the agreement between the offended God and the offending but elect sinner in which God promises salvation through Christ. A covenant of redemption is also usually included in the system.

---

32. For a presentation and defense of dispensationalism see Charles C. Ryrie, *Dispensationalism Today* (Chicago: Moody Press, 1965).

33. Ibid., pp. 29, 31.

34. For a presentation and defense of covenant theology see Berkhof, *Systematic Theology*, pp. 262-304.

This covenant was the agreement in eternity past between the Father, Son, and Holy Spirit as to each one's part in the redemptive plan of God.

The covenants in covenant theology—redemption, works, grace—must not be confused with the four biblical covenants discussed earlier. In covenant theology these biblical covenants are stages in the development of the covenant of grace. Dispensationalism, on the contrary, places primary emphasis on the biblical covenants without denying the covenants of covenant theology.

Some amillennialists who follow the fifth-century view of Augustine see the millennium as being fulfilled now on earth. Augustine's amillennial view is shown in figure 5. Others, following Warfield, believe the promises of a millennium are being fulfilled now in heaven. The diagram of Warfield's amillennialism is shown in figure 6. Both groups agree that Christ will bodily come again. When he comes the second time, however, he will not institute a kingdom on earth but will usher in the eternal state.

The future order of events embraced by most evangelical amillennialists is: (1) worsening conditions in the world before the second coming; (2) the second coming of Christ, accompanied by (3) the general resurrection and general judgment, and followed by (4) eternity.

FIGURE 5 **St. Augustine's Amillennial View**

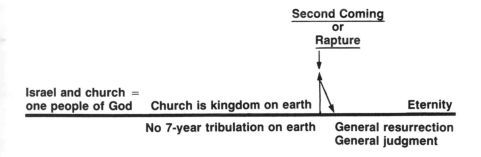

Premillennialism. Premillennialism is the belief that Christ will return before the millennium and, in fact, will establish it when he returns to the earth. Charles Ryrie, a distinguished defender

FIGURE 6 **Warfield's Amillennial View**

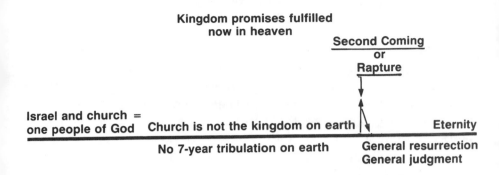

**Kingdom promises fulfilled
now in heaven**

**Second Coming
or
Rapture**

**Israel and church =
one people of God**   **Church is not the kingdom on earth**   **Eternity**

No 7-year tribulation on earth   **General resurrection
General judgment**

of the premillennial system of thought, defined it this way:

> In general the premillennial system may be characterized as
> follows: Premillennialists believe that theirs is the historic faith of
> the church; holding to a literal interpretation of the Scriptures they
> believe that the promises made to Abraham and David are
> unconditional and have had or will have a literal fulfillment. In no
> sense have these promises made to Israel been abrogated or
> fulfilled by the church which is a distinct body in this age having
> promises and a destiny different from Israel. At the close of this
> age premillennialists believe that Christ will return for his church
> meeting her in the air (this is not the Second Coming of Christ), to
> establish his kingdom on the earth for a thousand years, during
> which time the promises to Israel will be fulfilled.[35]

Premillennialists are agreed that when Christ returns to the
earth, he will institute the kingdom promised to David. Christ's
second coming in power and great glory is not followed
immediately by the eternal state. Instead it is the thousand-year
earthly rule of Christ which begins at that time. Old Testament
promises to Israel are then fulfilled. The covenants of God made
with Abraham (Gen. 12) and David (2 Sam. 7) and others are then
realized.

Will there be a seven-year period of unprecedented tribulation
which will be the outpouring of God's wrath upon the world? Will
this be what Jeremiah called the time of Jacob's trouble, a time of
divine judgment unlike any other (Jer. 30:7)? Did Jesus refer to this

35. Ryrie, *The Basis of the Premillennial Faith*, p. 12.

time when he told his disciples there would be "a great tribulation, such as was not since the beginning of the world to this time, no, nor ever shall be" (Matt. 24:21)? Premillennialists would be in general agreement in answering "yes" to these questions.

Will the church, the body of Christ, be called upon to go through the seven-year period of tribulation? Premillennialists give different answers to this question. They are not all agreed on the order in which some of the future events will transpire. For example, there are at least four different views of the relation of the church, which is Christ's body, to the coming great tribulation within premillennialism.

Pretribulationism. Some believe the entire church will be raptured, caught up to be with the Lord, before any part of the seven-year tribulation begins. Those who hold this view are called pretribulationists. John F. Walvoord, a widely recognized spokesman for premillennial pretribulationism, defines the position this way:

> The pretribulational interpretation regards the coming of the Lord and the translation of the church as preceding immediately the fulfillment of Daniel's prophecy of the final seven-year period before the Second Advent. Based on a literal interpretation of Daniel's prophecy, it is held that there has been no fulfillment of Daniel 9:27 in history and that therefore it prophesies a future period familiarly called "the tribulation." The seven years of Daniel bringing to a close the program of Israel prior to the Second Advent will, therefore, be fulfilled between the translation of the church and the Second Advent of Christ to establish his kingdom on earth. At the translation, before the seven years, Christ will return to meet the church in the air; at the Second Advent, after the seven years, it is held that Christ will return with his church from heaven to establish his millennial reign on earth.[36]

Pretribulationists find in Scripture a definite distinction between God's program with Israel and his program with the church. They also see a difference between Christ's coming *for* the church and

---

36. John F. Walvoord, *The Rapture Question* (Findley, Ohio: Dunham Publishing Company, 1957), p. 51.

his coming *with* the church. The coming *for* his church they call the rapture. Christ coming *with* his own to the earth is called the second coming.

Pretribulationists are dispensationalists, but not all premillennialists are dispensationalists. Premillennialism has been divided into the historic and dispensational varieties. Those who consider themselves historic premillennialists distinguish themselves from dispensationalists by insisting that premillennialism was embraced by the earliest church fathers, whereas dispensationalism with its literal hermeneutic which distinguishes Israel and the church as two people of God, was not.[37]

Basic to the pretribulational view is the hope that Christ could come at any moment. According to this view there are no prophecies awaiting fulfillment before his return in the air for the church. Among premillennial pretribulationists there is general agreement on the order of events in the future:

1 Increase in apostasy as this age draws to a close (1 Tim. 4:1-3; 2 Tim. 3:1-5).
2 Resurrection of the dead in Christ, the translation of the living saints, and the rapture of both groups (1 Cor. 15:20-24, 35-50; 1 Thess. 4:14-18).
3 Seven-year tribulation on earth (Rev. 6-16). Those resurrected and translated are with the Lord in heaven.
4 The judgment seat of Christ (1 Cor. 3:12-15) and the marriage of the Lamb (Rev. 19:7).
5 The battle of Armageddon and the end of the tribulation when Christ comes with his own (Rev. 19:11-16). When Christ comes, Israel will be regathered and judged (Matt. 24:37-25:46). The Gentile nations will also be judged (Matt. 25:31-46).
6 The millennial reign of Christ begins (Rev. 20:1-6). Before it starts, Satan is bound in the bottomless pit; after the thousand-year reign he will be loosed for a little season (Rev. 20:1, 7). He will deceive the people, lead a revolt against God, be defeated by Christ, and then cast into the lake of fire (Rev. 20:8-10).

37. For an excellent discussion of the contrast between the two viewpoints see *The Meaning of the Millennium*, ed. Clouse, pp. 17-116.

7 The great white throne judgment occurs, at which the unsaved of all ages appear and are then cast into the lake of fire (Rev. 20:11-15).

8 Creation of a new heaven and a new earth (Rev. 21:1).

9 Eternity (Rev. 22).

The premillennial pretribulational view is shown in figure 7. This is the most prominent view among premillennialists.

FIGURE 7 **Premillennial Pretribulational View**

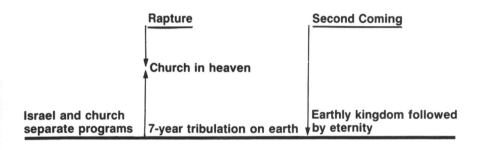

Posttribulationism. Some who affirm premillennialism question the belief that the church will escape the seven-year tribulation. They do not believe that the church will be caught up to meet the Lord in the air before the tribulation begins on earth. Rather it is their contention that the church must pass through the period called in Scripture the time of Jacob's trouble. God will protect or preserve his own through this time, they insist. This view is called posttribulationism. It is common among amillennialists and postmillennialists but is also held by some premillennialists. Alexander Reese gave this definition of premillennial posttribulationism: ''The Church of Christ will not be removed from the earth until the advent of Christ at the very end of the present age. The rapture and the appearing take place at the same crisis; hence, Christians of that generation will be exposed to the final affliction under Antichrist.[38]

38. Alexander Reese, *The Approaching Advent of Christ* (London: Marshall, Morgan, and Scott, n.d.), p. 18.

FIGURE 8   **Premillennial Posttribulational View**

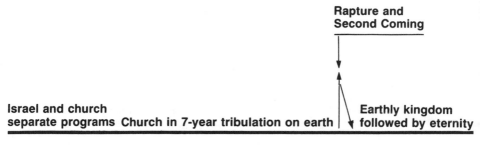

Posttribulationists are not dispensationalists, and they do not normally present an order of future events.[39] Christ's coming *for* his own and his coming *with* his own are seen to be at the same time. There will be a resurrection and judgment of men and angels before the eternal state begins. Figure 8 pictures this position.

Midtribulationism. Some premillennialists believe the church will pass through the first half of the tribulation. The last half of the seventieth week of Daniel 9:24-25 is seen to be far more severe than the first half. This view has the church raptured in the middle of the week, or in the middle of the tribulation, and is known as the midtribulation view. It is a rather recent explanation of the relation of the church to the coming tribulation, and midtribulationists do not usually use the term to refer to themselves. They consider themselves pretribulational since they do believe Christ will return to rapture his own before what they call the great tribulation, the last half of Daniel's seventieth week.[40]

To a certain extent the divine programs with Israel and the church seem to overlap in this viewpoint, since the church participates in at least part of the tribulation that is called the time of Jacob's trouble.

It can be seen in figure 9 that the order of future events is basically the same in the midtribulational view as in the pretribulational.

39. A recent exception to this is Robert H. Gundry, who argues for a posttribulational dispensationalism in his *The Church and the Tribulation* (Grand Rapids: Zondervan, 1973), pp. 12-28.
40. Gleason L. Archer, "Jesus Is Coming Again: Midtribulational," *Christian Life*, May 1974, p. 21.

FIGURE 9 **Premillennial Midtribulational View**

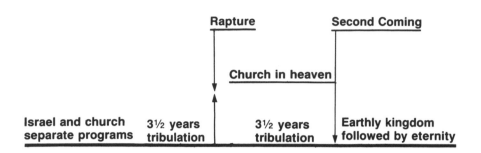

Partial rapture. A major difference between the partial rapture interpretation and the pretribulational view is the number of believers who will be raptured when the Lord comes. Partial rapturism is not a very popular view.

A contemporary exponent of the view gives three purposes for the future tribulation. It is to be a time of trouble for Israel and a means of destroying the wicked. His third purpose reveals his partial rapturism:

> Finally we would note that the purpose of the tribulation is also to be the testing of lukewarm, shallow, Laodicean Christians who will be left behind at the coming of Christ. No doubt multitudes who expected to be raptured will be disappointed because, like the foolish virgins they were not watchful. The tribulation then is for the purpose of trying the faith of these who profess to be Christians but who really never repented or are living in disobedience to the will of God.[41]

Only those Christians who are ready for the Lord are raptured when he comes. But how is one made ready for that great event? Believers evidence their readiness by looking for the Lord. Those who are not living spiritual lives will not be prepared and will not be raptured when the spiritual Christians are. Carnal Christians will be left to go through at least enough of the tribulation so that they will be made ready to meet the Lord.

The premillennial partial rapture view, figure 10, shows that the order of future events is the same as that of the pretribulation view except that some Christians remain to go into the tribulation.

41. Ray Brubaker, "The Purpose of the Tribulation," *Radar News*, Dec., 1968, p. 6.

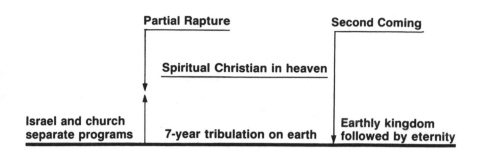

FIGURE 10 **Premillennial Partial Rapture View**

Eternal Punishment of the Wicked

Except for a few (Origen was a notable exception), the early church fathers held to the doctrine of eternal punishment for the unregenerate. The fathers of the Middle Ages held the doctrine and often presented it in extreme forms. The great Protestant Reformers believed it but did not stress it, no doubt because they said little about the broader doctrine of eschatology.

> In the eighteenth century a rebellion against the doctrine started. Caused in part by the extreme forms in which the doctrine was propagated by its adherents, this rebellion swelled into a mighty revolt in the nineteenth century, a revolt which continues to the present day. At the same time, many continued and still continue to hold the traditional doctrine, although rarely in the grotesque forms in which it was held during the middle ages.[42]

Within evangelicalism there is a small but growing movement away from the belief in eternal punishment for the wicked. At the present time this difference among evangelicals is not nearly as great as those discussed above, yet it does deserve mention. One evangelical describes the difference in these strong words:

> This issue of the duration of punishment for the unrighteous is *the* issue for professing Christians in the late twentieth century. Today there is hardly anyone feigning to be a Christian or assuming himself part of God's church who does not agree there is at least some judgment on the ungodly. But there is a growing number

42. Buis, *The Doctrine of Eternal Punishment*, p. 111; see also pp. 53-111.

who are insisting that, contrary to the obvious teachings of the
historic church, the Bible teaches only a temporary period of
punishment.[43]

Those evangelicals who question the eternal punishment of the
lost often do so by arguing the Greek word *aionios* means "aionic"
or "new age" rather than the traditional "everlasting" or
"eternal."[44] This understanding of *aionios* must, of course, be
squared with the fact that the same word, or a form of it, is used to
describe God the Holy Spirit and God the Father.

Leon Morris' comments highlight this reality:

> It is plain from the Bible that sin will be punished (Dan. 12:2; Matt.
> 10:15; John 5:28-29; Rom. 5:12-21), and the duration of this
> punishment is sometimes expressed in the NT by the use of *aion* or
> one of its derivatives (e.g., Matt. 18:8; 25:41, 46; II Thess. 1:9). *Aion*
> means "an age," and it was used of the never ending "age to
> come," which gave to the corresponding adjective *aionion* the
> meaning "eternal," "everlasting." These words are used of "the
> King of ages" (1 Tim. 1:17), of "the eternal God" (Rom. 16:26),
> and when glory is ascribed to God "for ever" (Rom. 11:36) and
> God is blessed "for ever" (II Cor. 11:31). The concept of endless
> duration could not be more strongly conveyed; the use of these
> expressions for the eternity of God shows conclusively that they do
> not mean limited duration. It is important that the same adjective is
> used of eternal punishment as of eternal life (Matt. 25:46 has both).
> The punishment is just as eternal as the life. The one is no more
> limited than the other.[45]

How Should We Then Live?

Holding to a particular view of eschatology is one thing. Living a
life in the here and now in harmony with that view is something
else. And yet if our conduct is not commensurate with our creed,
there is something seriously wrong.

43. Jon E. Braun, *Whatever Happened to Hell?* (Nashville: Thomas Nelson, 1979), p. 158.
Braun cited as one support for his contention an article by Edward Fudge entitled "Putting
Hell in Its Place," *Christianity Today*, Aug. 6, 1976.
44. See Fudge, "Putting Hell in Its Place."
45. Leon Morris, "Eternal Punishment," *Evangelical Dictionary of Theology*, ed. Walter A.
Elwell, (Grand Rapids: Baker Book House, 1984), p. 369.

The certainty of Christ's return, of future resurrection and judgment, ought to have its effect upon our lives. Believers do have hope, hope that is based on divine certainty. Death does not end it all. A day of reckoning and accounting will come. There is no second chance after death.

What about my life? Am I ready to have my works judged by the Lord himself? Have I been faithful in living for Christ and witnessing for him? What if Christ should come today? No matter which of the views discussed in this chapter one holds, questions such as these must be addressed.

Belief that Christ could come at any moment brings an added dimension to Christian living. If you really believe the Savior could return to take his own to be with him today, or before you finish reading this chapter, life should take on a vital new urgency for you. I submit that if what we believe does not affect our behavior, we are either believing the wrong thing or behaving in the wrong way, or both.

How should we then live in view of the biblical message about the future? We should live according to Scripture, live as though we would appear before the Lord in a matter of minutes or hours. As we so live, we should view every opportunity as though it might be the last one we will ever have. The Bible does not teach God's people to fold their hands and wait idly for Christ to return. Rather, it emphasizes the need to be actively serving while we wait for God's Son from heaven.

Questions for Discussion

1. Why do evangelicals agree on the doctrines of the immortality of the soul, the intermediate state, the future return of Christ, the resurrection of the dead, the judgment to come, and the eternal state?
2. Why do evangelicals disagree on the doctrines of the biblical covenants, the millennium, and the tribulation?
3. How do the biblical covenants relate to one's view of things to come?

4. Among premillennialists why are there differences over whether or not the church will go through the great tribulation?
5. How is one's daily Christian living related to one's view of future things?

Suggestions for Further Reading

Adams, Jay. *The Time Is at Hand*. Nutley, N.J.: Presbyterian and Reformed Publishing Company, 1974. Amillennial.

Bass, Clarence B. *Backgrounds of Dispensationalism*. Grand Rapids: Eerdmans, 1960. Antidispensational.

Berkhof, Louis. *Systematic Theology*. Grand Rapids: Eerdmans, 1968. Amillennial.

Boettner, Loraine. *The Millennium*. Philadelphia: Presbyterian and Reformed Publishing Company, 1964. Postmillennial.

Clouse, Robert G., ed. *The Meaning of the Millennium*. Downers Grove, Ill.: Inter-Varsity Press, 1977. Presents several millennial views.

Gundry, Robert H. *The Church and the Tribulation*. Grand Rapids: Zondervan, 1973. Posttribulational.

Ladd, George E. *That Blessed Hope*. Grand Rapids: Zondervan, 1956. Posttribulational.

Pentecost, J. Dwight. *Things to Come*. Grand Rapids: Zondervan, 1958. Premillennial, dispensational.

Ryrie, Charles C. *Dispensationalism Today*. Chicago: Moody Press, 1965. Dispensational.

Walvoord, John F. *The Millennial Kingdom*. Findlay, Ohio: Dunham Publishing Company, 1959. Premillennial, dispensational.

_____ *The Rapture Question*, Rev. ed. Grand Rapids: Zondervan, 1979. Pretribulational.

Wood, Leon J. *Is the Rapture Next?* Grand Rapids: Zondervan, 1956. Pretribulational.

Conclusion

This study has presented evangelical theology as a God-centered system of beliefs. The major doctrines of the historic orthodox Christian faith have been set forth. The treatment of these has included a historical overview of the doctrines, the major points of agreement, and some of the major areas of difference among evangelicals.

The Bible is not a system of theology. Some think Christians should therefore simply take the facts of the Bible as they are without attempting to systematize them. A system of beliefs such as has been presented in this book is sometimes viewed as unnecessary, if not detrimental. Doctrine divides, it is often said—so away with theology.

I submit, to the contrary, that God expects us to see relationships between the truths he has revealed in Scripture. The human mind is so constructed that it cannot help but strive for order. In fact, the full extent of God's truth is not known until the whole is seen in relationships. The study of doctrine produces healthy Christians. The study of Scripture's teachings makes God's people better and more useful tools in the hands of the Holy Spirit. Sound doctrine will also help keep us from embracing error.

If doctrine is to benefit the believer, it must be applied to life. Mere knowledge of the facts of Scripture, including all their relationships, is not enough. Apart from obedience to the truth this knowledge usually produces pride and a haughty spirit. What we believe does make a difference, just as how we behave does. Belief must be reflected in behavior.

In each of the chapters of this study a word of practical application was given. A review of these may be in order. Theology is, as we said, a word about God. Evangelical theology is theocentric in its emphasis. Those who embrace it ought also to live lives that are God-centered. At no time has there been a greater need for this than today in the face of the widespread influence of nontheistic humanism.

Name Index

Subject Index

Abrahamic Covenant, 259–260
Act of Supremacy (1534), 222
Adam: federal versus seminal view of, 181–182. *See also* Anthropology; Fall (the); Man
Adoption, into family of God, 203
Against Heresies (Irenaeus), 38, 219
aionios, 278
Alexandria, Catechetical School of, 68
Allegorism, 25–26, 39
Amillennialism, 248–249; on covenants, 263; future order embraced by, 270; nature of, 266–270; on present ministry of Christ, 97; as realized millennialism, 268
Anabaptist Free Church movement, 222-223
Angel(s): holy, 134–141; appearances of, 137–138; creation of, 134–136; designations of, 136–137; existence of, 135; humans and, 138; Jesus Christ and, 138–139; ministries of, 139–141; nature of, 135–136; number of, 137; orders of, 131, 133, 137. *See also* Angelology; Archangels; Demons
Angelology: doctrines of, 129–151; areas of theology affected by, 129–130; Christian response to, 150; evangelical differences over, 145–149; exorcism, 149; historical development of, 130–134. *See also* Angel(s), holy; Archangels; Demons; Satan
angelos, 136
Angels: God's Secret Agents (Graham), 133
Anglican Reformation, 222

Anointing by Spirit, 112
Anthropology, doctrines of: creation, 178–179; evangelical differences over, 178–182; historical development of, 153–156; human nature, 168–170, 179; image of God, 170–173; origins of man, 153–154, 166–168, 181–182
Apocrypha: nature of, 19; Old Testament, 19
Apollinarianism, 69, 72
Archangels, 131, 135, 140
Arianism, 41–42, 68–69, 72, 103
Arminianism, 59–61; anthropology of, 162–163; on divine election, 208–209; hamartiology of, 162–163; salvation and, 188
Ascension of Jesus, 90–91
Astrology, 134
Atonement, theories of, 70–71
Augsburg Confession, 106
Authority of the Bible, The (Stott), 31

Baptism: of Christ, 85–86; meaning of, 242. *See also* Spirit baptism; Water baptism
baptizo, 242
Belgic Confession (1562), 81
Bible. *See* Scripture(s)
Bishops, 233–234; perpetual succession theory of, 219
Body of Christ, church as, 217, 228, 237–239
Bondage of Will, The (Luther), 161

Calvinism, 59–61; angelology of, 133;

anthropology of, 161–162; ecclesiology
of, 221, 239–240; election theology of,
208–209; five points of, 60;
hamartiology of, 161–162
Canon of Scriptures, 16–22; close of,
21–22; New Testament, 19–21; Old
Testament, 17–19, 21; tests of, 17–18,
20–21
Celestial Hierarchy (Dionysius the
Areopagite), 131
Charismatic movement, 107–108
Cherubim, 137
Christology, 65–99; doctrinal
development of, 66–76; evangelical
differences over, 91–97; Lutheran, 72;
person of Christ, 76–87; Reformed,
72–73; sufferings and death of Jesus,
91–94; work and ministry of Christ,
83–91
Church, 217–246; Anabaptist doctrine
on, 222–223; Anglicanism on, 222; as
assembly of people, 217, 228; as
body of Christ, 217, 228, 237–239;
Calvinistic doctrine on, 221;
centralization of authority and power
in, 218–220; doctrinal development of,
218–227; evangelical doctrinal
differences over, 237–245; external
unity versus internal purity of, 218–
220, 239–241; Lutheran doctrine on,
220–221; necessity of, for salvation,
219. *See also* Ecumenical movement
Church (local), 232–237; governmental
forms for, 243–245; identity of, 232–
233; meaning of, 217; membership in,
233; mission of, 235–236; ordinance(s)
of, 234–235; organization of, 233–234;
practices versus precepts of, 232;
reality of, 232–233
Church (universal): centralization of
authority and, 218–220; denial of,
237–239; entrance into, 229;
foundation of, 229–232; foundations of,
239–241; meaning of, 227–228; reality
of, 228
Church-state relationships, 221, 222
Church unionism, 224–227; doctrinal
rejections by, 225
City of God (Augustine), 219
Communion, ordinance of, 234–235
Concord, Formula of, 106
Conference on Faith and Order, 226
Conference on Life and Work, 226

Conscience, 169–170
Consubstantiation, 243
Consultation on Church Union (COCU),
227
Councils of Church: Carthage (411–412),
156, 210; Chalcedon (451), 69, 104;
Constantinople (381), 103–104;
Constantinople (553), 69, 70;
Constantinople (680), 69, 70; Ephesus
(431), 69, 70, 104, 157; Nicea (325), 41,
68, 69, 103
Counterfeit Miracles (Warfield), 124
Covenant(s), biblical, 258–264;
Abrahamic, 259–260; Davidic, 260–
261; eschatological views of, 261–264;
nature of, 259; New, 261; Palestinian,
260
Covenant of grace, 269
Covenant of works, 269
Covenant theology: on church, 240;
definition of, 240n; on life sufferings of
Christ, 92–94; nature of, 269; on Spirit
baptism, 118–119
Creation, 167–168; fiat versus special
complete, 178–179; as work of Holy
Spirit, 110
Creationism, 155, 180–181; progressive,
178
Crisis theology, 8. *See also* Neoorthodoxy
Cur Deus Homo (Anselm), 158

Davidic Covenant, 260–261
Deacon(s), 234
Deaconesses, 242
Death: eternal, 174; physical origins of,
161–162, 173; spiritual, 174, 175–176
Death of Jesus: Holy Spirit and, 113;
as propitiation, 195; purpose of,
87–88; as reconciliation, 195–196; as
redemption, 194–195; as substitution,
88, 177, 194; as universal application
of, 209–210
Declaration of Sentiments (Arminius), 162
Demons, 143–145; activity of, 144–145;
Christian response to, 144–145, 148,
150; existence of, 143–144; exorcism
of, 149; final judgment of, 254–255;
limitations of, 150; nature of, 135–136,
144; possession by, 147–148; reality of,
131–132; as "sons of God," 146; as
"spirits in prison," 146–147. *See also*
Satan
De Trinitate (Augustine), 41

of, 69–70; preexistence and eternality of, 76–77; Presbyterian credal statement on, 73n; redemptive work of, 193–196; Resurrection of Jesus and, 90. *See also* Christology; Hypostatic union; Jesus Christ

God-consciousness, 180

Grace: Arminianism on, 163, 188; Augustinian view of, 156–167; common, 197–198; doctrinal developments in, 154–166; effectual, 199; efficacious, 199; election and, 208–209; as expression of divine love, 52; in Gnosticism, 154; God as source of, 192; Holy Spirit and, 105; irresistible, 157, 199; man as object of, 172; Pelagian view of, 156. *See also* Justification; Salvation, doctrine of

Guardian angels, 133

Hamartiology, doctrine of, 153–184; fall of man, 173–177; historical development of, 153–166; imputed guilt, 174–175; personal sin, 176–177; transmitted depravity, 175–176. *See also* Anthropology; Grace; Sin

Healing, gift of, 124

Heaven, 256–258

Hell, 147, 256–258. *See also* Eternal punishment

Helvetic Confession, Second (1566), 72, 106

Hermeneutics, 23–26; allegorical, 25–26; literal, 23–25. *See also* Scripture(s)

Historie v. *geschicte*, 8

History: as plan of God, 57–58

Holy Spirit, 101–127; attributes of, 109, 110; baptizing ministry of, 229, 241; Christian response to, 126–127; conviction of sin by, 198; deity of, 109–110; doctrinal developments on, 102–108; *filioque* controversy and, 104; foundation of Church and, 241; general work of, 196–198; gifts of, 117–118, 121–126; Jesus Christ and, 111–114; personality of, 108–109; in plan of salvation, 196–199; procession of, 104–105; regeneration by, 199; restraint of sin by, 197–198; Resurrection of Jesus and, 90; Roman Catholic de-emphasis on work of, 106; salvation and, 157; specific work of, 198–199; Virgin birth and, 78–79. *See also* Holy Spirit, works of; Spirit baptism

Holy Spirit, works of, 110–118; anointing, 111, 112; baptism (*See* Spirit baptism); creation, 110, 111; enablement for service, 111; filling, 111, 112–113, 116–117; illumination, 22–23, 106; indwelling, 111, 115; inspiration, 110, 111, 150; regeneration, 111, 119, 120; restraint of sin, 111; revelation, 110, 111; sanctification, 111, 113–114; sealing, 111, 116

homoousios, 41

Human body, 168–169

Humanism, biblical versus secular, 172–173

Hypostatic union, 81–83, 96–97; description of, 81–82; mystery of, 83; perpetuity of, 83; reality of, 82–83

Illumination of Scriptures, 22–23

Image of God in man, 170–173; meaning of, 154, 170–171; significance of, 171–173

Immortality: of God, 250; of man, 157, 171; of soul, 250–251

Imputation, 174–175

Incarnation, 73, 79–83; denial of, 74–76; description of, 81–82; mystery of, 83; perpetuity of, 83; reality of, 82–83. *See also* God (the Son); Jesus Christ

Indwelling of Holy Spirit, 111, 115, 150

Inerrancy of Scripture, 9, 26–32; arguments favoring, 28–32; inspiration v., 12–13, 26–28; modified v. total, 26–32; nature of, 12

Infallibility of Scripture, definition of, 13

Inspiration of Bible, 12–15; inerrancy v., 12–13, 26–28; infallibility v., 13; liberal theology on, 7; nature of, 12; plenary, 13; theories of, 14–15; trustworthiness v., 13; verbal, 13; as work of Spirit, 110

Institutes of the Christian Religion (Calvin), 42, 161

International Missionary Council, 226

Interpretation of Scriptures: allegorical, 25–26; literal, 23–25

Jesus Christ: angels and, 138–139; ascension of, 90–91, 253; baptism of, 85–86; birth of, 67, 78–80, 110; conception of, 112, 140; future return of, 252–253; historical, versus Christ of faith, 73; Holy Spirit and, 110, 112–

Scripture Index

Genesis

1—178
1:1—44, 46, 55, 134
1:1–2—168
1:2—110
1:26—48, 168, 170, 181
1:26–27—50, 167, 250
1:26–28—171
1:27—170
1:31—136
2—142
2:1—135
2:1–3—181
2:2—179
2:7—167, 169, 180
2:15–20—173
3—142, 173
3:1—173
3:1–3—173
3:14—174
3:15—79, 174, 190
3:16—174
3:17—174
3:17–19—174
3:18—174
3:20—174
3:22—48
3:22–24—174
3:24—137
4:1–6—143
5:1—170
5:1–3—170
6:1–10—143
6:2—146

6:3—197
6:6—51, 147
8:15–9:7—171
9:1–6—50
9:6—170
11:7—48
12—271
12:1–3—259
12:2—259
12:6–7—259
12:8—56
13:4—56
13:14–17—259
15—259
15:15—252
16:7–13—48, 77
17:1–14—259
17:6—259
17:7—254, 259, 262
17:8—259
17:13—262
17:19—262
19:1—139
12–13—139
22:11–18—48
22:15–18—77, 259
25:8—252
26:24—254
28:21—254
32:1–2—136
35:1—56
35:2—56
35:4—56
35:18—169
41:38—115

Exodus

3:6—254
3:14—51, 56
3:15ff.—56
5:2—45
12:3—94
12:6—94
14:18—45
14:31—45
20:2—52
20:7—56
20:10–11—168
25:17–22—137
31:3—115
31:17—168
33:19—56
34:5—56
35:31—115

Leviticus

6:30—195
8:15—195
11:44—62
13:21—56
17:7—144
19:2—51
22:2—56
22:32—56

Numbers

16:22—180

295